the movies of
racial childhoods

the movies of racial childhoods

Screening Self-Sovereignty in Asian/America

CELINE
PARREÑAS
SHIMIZU

DUKE UNIVERSITY PRESS

Durham and London 2024

© 2024 DUKE UNIVERSITY PRESS

Printed in the United States of America on acid-free paper ∞
Project Editor: Liz Smith
Designed by Matthew Tauch
Typeset in Garamond Premier Pro and Helvetica Neue LT Std
by Westchester Publishing Services

Library of Congress Cataloging-in-Publication Data
Names: Shimizu, Celine Parreñas, author.
Title: The movies of racial childhoods : screening self-sovereignty in
Asian/America / Celine Parreñas Shimizu.
Description: Durham : Duke University Press, 2024. | Includes
bibliographical references and index.
Identifiers: LCCN 2023015285 (print)
LCCN 2023015286 (ebook)
ISBN 9781478025658 (paperback)
ISBN 9781478020912 (hardcover)
ISBN 9781478027775 (ebook)
Subjects: LCSH: Children in motion pictures. | Asian American children. |
Asian Americans in motion pictures. | Motion pictures—United States—
History—21st century. | Stereotypes (Social psychology) in motion
pictures. | BISAC: SOCIAL SCIENCE / Ethnic Studies / American / Asian
American & Pacific Islander Studies | SOCIAL SCIENCE / Gender Studies
Classification: LCC PN1995.9.C45 S455 2024 (print) | LCC PN1995.9.C45
(ebook) | DDC 791.43/65230895073—dc23/eng/20230831
LC record available at https://lccn.loc.gov/2023015285
LC ebook record available at https://lccn.loc.gov/2023015286

Cover art: Nicholas Uglow, *Warm Pacific Waves*.
Courtesy of the artist.

Always with you, Lakas
For Bayan, with so much love

contents

Devastated Creator: Theorizing as Grieving Mother-Author-Spectator

I must take space and time to share that I write this book about racial childhoods as a grieving mother. I live in a deep piercing pain from the sudden death of my younger son, Lakas, that may bring up for the reader a discomfort with the sadness fueling my motivation to study Asian/American childhoods in the movies—which is to connect to my child who is no longer developing.[1] It may be too dark to come into proximity to my impossible undertaking as mother-author-spectator where creativity coincides with devastation. Lakas will come up again and again because this book is a willing for him to live, for me to feel his precious life as I experience movies about children at the ages he could not live in the past ten years.

Grief births this book, and the act of creating it helps me crawl out of devastation. As the mom of an older son who's left home for college and a deceased child who would be a teenager today, I remember anticipating with fear their violent birthing. The simultaneity of life and death in the opening of my body to give birth, with the risk of death ever present, scared me. Sigmund Freud conceived how "Eros, the life drive to preserve living substance and join together individuals to create higher organisms, families, and nations, is itself inseparably joined to . . . the drive to disjoin and dissolve all aggregates psychic, social, or organic."[2] I recognize this conjoining in the act of giving birth as one that teeters at the border of life and death when the body takes on a force of expulsion. Freud goes further, however, to chart his understanding of human existence beyond this moment. He argues that together the life and death drives, Eros and Thanatos, precisely capture how he perceived "human life itself . . . governed by a process of creation and destruction."[3] I recognize this phenomenon in the experience of the death of my child—as a mom who expected that in surviving childbirth, a particular natural order would ensue.

The physical disattachment in giving birth to my children—whom my husband, Dan, and I named Bayan (which means home, country, belonging in Filipino) and Lakas (meaning strength, both inner and of the people, also in Filipino)—came as a series of powerful oceanic tidal waves inside my body, teaching me about my physical and psychic capabilities. After almost two days of labor for our older child, my body was opened via emergency C-section, and my husband saw my insides before I was sewn up. Indeed, Eros and Thanatos, death and life, come together inexorably in giving birth.[4]

Almost three years later, after the delivery of our younger son, Lakas, the scar from my second C-section would not close, would not heal, so I was put on bed rest for six weeks. The scar ceaselessly oozed a substance that my doting husband would vigilantly pat dry to ward off infection. In those weeks, I could barely get up and could not walk. Holding our new baby, Lakas, and cradling our older son, Bayan, as a big brother nonetheless created this delicious joy I savor. We were alive even as we straddled the edge of death. Bed rest occurred at a time when our family saw no one else. I remember the warm, wonderful, purposeful, and focused feeling cradling our family. Still. I savor the experience of the complete four of us. We did not yet know what was ahead in our severing, our incompleteness in meeting death. I always thought I would die first. He did too. When he was alive, Lakas one time said, "When I am fifty, you'll be dead." I did not deny that would likely be the truth.

Lakas died on Christmas Day in 2013 at age eight, when I was forty-three. Today the memory of his body, character, and personality endures ever more in how I perceive mine. He remains undeniably part of my physical self-perception and my psychic self-understanding. Without him, I am not the me I recognize. It is not the me I intended or ever wanted. I stand at a crossroads onto a new self while a different self-understanding persists. My body knows his body. He was here, the scar under my belly his gateway into this world we share—where he lived and where he remains in us, of us, among us. In a child's dying, that is the thing to remember for me, that this is the world where he remains. I cannot go elsewhere to be with him. This is the place to stay. This is where he is.

Ten years since his death, I also know there is no dimension of time or space that can keep us apart. The best is when I feel his presence now. Christmas Day on the eight-year anniversary of the day he died, I woke up receiving five kisses from him on my face. Christmas was when he died, a confounding day I begin feeling on his September birthday, a three-month cloudy season of sensing a looming disaster is about to strike. To get through, I repeat our rituals, the things we did as the day of his death approaches soon after the day of his birth: communing with nature, baking his Halloween pies, baking the Christmas tree cookies he learned from his grandma, and our family hugging each other.

The physical awareness of my body that I experienced as a new mother, from the very physical encounters in the first days to the present, informs my reading of films as a grieving mother-author-spectator when I finally recognized in his death that I am a very attached mother as a conscious response to my own neglected childhood. Now I go through sorrow and mourning as a creative act of self-fortification (rebuilding the self) and flourishing (thriving, living anew) in making this work take place in the world that is his too. In this book, I am mother-author-spectator, devastated creator, asserting what I call an agentic attunement, a lingering and waiting awareness and anticipation of my children that started immediately when they were born. The anticipation of the children's needs awakens an alertness in me. It is a feeling I recognize in myself when a film begins: the senses alert and awake. This is the very way I pay attention to the movies of my study, for they help me to imagine Lakas at the ages he was and the ages he did not quite reach. Six-year-old David, a main character in the 2020 movie *Minari*, already evaluates others around him, assessing his parents' repeated fighting, judging his grandmother's rituals, and analyzing the white people around them as representatives of hostility or welcome. I remember Lakas, almost six, measuring the school playground on his first day of kindergarten before soon becoming so popular on it, in all his brown confident glory within his wealthy and predominantly white community. Observation, as psychoanalyst Fred Pine asserts, is the bedrock of psychoanalysis.[5] And Lakas's actions as well as David's occur within historical and social contexts: the demographics of the spaces can determine what is aspired to and actualized there. Surely practicing observation during kindergarten, Lakas landed on this personal philosophy: "I want everyone to be treated the same," which he practiced in his way of always including others and making kindness fun. Lakas likely assessed the predominant whiteness of his environs and decided he would be brown and proud, painting dark self-portraits every year for class. Because brown kids historically get short shrift in educational institutions, this is unusual and strong. Psychoanalytic methods of observation enable us to practice such agentic attunement to conceptualize relations on-screen or in a scene, interpreting how they shape our lived experiences.

Precarity and Inequality: Intimate Attachment

Precarity centrally informs this book about racialized childhood in the movies because racial and other inequities fundamentally shape childhood, as do privilege and security. We see it early, as pregnancy is itself a site of racialization, as Khiara Bridges argues in *Reproducing Race* (2011). Indeed, raising babies made me aware of the investments in different kinds of childhoods that, in turn, shape their experiences, as well as made me keenly attuned to my circumstances and surroundings. One example is the comfort of class privilege in having space for my children to cry (and I could attend to why) without worrying about shared walls. Indeed, access to advantages and resources is the terrain where unequal childhoods form. In giving my children heritage names as people of color in the United States, I placed value on their cultural inheritance, even if nonwhite ethnic names themselves have real consequences in the job market or in navigating the social sphere. I trusted in the strength they would gain from the affirmation of their cultural background as a source of pride to fuel and buoy them, even catapult them to wherever they wished to land with their history and heritage in tow. Lakas would tell new friends on the playground who would fumble his name, "It's easy. Just say it," as he patiently and confidently expected them to do it right then and there. While he may not have known it, the act of teaching claimed his belonging and his right to be addressed correctly. As a mother, I intended for my children's names to act as assertions of self-definition, cultural wealth, and strength in a world of racial and class discrimination. Their names helped to expand boundaries of knowledge and acceptance for themselves and for others who learned to say them.

For me, mothering is about shaping the present, the inheritance of the past, and actively forging the future without fear, so we chose those names to clear a path for them to claim their legacy. It is a form of "mothering as social change," as best-selling author Angela Garbes argues in *Essential Labor* (2022), where the work of caregiving contains within it not only the needed labor to enable other labor but the goal of creating a more just world. Indeed, the structural contexts of nurturing in the present involve concrete advantages and disadvantages. Still, I assert participation in the long arc of ancestors and descendants bound together in my expanded understanding of the diaspora, opportunity penalty from racialized names of color be damned.

The death of a child distorts that arc, makes life feel disordered and unnatural, leading me to accept there are things certain and uncertain, out of my control. Things happen for no reason at all. Theoretical psychoanalyst, philosopher, and film theorist Teresa de Lauretis theorizes the death drive as "the last avatar of sexuality, that agent of unbinding, negativity, unconsciousness, and resistance to the coherence of the ego that was the cornerstone and the discovery of psychoanalysis."[6] This does not quite feel like the opposite of Eros—going toward life. Grief is actional in the sense that living with an awareness of the force of the death drive is, for a living person, a creative act of making sense of the nearness and facticity of death.

Grief illuminates the position one holds to enact powerfully what it means to be born and what it means to mother and parent within these circumstances and conditions. That is, death leads to a grief that reveals the need I have for my child—not just his for me. The need I have to care for Lakas is a source of joy, a purposeful opportunity, and a relished responsibility. Encouraging curiosity and whatever his interest—baseball, diving, Legos, cooking, Scrabble—is a form of agentic attunement between me and him, and our family: to care for him generatively so he may launch well. Others feel its life-giving and life-defining power too. The amputation of the sensuousness of the physical relationship between caregiver and child, between me and Lakas? The elimination of physicality in hugging as an expression of care and love? That disappearance hurts, aggravated by the appearance of the casual cruelty that grievers face.

Things people have said to me in the aftermath of his death: *You will lose your life. You will die while alive. You will become a shell of yourself. Things happen for a reason. He is in a better place. He wanted to die. He was meant to die.* What I know above and through this noise is that he loved life. We loved life together. We did things. He would say, "I'm bored. Let's do something." It would inevitably be something easy and fun. A walk. Climbing the highest bars of the play structure. The beach. Digging deep in the sand and the waves he would inevitably dive into. Playdates with friends. Making dirt cake—crushed Oreos, gummy worms, and unlimited sprinkles. A pumpkin pie from a recipe he learned at the school library story time—of which he brought half (the first pie he ever baked) to the librarian (we continue to deliver them to her today). And he would always sit on my lap after a meal. Satisfied. He gave the best hugs. Satisfying.

Childhood and mothering involve acts of intimate attachment that describe the sensuous physicality of the relationship. I remember the peaceful connection when both my children strongly latched on to my lactating breasts, which released the milk through several holes in each nipple. In the descent of the milk, the process of its draining, and by the force of my children's suckling, I felt our energetic exchange in the entirety of my body. While milk from my body sustained life, psychoanalysts like D. W. Winnicott, who was also a pediatrician, say there is no interchange between mother and child at that moment: the breast is a part of the child, and the breast is a part of the mother.[7] They each experience and perceive the process as part of their own selves. It is fascinating to think about how the child perceives that act, which for me as a mother was indeed a giving of my body for the baby's sustenance, as I felt it physically affecting me. It is a very particular act of purposeful redirection of that body part for another who is apart from me yet is part of me. The attachment changed me in capturing my body not only in service of my offspring but also in how this relation of giving continues throughout the demands of the baby's new life (through the rest of mine even in his death, actually).

Mothering, for me, combines awareness along with the action that arises to sustain another toward their independence. And in the case of the mother-spectator-author there is the recognition of how film can help map the path toward healthy selves, which encourages my formulation of agentic attunement—*paying attention to the child's development with their future sovereignty in heart and mind*. The interchange from mother/parent/caregiver to child is felt then and throughout life as mutual, in the trust that my child learned and that I demonstrated as trustworthy in that experience. People would comment on Lakas's attachment to me and mine to him—joking that he was my appendage. I know it ultimately gave him confident independence to feel my attunement to his needs, helping launch him on a path toward better chances for successful self-sovereignty.

Parental attention to the child's demands—that everyday interchange—shapes children now and in their future. Meeting their needs strengthens our bond, and the self-satisfaction results from their dependency being met by others—even if they are unaware that it exists outside of themselves. The ability to meet their needs becomes part of how they understand themselves and the ease with which they move in the world. This does not mean that every need is met but that the broader parenting style—the repetition or dependability of receiving care—contextualizes child development in terms of the drives and instincts that exist in children and the role of the external (structures and relations) in shaping them. That refers not only to their desires, and whether they are being met, but also to their resulting self-esteem and self-confidence from the expression and meeting of those needs. Comfort in a changed diaper and being acknowledged by having their needs attended to matter in shaping the baby's confidence and achievement of peace. Persistent neglect and repeated disregard can build feelings of insecurity and undervaluation. A child's need for care is immediate, urgent, and impactful—and it makes them intensely and breathtakingly vulnerable. If a child is neglected and does not feel attended to as part of an overall caregiving approach, where they cannot achieve ease, what happens to their sense of themself as valued?

Psychoanalyst and pediatrician D. W. Winnicott coined the phrase "going on being," which can refer to the peace an infant achieves in being able to trust that their caregiver is meeting their needs. If there are deficits in the care they receive, then this state is hard to come by. In the earliest stages of life, babies possess the drive to live, to eat, to defecate, to breathe. These drives, however, are relational as the baby experiences whether their needs are being met by a caregiver. Needs are shaped by relations and cannot be understood outside of them.

A central tenet in the four psychologies—drive, ego, object relations, and self psychology—is indeed "the patient's contemporary and remembered relations with significant others."[8] This begins early in life and continues. Not only does psychoanalysis show how the development of the self relies on interactions with the external world from the very beginning of development, but the four psychologies work together to determine how urges, drives, and ego find themselves intertwined with objects and self-formation. That is, psychoanalysts listen to patients describe their relationships and help them interpret them in order to shape their self-understanding and life experiences. Winnicott identifies the self as always in relation to the other, and he works squarely within the dyad or dialectics between mother/caregiver and child—focusing on the relationship as significantly constituting both. In my analyses I incorporate object relations theory and self psychology without forsaking drives and ego psychology. I want to make room for what of life's choices can be of "our own making" in interpreting the inventory of our experiences through both psychoanalysis and filmmaking.[9] Agentic attunement captures the power of paying attention to experiences—as spectators, film scholars, and filmmakers—and how we can interpret them to establish helpful narratives in child and adult development.

Indeed, conditions and circumstances in capitalism—such as the lack of universal childcare and an inadequate minimum wage—may violently prevent parents from caring for their child adequately by requiring their separation early in parenting and childhood. Political and social factors shape object relations. Nevertheless, an agentic attunement between parent/caregiver and child can still be cultivated. Constant presence is not required; being away does not preclude an agentic attunement that leads to security. As a working mom, I wanted my infants to receive care that followed my own philosophy, which not every working parent can afford or have the privilege to contract or choose. My boys' caregivers and I worked to build their confidence and independence.

For me, the carnality of wiping feces off the babies, how the smear at times went up their backs, and how the urine would occasionally fountain into my eye demonstrated the physical attunement that occurs between child and caregiver. I recall these experiences as the tethered dynamic between me and my infant children, where I learned how to detect when they wanted to stop eating, or became aware of when the poop came, or the burp, or the cry. We communicate and develop a forceful attachment. Yet, I recognize that the experiences children undergo are their own; as a parent or caregiver, I am merely attempting to decipher their needs as separate entities from my body.

As the mother of a teen who just left home, I was never forewarned about how painful releasing him would be and how it is all worthwhile—simultaneously. I want to hold on as I let go. Everything we do to raise him results in this confident self-sufficiency and readiness to contribute to the world through talents, skills, sense of responsivity to self and others, and more. The dreams of my older son, Bayan, entail a departure from our home and a physical detachment that gives us light in this life, a feeling of helping to shape the future, and his independence is a physical manifestation of the love we gave and continue to give. His departure is not a death, for it coexists with the joy of his autonomy and the launching of his self-sovereignty. He now makes his own way at a developmental stage that feels right. It is an affirmation of our family continuity as he pursues his own goals. In contrast, I could have died when my younger son, Lakas, died. The stopping of his life threatened my own continuity, my own very living. In counting how old he would be today, imagining his needs and his desires, and in honoring his life through writing this book, I still mother him.

My film *80 Years Later* (2022) focuses on racial inheritance and what gets passed on within a family. A key collaborator on the film, who did not know me before Lakas died, said he did not know how I was as a mother—whether I was a good mother. I do not know how he defines good mothering—to me it is about agentic attunement while maintaining awareness of our separate yet bound selves. That is, a devoted mother remains nearby, making sure not to smother the child with intense infantilization or premature adultification so that they can achieve independence with their full selves—heritage and history included. The child is not her/them, nor a mere extension of her/them, and is at a specific developmental stage that any parental expectations should recognize. For me, the goal of motherhood is to raise a child with an independent self. Agentic attunement recognizes that separation.

I write this book, then, from the perspective, practice, and position of an attentive mother-author-spectator to the child on-screen as I long and yearn for one child who no longer lives at home and for another who is no longer alive. Devastated creator. I write this book as a way to imagine how Lakas would have grown up and how he would be growing today. To be clear, I write to affirm the preciousness of those years—that I know uniquely from profound loss—so that it is not simply a projection or displacement of grief onto the characters in the films.

The ages of the children and young people in the movie are the ages Lakas would have been in the decade after he had died. He would be eighteen years old now. As viewers, we are situated subjects, and I view films as the mother of a dead child for whom art can provide life-affirming connection, about how to live without his physical presence, especially in helping to imagine what could be, in the face of what cannot be, for a child no longer progressing into his own life except through what he left behind—his own friendships and his family in the way he imprinted us and in continuing the impact he made on us.

acknowledgments

For reading the entirety of the manuscript with generosity and care, heartfelt gratitude to Bakirathi Mani, who always affirmed the mothering in this work. My loving thanks to J. Reid Miller for helping me to think deeper, read harder, and write better in key moments throughout the book. I thank Jennifer DeVere Brody, Shelley Sang-Hee Lee, Ricky T. Rodriguez, and Clare Sears for reading and responding to parts of the manuscript so I may benefit from their needed brilliance and expertise. Nicole Fleetwood and Rachael Miyung Joo give good company in writing with purpose and pleasure. Working with Anitra Grisales for the past fifteen years helps me actualize more precisely my ideas. I am thankful for our long and deep connection! For their engagement, I am grateful to Linh Thuy Nguyen, the University of Washington and the Simpson Center; J. Reid Miller and Haverford College; Richard T. Rodriguez and the University of California at Riverside; Purnima Mankekar, Akhil Gupta, Lata Mani, Miriam Ticktin, and Shannon Speed at the American Anthropology Association; Jasmine Nadua Trice, Grace Hong, and Zizi Li at UCLA's Thinking Gender 2023 conference; and the audiences at the American Studies Association, Society for Cinema and Media Studies, and Association for Asian American Studies.

From the despair of the early times as a grieving mom to now, my therapist has helped me every week since the third day after Lakas died. My family keeps me, including my father-in-law, Tadashi Robert Shimizu, who stayed with us and cared for us in the months after Lakas died. Our siblings cared for us: Rolf and Sharon Parreñas, Rhacel Parreñas and Ben Rosenberg, Rhanee and Claudio Palma, Cerissa and Ian Piamonte, Juno Parreñas and Noah Tamarkin, Aari Parreñas, Mahal and Nick MacNeill, Jenny and Gerald Risk, and Susie Shimizu McCobb. My *pamangkin* and *inaanak* Ciara, Isabella, Javi, Brady, Mica, Caleb, Malaya, Mayari, Sebastian, Ronin, Nolan, Matthew, and Daniel know and share the loss of Lakas while so young themselves and love and remember him now; even the youngest ones who did not meet him yet know him and love him too. Our community's feeding and loving us include my grieving mom's book club—where friends courageously read with me to better understand the loss of a child whom they loved too. I am grateful for the love of the friends of our son Lakas who help me imagine and feel his growth today. In the year after Lakas's death, Melissa Michelson, Crisanta De Guzman, Patrice Wilbur, Claire Sheehan, Cameron Hecht, Jenny Shimizu Risk, Ina Sheynblat, Pauline Masterson, and A Runner's Mind helped me run two half-marathons per month, culminating in the Skyline to the Sea Marathon with the 6K up-and-down course I completed in 7 hours 55 minutes and 59 seconds (4 minutes and 1 second under the cutoff). Thanks to the strangers who kept asking if I was OK, offering me Gu energy gels and water, and cheering me on as I cried and screamed while running up and down mountains, through forests, and finally to the ocean. Running, like writing, expresses externally the internal pain, calls forth my body/mind/soul/spirit to continue to live, and thus captures the grief journey itself. Finishing the race, like finishing this book, is a testimony to living in the aftermath of the death of my son whose life I honor here. And finding worth in my own.

For helping our family care for our boys, I am most grateful to Patty Barnwell, David Wanderman, Albert Kasuga, Terrence Lau, Silvia Argenal, Ster Vogel, Paula Foscarini, Mahealani Furukawa Lee, Monica Salamy, Genna Joseph, Noura Bou Zeid, and Joy Lockhart. Robyn Chamness, Tessa Rosa, Marcia Ginsburg, Sally James, Carol Welte, and all the boys' teachers, parent volunteers, classmates, and administrators at South, Crocker, and Nueva Schools who really helped our family. An Huang Chen, Christina McCleary, Leslie Ragsdale, Kristen Patel, Alice Chang, Emily Kenner, Renee Fitzpatrick, Dounya Matar, Laurel Miranda, Mina Morita, and more ensured my ongoing work as a parent volunteer in ways that helped me honor Lakas all over the Bay Area. KARA-Grief in Palo Alto, especially Jim Santucci, Kathleen Weed, Donnovan Ysrael, and April Espaniola and Children's House in Sydney, provided much-needed help and community that centered children and the ongoing memory of Lakas.

My colleagues and students at San Francisco State University and the University of California at Santa Cruz all inspire me to create, teach, learn, lead, and serve while talking about and knowing Lakas. For their support, I thank at SFSU, President Lynn Mahoney and Provost Amy Sueyoshi; and, at UCSC, Chancellor Cindy Larive, Campus Provost, and Executive Vice Chancellor Lori G. Kletzer. Thanks to my team in the UCSC Arts Division, especially Karen Meece, Maureen Dixon Harrison, Lindy Boisvert, Stephanie Moore, and Dave McLaughlin, for helping me concretely as I finished this book.

I am grateful to my dear friend Rachael Joo, who introduced me to Miok Snow, who connected me to Karen Elizaga, who enabled my interview with Diane Paragas.

The three anonymous reviewers galvanized depths of possibility in me and made this book better. My editor, Ken Wissoker, believed in, supported, and trusted me for the book to be born. Publishing with Duke is a homecoming full of recognition that I cherish. Ryan Kendall helped me through the production process, and Liz Smith shepherded me to the finish along with the creativity and attention of the production and marketing team at the press.

An earlier version of chapter 3 was published in the *Journal of Cinema and Media Studies* 62, no. 3 (2023): 170–75.

Our family lives every day in the ebb and flow of the pain from the death of Lakas and our wish for him and us to experience the joy of his life. My older son, Bayan, remains the light of my life and the love of my world. And as he writes, creates, and thinks through the world's pressing issues, with his overflowing talent, brilliance, courage, and immense determination, my admiration for him soars. He is the one who gives me hope for the future overall. Undoing trauma from my own childhood into the fold of our loving marriage, in our delicious and juicy creative collaborations, in our communing with nature's forests and beaches, and in our growing stronger together as grieving parents, Dan Shimizu reveals the immense beauty and boundlessness of life together. Dan, I love and need you even more deeply.

Lakas lives on infinitely. Gives us happiness abundantly. We love you forever.

Introduction

On Korean American Day, January 13, 2021, two prominent Hollywood production companies presented Korean American filmmaker Lee Isaac Chung's *Minari*, winner of the 2020 Sundance Grand Jury Prize and Dramatic Audience Award. Tickets for the Wednesday night online presentation disappeared fast as people shut in during the COVID-19 pandemic jumped at the chance to watch the buzzed-about independent film at home. The screening was followed by a Zoom panel with the director and cast, moderated by Sandra Oh. The award-winning film and television actor cried as she spoke from the perspective of a spectator about how much she did not know she had needed to see on-screen the particular gestures of her own embodied experience as a Korean American: "I never knew I needed that gift until I opened it."[1] Her visceral identification with the actors' performances—particularly the way they ate Korean food, their facial expressions, or even the way their skin made her recall that of her grandmother—was healing for Oh: "It's like a salve. The entire film is like a salve." She attested that in being "Korean American, seeing this film, you just did not realize you are sitting in so much grief. And watching this film lets it go a little bit. For us, it is really something to celebrate."

The conversation with Sandra Oh, the director Lee Isaac Chung, and actors Steven Yeun, Han Ye-ri, and Youn Yuh-jung was punctuated by choked-up silences as the participants struggled with words, which led to different kinds of crying in the Zoom gallery. Lead actor Steven Yeun talked about his personal work reconnecting to the trauma of moving to the United States as a four-year-old and of being severed from homeland, culture, language, and family. In recollecting this time from his childhood, he could barely speak, stopping to gather himself by closing his eyes, lowering his head, and pursing his lips to keep them from quivering. He described the powerful emotions that intimately informed his performance decades after that traumatic time, particularly in terms of an immigrant childhood steeped in "deep isolation." As an adult in the filming process, the most difficult part for him was having to "let go" of his own "will and desire to be deeply seen." But once he submitted to that extremely painful process, "the beauty of doing that" led to a "deep reconnection" to his childhood and a "recontextualization of understanding" the trauma of having his life "turned upside down." Playing the role of the father allowed Yeun to, as he thoughtfully and emotionally articulated, "overcome the gaze of my own internalized understanding of my parents and . . . overcome even the infantilization of them. . . . Oftentimes, because we're in some way severed from them through communication and through cultural boundaries . . . we remember them either through their suffering or in the ways that we miscommunicate love to each other." The most difficult part of making the film for him was going through that pain of, in his words, "servicing something larger than you . . . and just opening it up to everybody." His voice quivered as he admitted, "It actually allowed us to see ourselves a little clearer."[2]

I begin by describing this discussion between some of the most prominent Korean American and Korean creators to dissect where these deep, and perhaps surprising, expressions of emotion came from, especially as they relate to childhood trauma, race, and representation. These creators' jubilance in presenting a film that finally brought Asian American narrative cinema to the greatest prominence cannot be separated from the grief and isolation of their childhood and now adult experiences. *Minari* was nominated by the Academy of Motion Picture Arts and Sciences for

Best Picture, Best Director, Best Original Screenplay, and Best Original Score—the highest categories in one of the most important film awards in the world. Its lead actor, Steven Yeun, was nominated for Best Actor (a historic first for an Asian American male lead), and Youn Yuh-jung actually won for Best Supporting Actress—the first Korean in history and only the second Asian, following Miyoshi Umeki in 1958. The film's accolades included recognition not only at the Oscars but also at the Golden Globes, where its nomination was mired in controversy when the sponsoring organization, the Hollywood Foreign Press Association, placed it in the Best Foreign Film category. The organization claimed this was because English was spoken in less than 50 percent of the film's dialogue, essentially rendering the immigrant experience unfathomable as American. But this misrepresentation is exactly what this film challenges, especially because it is based on writer/director Chung's own Korean American immigrant childhood.

The *Minari* director explained how the film originated from his memories of what it was like to grow up in the rural American South. One afternoon, as an adult, he decided to write down everything he could remember about being six years old, the age of his own daughter at the time. The first memory that came to him was of being afraid that a tornado was going to hit his family's trailer, which, as in the film, his father moved them to without telling his mother. Even so, his memories were just a starting point, and the story continued to evolve throughout the filmmaking process, with input from the Korean and Korean American actors. Chung said the act of making film is to "create something completely new; we're not trying to capture something . . . we're trying to create something." When memory becomes film, then, it comes to life through collaboration, and the incorporation of others. Yet, by the time they reached the end of the process, he said, "I felt like it still retained so much of the spirit of what I remember from growing up."

Beginning this book on racial childhoods with a discussion of this lauded Asian American film is fitting because Chung puts the perspective of children at the center of the American family melodrama—particularly in the loss of home as a place of security, familiarity, and safety and in the threat of looming death for the six-year-old main character, David, portrayed by Alan Kim, an important narrator of the story. Critical to the film's narrative, David and his older sister, Anne (Noel Kate Cho), are central protagonists who actively make sense of their experience in the desolation of the rural South. In centering their agency as children, Chung recognizes how childhood can help the viewer understand the power of the film's premise. Moving from Korea to Los Angeles and then relocating to Arkansas impacts these young people's formation in ways worth distinguishing from the impact on their parents and grandparent. And we witness the critical events in their lives unfold in ways that we know will matter to them as adults. This was even reflected in the filmmaking process, as the writer/director and the actors themselves reached into the archive of their own childhood memories and personal struggles to tell this Korean American immigrant story.

Racialization works differently across generations, and the experiences of young people are critical to completing our understanding of it. The grandparent, the parents, and the children in the film each have their own subjective experiences. And the writer/director makes sure to include how kids themselves sort out and analyze their perceptions. What is fascinating here is how we do not learn about the early events, experiences, and relations in the grandparent's and parents' lives. Instead, we see the children's experiences and imagine what of these will be repeated and revisited as they get older. Indeed, the children's continuity organizes the film. David's heart murmur becomes the family's central concern, especially his mother's, in determining their viability in this new home. Prioritizing his health also becomes the basis for the parents' conflict and the reason their marriage may fall apart. In the film, and beyond, children's experiences and well-being are crucial; we must listen to them so we can more fully access Asian American immigrant stories.

Choosing Our Inventory: Psychoanalytic Approaches to Asian/American Childhoods in the Movies

As for the filmmakers and actors involved in *Minari*, as spectators our minds are never blank. Films enter our lives within the context of our entire lived experience, from our childhoods with our families to our histories, desires, and relationships now. We analyze film as we experience it: How does this make sense, what of this world do I recognize, what does the film hail in my world? We witness our own lives when making sense of a movie. We study characters as the agents of their lives, *asking ourselves if we too are agents in our own*. Films relay subjective experiences of events that we can analyze and relate to as we evaluate and measure our own autonomy then and now. Choices and actions are building blocks of film directing and film acting in ways that are paralleled in spectatorship and psychoanalysis. Both entail interpretive acts of forming oneself and others through an evaluation of our representations and our relations.

Lee Isaac Chung used the psychoanalytic approach of free association, a method Sigmund Freud established over one hundred years ago, to create his film about racial childhood. In taking inventory of his childhood memories, intently listening to and evaluating himself to generate the narrative arc of the film, Chung shows the link between psychoanalysis and (film) fiction. Both interpret and prioritize the power of childhood experience and early childhood memory. In creating a narrative arc, we then make sense of these events as not only of the past, but also what is currently real and actual, to hopefully improve our lives today.

I evaluate Asian American films that represent childhood by using the philosophy of psychoanalysis. I came to psychoanalysis for the centrality of sexuality and aggression in its philosophy for my first three books, which contend with power relations across race in sexual representations. I return to psychoanalysis for different reasons now. Here I expand my approach to racialized sexuality by moving away from racialized sex acts and power relations toward the sensuous experience of mothering/parenting and how that experience of becoming a mother/parent changed the way I moved in the world as I cared for others more than myself. My inner world—and what was important to me—changed too.

The inventory of events Chung constructed reveals how the child's relationships to significant others such as parents, grandparents, other adults, and peers shape self-perception. *Minari*'s mother and father fighting about whether they should stay, grandma's fun-filled exploration of their environs, white adults highlighting the family's racial difference in a homogeneous town, and white children questioning or accepting their presence across difference: these experiences narrate well what we may feel as constitutive. Social forces act on characters, and characters act and react, showing how they navigate others' narrations as they form themselves. We see David asserting belonging by enthusiastically joining other children socially, or defining his grandmother's foreignness to emphasize his own Americanness. Both acts—self-assertion and self-definition—are creative and teach us the importance of children as social agents.

They also show us the similarities of psychoanalysis and film: both interpret reality and work with historical events to assess what things mean and how people fashion themselves. The filmmaker analyzes the subjective experiences of the child in constructing the film, and film psychoanalysis renders them analyzable through our interpretations. It is in the act of the film's symbolizing and our interpretation that we can feel the child grappling with themselves as they enter and interact in the world not as separate from it but dependent on it in an ongoing way. That is, as children experience their emotions in conflict, which the film aims to dramatize, we see how they act, cope, and create, and how they may risk rehearsing these same dramas into adulthood, for Freudian reasons of reenacting pleasure or mastering trauma. Through their experiences and their subsequent interpretive choices, children shape the world as they feel it and occupy it. When we watch the experiences of children, we also see how they establish their autonomy through their subjective relationship to the objects around them, including place, space, and people.

Minari thus enables me to clarify the kind of psychoanalysis that informs this book, one that departs from the centrality of drive, ego, and instinct that is most associated with Sigmund Freud, to approaches that have developed since his philosophy and practice were established in the early twentieth century. Freud's clinical practice of attuned neutral listening to the patient on the couch was expanded to methods of child and infant observation by Melanie Klein and D. W. Winnicott (with object relations) and Heinz Kohut (with self psychology), who worked in the early-middle to later-middle twentieth century. Object relations and self psychology address the optimal conditions for well-child development. The central difference in these later psychoanalytic approaches that stem from Freud is in the focus on the independent role of others in relation to the formation of the self. Indeed, as psychoanalyst Fred Pine argues, Freud "had his object relations theory," but "the formal status he gave to the object was drive based—that is, the object was that person, part of a person, part of the self, or the thing through which gratification of drive was attained."[3] Rather than center drives as urges, and the gratification of those drives as the end point, object relations and self psychology evaluate the intrapsychic and interpersonal role of the other in developing oneself. And self psychology prioritizes self-formation as different, separate, and with one's own agency and self-esteem.[4]

Fred Pine identifies four psychologies in psychoanalysis: drive, ego, object relations, and self psychology. All are related, overlapping, and different, yet they all are useful because complex humanity requires the multiple angles they present.[5] The central concern that distinguishes the four approaches is in how we account for what is born instinct or developed in relations with others, such as caregivers or loved ones. The difference, however, between various psychoanalytic approaches is not a matter of biological versus relational. According to feminist psychoanalytic film theorist Teresa de Lauretis, even Freud would find that "not acceptable," since his "foremost intuition and lifelong effort was to define a new conceptual category, the psychic, and a theoretical domain, metapsychology or psychoanalytic theory."[6]

I am interested in how we have a hand in the forces that shape us. I answer this question through the act of interpretation that this book centers on, which I call *agentic attunement*—the act of attending to a child with their sovereignty, at that moment and in the future, in mind. I am interested in how "the view you get depends on when you are looking."[7] For me, the development of children is particularly important to emphasize because film dramatizes so much of our adulthood through our experiences as children. So much happens in childhood, which we remember as core events and memories in adulthood, that shapes our decisions and choices today. What would it mean to recall the feelings we possess as children and our own subjective experience to understand how we actualize ourselves as adults, and to interpret them not only in a film but also in how we talk about the film experience?

All psychoanalysis is relational by virtue of the analyst-patient relationship. However, even more relational models emerged due to the limits of Freudian drive and ego psychology, which considered the other as derivative to the goals of self-gratification. For Freud, the other is an object "defined as the end point in the search for gratification."[8] I move toward a less self-focused and more relational approach that emphasizes the other as a continual force in one's self-development, especially those relations and events instantiated in the early lives of children that resonate in adulthood. In my study, the later psychologies of object relations and self psychology add to, rather than supplant, drive and ego psychologies. The connection to the other can remain an attachment in itself, a comforting or grating memory throughout life, rather than in the instance of establishing the self. One of my main contributions with this book is to foreground these underutilized theories, especially in the analysis of film childhoods overall.

The development of object relations and self psychology is also grounded in changes with methods in a clinical practice that lends itself to film. Psychoanalysis developed from the "hovering" kind of listening Freud did, where the analyst listens attentively to the patient on the couch to better understand them and their inner world. Winnicott's and

Kohut's child and infant observation expanded that approach to new patients and methods. My approach thus utilizes Winnicott's object relations and Kohut's self psychology to make sense of the development of self-sovereignty in childhood films through the keen observation of child development. Others, like Anna Freud, Melanie Klein, and W. R. D. Fairbairn, also attend to questions about the impact of childhood events. Thus, in this book I do not ignore Freud's and Lacan's drive, instincts, and ego psychology, which we in the field of psychoanalysis and film usually emphasize, but I do put a stronger focus on object relations and self psychology due to the different ways these psychoanalytic theories approach childhoods.

To be clear, it is not that the social environment does not matter in drive, instinct, and ego psychology. Fred Pine argues that Melanie Klein's conception of object relations uses drive psychology to discuss how the child incorporates or expulses the object, which is thus tied to drives. D. W. Winnicott furthers Klein's object relations to anchor this relationship in actual parent-child relations and the specific dyad there.[9] Thus, Winnicott and Klein illustrate how the combination of the child's wishes and the parent's attunement and attachment remains formative in their lives. Because I am concerned with the self-formation of the child and how object relations with parents haunt and shape adulthood, this focus is necessary.

The Power of Representation and Emotions in Asian/American Cinema

In the Zoom session with the actors and director of *Minari*, Sandra Oh began the conversation by linking the power of the film's images to her perpetual yet unanswered need to experience on-screen her particular culture, manifested in the Korean language, hand gestures, bodily positions, and facial expressions. Her own face aghast at the shock of her need, she identified a long-standing hunger that found expression in tears, intermittently streaming from her eyes as she moderated. Steven Yeun's crying was different, for it referred to and emerged from the trauma of loss. It took him aback, sharing the quality of surprise in Oh's experience, but it disabled him into a long silence that compelled him to turn away from our view and bow his head.

I welcome all this crying as a kind of return to childhood need, made especially acute during the pandemic. I recognize the feelings emanating from their sounds, both the slow cry of hunger and the disabling cry of pain. And as we are all immersed in the pandemic, to cry together in the face of our loneliness, our losses, and our suffering from the deaths and deprivations we continue to endure feels right in nonlinguistic form. Yet, the panel's crying on-screen is about ongoing feelings Asian Americans hold in relation to representation, as a loss and sorrow, and as a vehicle of collective trauma that has lasted more than many lifetimes: we who have not experienced ourselves as the center of our cinematic stories. Sandra Oh highlights this when she asks the Korean actors on the panel, who have not experienced the trauma of a lack of representation in their home country, if they understand why the Korean Americans are crying. The cultural theorist Stuart Hall identifies the work of representation, or the depiction of people and events, as providing cognitive maps of who we are in relation to others.[10] Meanings produced in movies shape how we perceive and behave in the world. Since the inception of moving images, Asian Americans have occupied screens as fraught terrains of invisibility, distortion, and simplification, commingling in what Teresa de Lauretis calls the public and private fantasies of our popular culture.[11] Movies are technologies of harm for Asian Americans in our systematic exclusion from their authorship.

Thus, the reactions that the *Minari* conversation revealed are not new. Asian American moviegoers and moviemakers have expressed an unrelenting hunger for recognition on-screen since the beginning of cinema. Dating back to the birth of film itself, similar to when African Americans created content and engaged the technology of the new medium of cinema, Asian Americans like Anna May Wong deployed their emotions on-screen, presenting them as cultural practices worth celluloid, for they, to follow Sara Ahmed in *The Cultural Politics of Emotions* (2004), "produce the very surfaces and boundaries that allow the individual and the social to be delineated as if they are objects."[12] We have a right to the screen as a place for expressing emotion. As I explore in my experimental documentary *The Fact of Asian Women* (2004), which dissected the structure and grammar of her performances as well as her commentary, along with the stars Nancy Kwan and Lucy Liu, Wong knew that her acting on-screen registers Asian American women out of marginalization into new terrains of meaning. And she recognized the power of film to secure her critical intervention in the historical record.

A long and deep archive of Asian American actors have challenged, since its beginnings, the industry's commitment to racial stereotypes—or the repetition of what Homi Bhabha defines as "arrested representations."[13] Lauded Japanese American immigrant actor Sessue Hayakawa, who played a Hollywood villain from the 1910s to the 1960s known for violent misogynistic acts, such as branding a woman's back in the film *The Cheat* (1915), began his own film production company in Los Angeles. According to film scholar Daisuke Miyao, Hayakawa produced numerous films focused on Asian American and other racialized experiences.[14] In his own films, Hayakawa's characters bypassed his Japanese American ethnicity to play more fully realized characters of Arab, Indian, Latinx, and Native American backgrounds. He rewrote his villainous violence against women, too, by giving up his own future for their safety, even if it meant his own character's death. Through film, he aimed to generate a new narrative to distill trauma.

We need stories unique and specific to Asian American experiences and racializations, like the ones Anna May Wong, Sessue Hayakawa, and *Minari* project, so that the medium of film can do its work more effectively. That work, I insist, is to make us feel, especially for children who are at the cusp not only of accessing their autonomy but of navigating conflict, feeling emotion, and forging their self-regard. These feelings include grief, mourning, and alienation in ways both social and psychic, as identified in works on racial melancholia by Asian Americanist psychoanalytic literary scholars Anne Anlin Cheng, David Eng, and Shinhee Han and on Asian American affect in popular culture by writers like Cathy Park Hong.[15]

I cannot imagine Hayakawa crying, though, about the roles he had to take. What I sense from his own films is a *rallying* cry, one filled with anger that reveals a binding relationship to images that defined his legacy. In his lifetime, he wished to unshackle himself from his ill-famed roles, illustrating what documentary filmmakers Loni Ding and Renee Tajima Peña make with their *self-defining* images as a counter to what African Americanist sociologist Patricia Hill Collins calls "controlling images."[16] Following Collins, Asian Americanist media scholar Darrell Hamamoto extends her term to refer to Asian Americans as well.[17] In identifying how structural racism is manifested in industry images, Collins argues that dominant groups determine our cultural understanding of marginalized groups that, in turn, shape intergroup and cross-individual perception. To apprehend relations through media communication, however, we must take into account how images deploy emotions, encourage mutuality, and contain the possibility of empathy—including what I have argued in my previous books as the simplification of the complex process of representation where the identification with one's own subjugation occurs. That is, spectators of color read films critically and contextually as well as being deeply formative in our subjectivities, as scholars like Jacqueline Stewart and J. Reid Miller well argue. Images are relational, and power dynamics at the sites of production and spectatorship are analyzable, especially in terms of our complex cognitive and affective responses and relations to our objectifications.

Because the Asian American story is so broad and wide-ranging, this collective call to be seen within structures of representation resonates with contemporary Asian American creators working with a productive and creative anger online today. They literally claim rage through self-naming, like Phil Yu's *Angry Asian Man* blog and its companion podcast branded as a service for "the media-savvy, socially conscious, pop-cultured Asian American," and Lela Lee's *Angry Little Asian Girl*, a comic and cartoon series focused on Kim, a Korean American female child who rails against racial and gendered injustices, replete with rude hand gestures and curses.[18] Both of these examples deploy anger—claiming it as an emotion proper to Asian Americans who are constructed as the quiet minority who lack the capability and capacity for it. If Asian Americans do not have access to anger, how can they have other emotions, especially in conflict—the basis of psychoanalysis and movies both?

The Movies of Racial Childhoods harnesses the power of emotion, not only in the demands of Asian Americans for representation but also in how three fields—psychoanalysis and sexuality, Asian American and ethnic studies, and film and media studies—have the special ability to contend with and deploy emotions. The book's focus on Asian American childhoods addresses the lack of representation both in film and also in cultural studies approaches to childhood. It also identifies a field of study within Asian American cinema from which film, race, sexuality, and psychoanalytic studies may benefit by coming together, extending their lessons and expanding their purviews. While Asian American studies' engagement with childhood has largely focused on literature, ethnic and diaspora studies have begun to talk about the role of the child in narrative cinema in ways that I am further advancing.[19] For example, in talking about childhood sexuality—which is a focus of psychoanalysis but a topic that film studies shies away from, while it also remains an understudied field within Asian American studies and ethnic studies—I engage critical questions about desire and orientation, autonomy and overdetermination, and I identify how self-sovereignty and power dynamics appear early in one's formation as a citizen and subject.

Agentic Attunement and Other Key Concepts

In addition to applying the key concepts of object relations and self psychology in my film analysis, I also incorporate D. W. Winnicott's notions of the "good enough mother" and "true and false selves." The good enough mother figure focuses on the needs of her infant attentively until she begins to fail the child in small ways in order to prepare them for self-sovereignty. The true self is present and able to be in the moment, whereas the false self can only engage in superficial relations in defense against the world. Like Winnicott's concepts, Heinz Kohut's notion of selfobjects also emerges from child observation. Selfobjects capture the role of others in giving a child confidence and self-esteem through reliable care. Selfobjects are representations of the parent and caregiver on whom the infant and child depend; the child develops an attachment to that parental relationship, thereby forming the self. Kohut also gives us the concepts of the grandiose self and healthy narcissism to describe how children learn to preserve what is good and reject what is not for their own well-being. The subsumption of the grandiose self leads to a kind of healthy narcissism that helps regulate unrelenting attacks on an individual's self-esteem. In my study, these come from racism, sexism, heterosexism, and other forms of discrimination as they relate to children and young people of color's senses of self, in a world where they are perpetually and systematically managed as subjects.

I utilize these concepts from object relations and self psychology with the goal of showing how youth forge autonomy in the face of grief, especially over the loss of parents and homespace, as the loss of familiarity, safety, and love provides opportunities to rebuild the self. The goal of the book is to show how films are analyzable in ways that growing up can be. In our development, we choose which memories to repeat and revisit, either to confirm and elaborate on our pleasure or to learn to master our pain by rehearsing the same scenes and relationships. It is the act of evaluating and understanding our experiences through interpretation that I hope to gift the reader through a process I call *agentic attunement*. This concept incorporates a generative understanding of agency as acting for the sake of self and others in the face of obstacles. Here I am building on the ideas of anthropologist Saba Mahmood, for whom agency is the ability to act within constraints. Mahmood defines agency counterintuitively in how the unfree may find freedom and independence in the performance of the very roles they are subjected to and constrained by, such as when Islamic women "treat socially authorized forms of performance as the potentialities—the ground if you will—through which the self is realized."[20] As I argue in my previous books, self-cultivation cannot be removed from the formative power of the social, including how images intervene in one's most intimate desires. Similarly, Mahmood asks how "submission to certain forms of (external) authority is a condition for achieving the subject's potentiality."[21] I interpret her definition of agency to be generative in the sense of finding freedom within the engagement of and resistance to one's subjugation.

In terms of my concept of agentic attunement, I define attunement as the attentive practice of observation that spawns from the position of a watchful mother-author-spectator. From this role, I diagnose how movies help us mold and further develop ourselves through the process of interpreting key events, moments, and relations. Agentic attunement teaches us to take stock of and thoughtfully identify our formative experiences so we may transform and actualize ourselves to be who we wish to be: agents in our own lives, starring in our own movies. Agentic attunement relies on the keen observation of children's development now toward the goal of their self-sovereignty, autonomy, independence, and healthy adult futures.

I extend agentic attunement's purview beyond the interior world of the film. I am interested not only in diegetic relationships between parents and children but also in our affective relationship to the images on-screen for their potential to calm suffering. Films capture embodied feelings that words may not solely express. Psychoanalyst John Bowlby, founder of attachment theory, who studied relations between children and their parents, says there is no stronger feeling than the behavior of attachment or how children know to depend on their parents or caregivers in achieving security and confidence. One way to measure the child's attachment is through assessing the different kinds of crying and the response of the mother or parental caregiver. For Bowlby, "crying is elicited by a number of quite different conditions," including hunger and pain. Which of these is more powerful is hard to tell: pain stimulates hurry; hunger, a more "leisurely" response, the sources of which indeed are anxiety that can also lead to anger.[22] I write about Asian American cinema and the traumas addressed in childhood representations to make sense of these feelings as racial ones, where images hold and contain trauma as well as address it. Agentic attunement asks us to dissect images within their social context—noting family roles and dynamics as a site where emotion in performance can produce emotion in the spectator—as I do with *Minari* now.

Minari opens with a close-up on David, a six-year-old Korean American boy, in the back seat of his family's station wagon as his youthful mom, Monica, and sister, Anne, drive on desolate country roads in the middle-of-nowhere Arkansas. They follow a moving truck just ahead of them, which we find out is driven by the husband and father, Jacob. The mother is anxious as she absorbs where they are. She looks at her children in an attempt to gauge their well-being. She glances at the daughter, who reads alongside her in the front passenger seat, and in the rearview mirror, where she notes her son falling asleep in the back. When they arrive at their destination, Monica asks, "What is this place?" with worry and concern, looking at the nowhereness of their surroundings. The husband announces, "This is our new home," with confidence and even a smile. The kids run toward the trailer home parked on stilts. We soon discover, when the parents and sister dote over David, that he has a heart murmur, and his parents are trying to find a home where they can establish economic security. After moving from Seattle to Los Angeles, where there were other Korean Americans nearby but also a lack of opportunity, they have ended up in a place without an ethnic community or a good hospital. But what we see of their parenting depicts dimensions of agentic attunement.

The parents are attentive; they listen to their children's wishes and create opportunities for fun, even amid their own fear. They explain life lessons, including what they are doing in this unknown area with no malls and no schools nearby, and they ask questions about how the children feel. The mother worries about the hospital being an hour away as the father dreams about farming fifty acres of land. "Think about the kids," she says to him, to which he replies, "They need to see me succeed for once." The conflict between the parents is about the children's future and their role in providing safety versus the prospect of prosperity. Nonetheless, the fighting is frequent, and the kids cope by coloring and making airplanes that send messages that read "don't fight" to their parents in the other room, or by reading the encyclopedia while their parents work at their jobs in a chicken hatchery. The move is both an aspirational act for their children and a risk to their health. The film captures the stakes of the story by rendering the children's future legible in the parents' choices.

The children's experiences and active process of making sense of their lives are central to the immigrant family's narrative—in David's hiding his soiled underwear after he wets the bed so he won't add stress to his family, or in the kids' curiosity about why their father insists on growing Korean vegetables. The father, Jacob, tells his son they will cater to the "thirty thousand Koreans who immigrate to America every year." David also makes sense of how generations relate; he reacts to the news that his grandma Soonja is coming to live with them by observing, "Grandma is why you fight." His mother attempts to explain family and the bond between generations. When the grandma arrives, they attempt to overcome the language barrier along with the grandchild's perceptions of who grandparents are or should be. The way she looks and behaves puzzles him—she "does not look like a grandma. . . . Grandmas don't wear men's underwear." He is repulsed when she gives him a snack from her own mouth. He is baffled by her gift of Korean playing cards and the spirited way she plays, as if among adults rather than her grandchildren. While the film does not explain how he measures her strangeness, the focus and attention on the Korean immigrant family expand our definition of grandmotherhood on-screen. This is especially vivid when Soonja teaches her grandkids to play cards, yelling at them, "Sucks for you! Damn it. . . . A plague on you!" In an interview, Youn Yuh-jung said she identified with how the grandma character takes to the new location, finding in its soil a healthy place where minari, a Korean plant, could grow, "and that's obviously how she sees her grandson. And that's something his parents can't really see."[23]

What I find powerful and promising in the Asian American cinematic childhood representations in *Minari* and the other films I analyze in this book is how they regard racialization as foundational to growing up. Steven Yeun, in an interview at Lincoln Center on December 21, 2020, said that *Minari* is "an inside view of the family from our perspective as we lived it . . . liberated from the mainland home gaze . . . and the majority American gaze . . . the immigrant experience is its own thing."[24] I underscore this assertion that motivates Asian American filmmakers and film scholars then and now. The dramatization of racialization, the particular experience of being subjugated as a confrontation in this historical moment, highlights how so much emotion still needs to be expressed and explored on-screen. We have not yet felt all that we can feel in movies, especially if we don't undo cinematic harm with pleasure, affirmation, and relief. And these feelings are grounded in childhood, as Yeun reached all the way back to his own four-year-old immigrant experience to inform his acting and Lee Isaac Chung dug deep into his six-year-old experiences relocating to Arkansas to write the film.

Films are vehicles to help us feel collective trauma, pain, and representations of childhood explicitly so we can unflinchingly address them as both formative and changeable. This is why we must tune in to them to act and become agents. In experiencing these images that hold and contain both deep distress and joy, agentic attunement—especially toward the young—can make lived inequities known so we can address our woundings, seek justice, mobilize action, and encourage healthy paths toward adulthood. Asian American representations on-screen have been sites of harm, but they are the very same sites where we can address those injuries, to help us live happier, healthier, and fuller lives.

Indeed, Chung described how he showed *Minari* to his family over Thanksgiving. Through viewing it, he said, "we recognized our struggle with each other and how we made it to the other side. We have a better relationship because we now see each other."[25] Lacking the capacity to verbalize their experiences of immigrant struggle over decades, he had to go to moving images to represent his family's trauma and grief. The stories of Asian American children and youth, silenced subjects, deserve our fearless attention to help us toward similar goals of coherence and reconstitution. We must see their lives as worthy of the power of the movies and through the feelings and actions they ignite and inspire.

As a filmmaker and film scholar who practices agentic attunement in creating narratives that undo the harms cinema has wrought upon communities of color, I also show how films help us examine childhood attachment and how children can forge self-sovereignty as a rehearsal for adulthood. As Bowlby argues in his foundational work on attachment, to be able to relate to and depend on our caregivers is critical for success in future relations and overall life experience.[26] And while there are no guarantees, within the context of capitalism, that secure attachment will lead to successful well-being, films help to show us paths where we can undo trauma and redirect pain to find what Mary Main, Nancy Kaplan, and Jude Cassidy called "earned secure attachment"—that is, to produce at least one secure attachment relationship that moves consciously and deliberately away from the insecurity that the trauma of childhood inflicts.[27] While there are no absolute assurances that secure attachment results in well-being, it poises the child to launch on a healthy beginning with self-esteem and confidence. Psychologist Mary Ainsworth, a colleague of Bowlby, pioneered the Strange Situation, a laboratory procedure for assessing attachment security between infants and their mothers to iden-tify patterns of attachment, including insecure and secure attachment styles.[28] A student of Ainsworth's, Mary Main advanced this work to iden-tify how secure attachment led to more confident behavior, exploration, and play for infants.[29] Out of the traumas from one's childhood, earned secure attachment emerges when one explicitly creates new relations and new narratives in adulthood. In a sense, throughout this book I study pre-cisely the ways in which attachment succeeds and fails as characters relate to their childhood traumas in the formation of their future selves.

And in agentic attunement, I extend this inquiry to what race and representation inflict, to continually look at and make images that let us imagine something different. Especially in confronting power relations among marginalized voices within marginalized communities, we may experience what the imagistic can do beyond the linguistic. Trauma de-mands representation so as to create new realities.

Race and Childhoods in the Movies

The Movies of Racial Childhoods studies early twenty-first-century tele-visual and cinematic narrative representations of racialization and its impacts on the sovereignty of children, particularly Asian American and Asian children in independent global cinemas. Devastation and ex-ploitation are not the dominant themes in the stories of Asian/American childhoods and young adulthoods that we read about in this book; in-stead, we see a richer and wider range of childhood experiences.[30] Thus, my conceptualization of agentic attunement makes an extremely hopeful intervention, in identifying how the child and young adult embark on the process of raising themselves. They do this by taking seriously the project of tending to their own emotions and centering the self, both empowering and enabling actions.

Across each chapter, we witness how growing up as Asian/American entails grief and mourning, as children and young adults contend with the bonds of attachment, feeling the racialized forces that construct Asian Americans as model minorities (including premature adultification in breeding overachieving children who don't play, with parents already see-ing them as doctors and lawyers in their childhoods), the contestation of their sexual autonomy in the face of premature sexualization, and the literal loss of a parent or a home. While the parent or place appears as the object in key moments of one's life—events that have ramifications for confidence, self-assurance, and more—their death and loss mean a re-alignment of the world. There is a loss of confidence, loss of certainty, loss of the sense of omnipotence and autonomy that can come from secure attachments to person and place. Throughout this book, a parent's death may be a turning point in the film, or a child leaves home just as they hit a critical crossroads of development. Beyond interpersonal and intrapsychic loss, children's autonomy and self-mastery in these films are fraught with the structural forces of racialization and sexualization and the particular structural circumstances of their families that shape and form individual subjectivity. However, the children emerge as agents of their own lives, starring in their own narrative stories due to the agentic attunement their caregivers practice (or don't) or that they take on for themselves as young people.

Bringing together psychoanalytic methods with an agentic attunement to the body and psyche via race, gender, and sexuality studies, I study cinematic childhood as a set of experiences impacted by others—relationships, objects, and structures of inequality—to show the importance of forging oneself through the conscious act of interpreting one's own experiences. This means not simply accepting them but laundering them through a process of evaluation and interpretation, including of the social forces that shape and limit experience.

The bond between mother and child is not only racialized but also dependent on the structural conditions and historical circumstances where this relationship resides. The bodily and psychic connection between me and my sons, and any other mothering or caregiving, does not exist outside race and racism. The precarity of the mother's life, for example, is informed by the assumption that women of color have a higher tolerance for pain, by a history of forced sterilization in medical practices, or by the determination that they should not have ownership over their reproductive capacities or their own children.[31] For Asian/American women, as I present in my first book, the sacrifice of children to white men who forsake them in the opera *Madame Butterfly* (1904) and the musical *Miss Saigon* (1989) is also a form of perverse sexualization—that they are partners for fornication but not motherhood (reproducing bloodline) or wifehood (acceptable partnership). There is also the reality of the fear Black mothers face regarding the racial targeting of their children—from Trayvon Martin to Tamir Rice—that most white mothers do not experience; this is what visual studies scholar Nicole Fleetwood refers to as the "casual violence of whiteness" in her article "Raising a Black Boy Not to Be Afraid."[32] For me as a woman of color raising brown boys, and as a Filipinx American immigrant, the experiences of racialization and the work I do to prepare them for it start early as well. Racial identity impacts mothering not only in terms of social and cultural perception but also in self-perception and practice. Similarly, deaths of people of color are racialized, as we see from the disproportionate number of COVID-19 fatalities for Filipinx American, Latinx, and African American people.[33] As with the pandemic, we experience childhood and parenting unequally.

In our family, my first son takes after my husband's mixed-race Japanese and white heritage in his features and color, while my younger son takes after me—Filipinx and deeply brown, though his hair, eyes, and mouth are just like his dad's. Our varying appearances in terms of racial identity are differences that matter as much as my racialized experience of birthing, breastfeeding, and letting go as a parent. Mothering is also not equal across difference, nor is the experience of childhood when infantilization and adultification happen simultaneously as a child grows up. Thus, my attention to racialized sexuality in representations continues in my approach to motherhood and childhood, and in my refusal to universalize white experiences of innocence when addressing the experiences of childhoods of color.

Beyond Sex Acts: Sexual and Racial Innocence in Childhoods

While my first book engages the mythic representations of Asian/American women as hypersexual beings, my second book addresses the Hollywood images of Asian/American men as tethered to a straitjacketed definition of sexuality, and the third looks at transnational intimacies between radically unequal subjects across race and sexuality, this book looks at the narrative of growing up within precarity and grief for different kinds of racialized Asian/American sexual identities and capacities.[34] A different form of sexuality emerges in this book as well.

One of Freud's most controversial theories is that from the very beginning, children not only possess sexuality but also invest in their own sexuality. In *Three Essays on the Theory of Sexuality*, he argues that during the latency period children have a polymorphously perverse sexuality that manifests in sucking and touching themselves as forms of self-pleasure.[35]

As we develop and grow, our ability to take pleasure channels, concentrates, and focuses on specific desires that are most often focused on genital sexuality. What happens to the possibility of our polymorphously perverse sexual past in this narrowing? The adultification of these pleasures renders them beyond an innocence that all children possess. When I speak about childhood innocence, I am not referring to children starting out asexually and then becoming sexual or getting pulled into sexuality by adults. I am talking about the social imposition of adult sexuality onto this model of polymorphous perversity. For Freud, there is never a moment when children are not sexual for their own pleasure. For Freud, adults should and can get pleasure from more actions and kinds of people beyond the limits on gender identities and sex acts. When does the narrowing or closing of sexual infinity happen? When kids are forced into heteronormative ways of being and imagining their future sexual selves?

As they grow up, children possess themselves, including their sexuality—which I define as an inkling, a feeling, and an expression of their own desires, wants, and preferences—including a lack of interest in others. However, this does not occur in a vacuum; their racialized and sexualized character informs the meaning of their expression and reception by others. I think of the fourteen-year-old Laotian boy Konerak Sinthasomphone, who, bleeding, distraught, and with a hole drilled into his head, essentially lobotomizing him, fled the apartment building of now infamous serial killer Jeffrey Dahmer. To the horror of Glenda Cleveland and her daughter, among the Black women neighbors standing by attempting to protect the boy, the police believed Konerak to be a consenting adult lover based on the explanation of the white male serial killer, who soon after strangled the boy to death. The policeman later explained, in defending his action, that to his trained eye, he did not see anything improper in handing over the incapacitated brown child to the white, adult man.[36] In this situation, the Southeast Asian boy is overdetermined by fantasies about him, as Eng Beng Lim theorizes in *Brown Boys and Rice Queens: Spellbinding Performances in the Asias* (2013), in a kind of pornographic adultification. Indeed, there is a long transnational history of brown Asian children facing interpellations of, not only interruptions in and disruptions to, their sexualities as they grow into adulthood.[37] The policeman, egregiously uncaring, refused agentic attunement to the child in the face of a calm, white-skinned, blond-haired, and blue-eyed psychopath narrating a different story about the adult status of the Laotian American immigrant child who was clearly suffering, distraught, and in physical pain right there in front of him. An abject subject's pain remained invisible and his future did not matter. Of these differently valued subjectivities, the white male serial killer's prevailed.

What would happen if children of color were granted agentic attunement, the same nurturing and protection typically accorded to white children, so they may fashion their own adulthoods without undue constriction? In her book *Racial Innocence: Performing American Childhood from Slavery to Civil Rights* (2011), historian Robin Bernstein studies popular-culture representations of childhood according to how racial hierarchies impact them. Innocence is afforded to white children, which manifests as an incompatibility with labor and a rightful access to protection from the responsibilities of adulthood. Black children's purported lack of innocence is naturalized as "insensateness," or an inability to feel pain, which justifies their exploitation as adultified forced laborers.[38] In "A Lesson in Moral Spectatorship," philosopher of race and ethics Reid Miller describes how a high school class of predominantly Black children participated in a field trip to see the movie *Schindler's List*. Their responses to the film—laughter, jostling—were rendered inappropriate and used to support the notion that they cannot understand, empathize with, and experience cinematic historical trauma. The ensuing media spectacle following the incident racially constructed the young Black high school children as insensitive to representations of trauma due to their circumstances of poverty and living in what is perceived as the urban slums. Miller writes, "Such ascribed detachment, rather than being unique to this occasion, belongs to a larger depiction of black people as disconnected from the ethical implications of their historical subjugation."[39] Beyond their purported distance from empathizing with their own historical lot or analyzing their own subjugation, they are also presumed to be far from concerned for or analytic about their own freedom. The racialized claim that Black children cannot feel for themselves or for others is constructed in the media as insensitivity, or a lack of a critical perspective regarding their own history of enslavement or aspiration for their own freedom.[40]

Children's pain, according to Bernstein, is directly related to the innate identity their racial subjection affords them. That identity is composed of characterizations of not only their physical abilities and emotional capacities but also their compatibility with freedom itself or morality, in the case of Miller's study. This access to freedom, then, is determined as early as childhood. The process of racialization is the process of justifying whether one can access freedom. Bernstein argues, "To combat the libel of black insensateness, abolitionists showcased the physical, emotional and spiritual suffering of enslaved people. . . . [T]hey based an argument for human rights on the ability to suffer."[41] Extending Bernstein's argument to film studies and the racialization of Asian/American children and young people, *The Movies of Racial Childhoods* investigates contemporary films in the new century that feature childhood as a site where their sovereignty is seized by others, enforcing a lack of freedom evident in their sexualization as adults that I discuss in my previous books. Children's own actions are inflected and impinged upon by structures and forces of not only adult power but also the race, class, and gender that support them—so much so it is not only within representations but also in popular culture and everyday life itself that suffering and pain are not seen and not sensed. They are sidelined for the benefit of others—whether the adults in their lives or children with more racial, gender, and class privilege and cultural citizenship. The well-being of brown children is sacrificed for the comfort of more privileged and heard others.

Racialized childhood is an aggravated site of struggle for self-sovereignty, which I define as confident independence, self-possession, autonomy, and the ability to access self-determination within the context of specific Asian and Asian American narratives. My previous books, like this one, attend to the local, global, and diasporic; the rural and urban; the historic and present as all infusing each other in a vision of a global Asian and Asian American world, reflecting the migrations and movements of people, as well as the relentless questioning of their citizenship in the United States, where they have been for multiple generations.

In this book, I look at the lives of individuals as shaped by historic, political, social, and economic structures, which they also resist and critique even as children. I center their perspective as children in dealing with the imposition of adults on their self-perceptions, including their desires and how they wish to grow up. I am interested in viewing these perspectives as if they were the children's memoirs in the films, or what Diana Taylor calls a "repertoire" of embodied memory, in relation to the "archive" of recorded history, which represents the adult version of the same childhood.[42] I show the entanglement with the young people's interior desires and the external forces that define them in films made by adults that represent racialized and sexualized childhoods. Films that focus on Asian/American children can help us identify the ways in which they do or do not experience nurturing and protection in agentic attunement. And if they experience ambiguous and open-ended narratives that enable them to have freedom and an infinity of possibility, the better for achieving future freedom.

Practicing Agentic Attunement as Filmmakers and Spectators

This book continues my scholarly goal of amplifying the voices of filmmakers of color, characters of color, and performances by actors of color. What is delicate about this new step and new direction is that movies are mostly made by adults, and the representations of children's experiences are limited by recollections or projections over what can be vast amounts of time for the adult authors representing younger people. Thus, our cinematic understanding of childhood and infancy can only be made through inference and assumption, as Kathryn Bond Stockton also theorizes. We are limited in what we can know due to the complexities of representations. For the past twenty years, my books, articles, and films have addressed the complexities of moving images in relation to the problems and politics of sexuality and gender in Asian American and diasporic contexts. The intervention in my work is threefold: I address the power of representation in shaping our social institutions, our interpersonal and group relations, and our intimate self-understandings. Simultaneously, I expose the dangerous lack of diversity in film and media production and in the critical voices that frame our discussions. I look directly and unflinchingly at challenging relations on-screen in order to offer new ways of thinking about and imagining anew our relationships off-screen. Finally, I am invested in the ambiguity of cinematic language to enable an infinity of meanings for subjects of color who have been colonized on film as knowable, secured by the tradition of limited images where people of color are antagonists in relation to white protagonists. As spectators and filmmakers of color, we need access to the inexpressibility of complex experiences that cinema aims to represent (this is what it means to access representation) not simply for visibility, but for how cinema can represent inexpressible things—verbal, aural, or any singular version of the senses.

Representations of childhood are inherently speculative and partial, reflecting an unknowability that should be maintained.[43] Childhood is rendered within the limits of memory not by the people living this important age but by those who may still be affected by their origin stories and seminal memories as adults. What is crucial, too, is whether they have contended with the meanings of their experiences consciously, through agentic attunement, or if these experiences remain unprocessed and confusing, with continuing ramifications for themselves that then appear and continue in their work. This is the dilemma that my book addresses in advocating for conscious engagement, analysis, and interpretation in agentic attunement, to encourage filmmakers and spectators to become agents in their own lives.

From the filmmaker's perspective: in the sense of inference regarding one's own childhood, filmmakers are like the parents of the children they represent on-screen, even if they are making stories about their own childhoods as adults. They parent themselves with agentic attunement in how they study that former self, that earlier self, to make a work that helps our understanding of child subjectivity. I am also referring to the particular directorial process wherein the adult works with an actual child (or an adult who looks like a child) to create motivation, to mobilize meaning through the actor's emotion, and in the screenwriting process of creating scenarios to communicate a child's perspective. As a recuperative act from the perspective of adult authorship, it is a sensitive space wherein exploitation of the child can occur while the adult works to make sense of one's development, as an act of looking back and making sense of memory. This act is complicated; without the work of undoing power, harm can be reenacted. And without the acknowledgment of power in this directorial relationship, abuse can too easily take place and traumas be revived. My task is to distinguish what the filmmakers are able to capture in their representations of children—not only how they define childhood as both always already racialized and sexualized but especially in relation to adultification, or their premature assignation as "grown up," in the sense of responsibility and desire. I am interested in how the filmmaker, in practicing agentic attunement, can help viewers consciously unlearn lessons from childhood that form adults who are unable to thrive and lead healthy lives.

From the spectator's perspective: too many times we see those who have lived through brutality in their childhood justifying it—I am fine, I survived—versus engaging with it through agentic attunement, whereby they identify and confront it in order to undo or redirect it. In avoiding the potentiality of redefining the suffering, it gets reenacted and repeated as natural and inevitable. Rather than listen to the disciplining adult, we should center the experience of that discipline from the child's perspective. What did it feel like to be punished? Then, through agentic attunement, we see that unfairness as changeable.

A child's racial, sexual, and other senses of their individuality are psychic and physical realities that they own, even when they are imposed on them by others in our shared social worlds—filmmakers, viewers, and adults alike—in specific historical and political contexts. As a person grows, they experience in their childhood the development of desires that meet a transformative series of impositions, including rules of the home, intimate relations not immune to structural power dynamics, or external forces of social life that often disregard children's understandings of their own bodies and identities. When adults take over, they can interrupt and impose, then reshape, redirect, and even traumatize. I pay attention to this process as part of a larger vision that understands how childhood experiences can curtail development in damaging ways that can extend far into adulthood. The coming-of-age that occurs in childhood and adolescence is crucial to the development of an adult self who aspires high, dreams big, encounters disappointments, experiences punishments, and forges ways of coping and living. Agentic attunement to movies, from the spectator's perspective, can show us better ways of understanding our racialized and sexualized childhoods and our adult selves.

When movies represent children, the phenomenological response of caring spectators concerned for the welfare of children and our spectatorial relationship to childhood itself are powerfully exposed. Reflecting on one's own childhood involves, according to Freud, "the distortion and refurbishing to which a person's own past is subjected when it is looked back upon from a later period."[44] Utilizing that construction of childhood, even one's own, serves as a way to narrate differently one's past experiences depending on one's priorities now. While I do not conduct childhood biographies of filmmakers, I do consider how they construct childhood as adults—privileging the child's perspective—and acknowledge how we as adults perceive that experience, both as makers and spectators, in limited ways. What we know of or learn about children in movies is already so narrow.

There is an immense filmography that renders white childhoods visible, from François Truffaut's *The 400 Blows* (1959) to Wes Anderson's *The Royal Tenenbaums* (2001) and Richard Linklater's *Boyhood* (2014). The lives of the filmmakers—white men—do figure in a mythical way in the making of these films. Truffaut's film is somewhat autobiographical, and his direction of the young actor Jean-Pierre Léaud spans several years and several films. Wes Anderson exemplifies a white boy-wonder filmmaker whose unmarked whiteness—where white racialization is unacknowledged, in the sense of Ruth Frankenberg's notion of whiteness as default American-ness—of filmmaking and film subjects has warranted critique.[45] Similarly, Richard Linklater spent twelve years making a film in Texas about a young boy, located in a place that is not and never has been so white or, as *Los Angeles Times* columnist Amy Kaufman argues, lacking in Latinx people, and where the single one who speaks is rendered as one in need of saving. This book won't continue that universalizing of childhood as white, as it never was in the first place. Like Frankenberg, I approach race as a "process" rather than a "thing" that is involved in parenting and other acts, identities, and behaviors in film and culture.[46]

Filmmakers do figure in their film authorships, but not as much as they should in the conversation about their films and their filmmaking—especially in terms of the assumption of whiteness they propagate. I have discussed the importance of acknowledging whiteness in my previous scholarship and ask filmmakers to imagine spectators encountering their work for the first time.[47] How does their work rebut, reshape, and reimagine the spectatorial relationship to children as well as the psychic tie between the filmmaker and the children they represent, without an acknowledgment of whiteness or the racial context in which one grows up as white? Why does whiteness remain unmarked, and what are the consequences, not just for how nonwhites are spoken for but in exposing the factual privileges of whiteness? In this cinematic act of recollecting childhood with agentic attunement, we can read and analyze the formation of identity then and now as undeniably raced—and in ways that shape sex, sexuality, and other aspects of growing up.

Film and Psychoanalysis: Externalizing the Internal

The creative writing focused on Asian American childhood sexualities is robust and unafraid to confront the impositions that impede self-sovereignty, sexual self-definition, and autonomy, such as in the award-winning work of Jessica Hagedorn in *Pet Food and Tropical Apparitions* (1981), which embraces fantastic practices deemed perverse for her immigrant Filipinx teen protagonist; Evelyn Lau in *Runaway: Diary of a Street Kid* (1989), which includes the relentless policing of the Chinese Canadian female body, childhood rape, and men's continual assumption of racialized sexual availability even if there is none; R. Zamora Linmark in *Rolling the R's* (1997), which presents a bullied adolescent who exerts control over his own body, accompanied by his friends, who also contend with sexual forces and social structures as they forge their own self-understandings in their Filipinx Hawaiian community; Jhumpa Lahiri in *The Namesake* (2003), which chronicles an Indian American immigrant community's investment in individual sexual desire from childhood to adulthood; and Ocean Vuong in *On Earth We're Briefly Gorgeous* (2021) and Anthony Veasna So in *Afterparties* (2021), in which scenes of sexual exploration and exploitation abound in Vietnamese and Cambodian American refugee communities in Hartford, Connecticut, and Stockton, California, respectively. These works include exploring one's bodies and psyches for carnal and drug-induced pleasures, pursuing pleasure from disapproved bodies and desires, confusion about the intersection of race and sex in terms of interracial desire, and abuse by elders that leads to a persistently vexing understanding of adults and even family.

Unlike fiction and nonfiction on paper, the fictional moving-image representations of Asian and Asian American childhoods that I study physically enact these scenes through the visual language composed by many components—cinematography and production design, including costume and sets; the sonic language of the musical score; sound design; rerecording and mixing; and the performances of the cast—rather than through description in the written form by a single author. The direction of intimate scenes requires not only the choreography of bodies and expressions but also an engagement of real people's histories of sexuality as they physically entangle on-screen—for actors, indeed, and for the screenwriters, directors, and others involved in the storytelling. Harm can occur if we do not acknowledge the power of sexuality when performing. Part of film's power is its ability to conjure our own sexual histories in our performance, interpretation, and consumption of the sexual acts and sexual lives depicted on-screen. Psychoanalysis lends itself well to the medium due to the way it externalizes the internal life.

In my use of psychoanalytic concepts, race is intrinsic to and inseparable from sexual identity and experience. Race—along with its visual manifestation and marking—acts as a social force that structures sexuality and grief in representation, too. I delve into how filmmakers represent racialized childhood within contexts and structures that shape various experiences, including mourning, loss, and connection, specifically in terms of the child's sovereignty and self-governance. I examine the development of the self by reading the emotional and sensational conflagration captured in psychoanalytic vocabulary. As I begin to develop these ideas, all four investigatory sites of psychoanalysis—instincts and drives; ego, id, and super ego; object relations; and self-experience or self psychology—are useful.

Expanding from Freudian instinct and drive, other schools of psychoanalysis formed to explain the variety of human functions—how individual psychologies work in terms of seeking gratification, repeating particular relationships or patterns of the self squarely and undeniably within a larger relational field. Because I am interested in childhoods, I am thus employing the psychoanalytic areas that develop out of infant and child observation to show us how the self is socially and historically situated, such as in object relations theory and self psychology. I am particularly interested in how they illuminate the medium of film, as it is invested in conveying the inner life of its subjects but through a language of world-making that involves social structures and historical realities—not as part of the self's drives and urges toward the goal of gratification but as an ongoing relationality in the world as one constantly works to determine the parameters of the self in seeking empowerment.

Object relations theory, formed by psychoanalysts including Ronald Fairbairn and Melanie Klein, aimed to bring together, through studies of the mother-child relationship, the primacy of the object as the goal of satisfaction, or the role of internalized objects in the making of oneself or "internal mental representations of self and other."[48] Object relations theory, then, is about how the individual develops an internal representation of oneself through objects, which then shapes how one relates to the world, in a pattern of repetition based on the internalization of objects, whether good or bad. Psychoanalyst and pediatrician D. W. Winnicott, in the 1920s through the 1960s, and psychoanalyst Heinz Kohut, in the 1960s and 1970s, working through the mother-infant relationship, formed influential ideas about the self in relation to other psyches and other objects in self-experience and self psychology. They were both invested in the formation of healthy selves into adulthood through their studies of the psychoanalysis of childhoods.

Winnicott develops the notion of the true self and the false self. He says that when the child's needs are not met as an infant, their authentic self is compromised toward a more destructive and defensive false self, versus a more creative, present, and responsive true self, which both matter in adult development. Their original expression of need is "replaced by actions of the child that are meant to accommodate to the world, at the expense of inner expression—the beginnings of a 'false self.'"[49] At this early stage, the environment clearly influences the expression of one's innate urges and disciplines or enables them to blossom. Heinz Kohut's self psychology emphasizes how the development of the self is very dependent on experiences with others and within the context of how the "environment we choose and create for ourselves altogether, [is] very much influenced by who we are, by our central motives and mechanisms."[50] I appreciate all of these psychoanalytic contributions from Freud to Kohut because they are interrelated and depend on each other while emphasizing different functions within an individual's complex self-formation, from narcissism to attachment. I emphasize the importance of object relations and self psychology for two reasons: the relational aspects that determine personality outside of drives (bigger than drives in that the attachment to the object is a thing throughout life) and the focus on the development and maintenance of the self and narcissism that were not so prominent in Freud.

We are not independent of each other or the objects we rely on. This was made so undeniably clear to me during the COVID-19 global pandemic, when we had to be alone with ourselves so much more. The relations with others that we could not have as intensely during shelter-in-place restrictions were revealed to be so truly satisfying and so necessary. And this to me affirms why I make films and read, analyze, and write about films like an addict. I make nonfiction films based on family and historical archives, while I teach narrative film. In both fiction and nonfiction forms, films aim to express emotions and the internal life, the psychic life, which, as we know when we storyboard or dissect films, require relationships, actions, objects, and settings. Thus, object relations illuminate the unique power of cinema to externalize physically the internal psychic life in order to reach others. What is fascinating about the focus on the self, or narcissism, in relation to objects is how one undergoes a process of self-centering in growing up: what does one keep and take away, what does one focus on and what does one let go in forging the adult self? This is my interpretation-of-inventory method that agentic attunement recommends.

In object relations and self psychology, Fairbairn, Klein, Winnicott, and Kohut theorize childhood, but not the role of race in it. In this book, I fill that gap by paying attention to the psychic and physical realities of children's racialized sexuality and grief, and I use close readings of Asian American childhood representations in film to interrogate how they work together. I build further from the theorists of psychoanalysis to better understand how film can advance their work—and do what only film can do—in the relationships that can be seen, felt, and experienced by spectators who then absorb and learn from the movies.[51] My close readings aim to detect, reflect on, and receive instinct, drives, ego, objects, and self in the lives of racialized childhoods and mourning presented in the movies. Race and racial experience provide the ground for my analysis of these internal forces of identity that are shaped by historical and cultural context.

My work as a feminist Asian Americanist scholar and filmmaker aligns with other theorists of color in dialogue with Freud and other principal thinkers of psychoanalysis. Contending with the imbrication of race and sexuality in subjectivity, race and psychoanalysis scholars include David Eng and Shinhee Han in *Racial Melancholia, Racial Disassociation*, who theorize loss for Asian Americans in the experience of immigration and assimilation. The engagement with race and psychoanalysis substantially arose with the publication of Hortense Spillers's classic essay "Mama's Baby, Papa's Maybe: An American Grammar Book," along with works that helped to establish the field, such as Christopher Lane's *The Psychoanalysis of Race: An Introduction*, Anne Anlin Cheng's *The Melancholy of Race*, and Kalpana Seshadri-Crooks's *Desiring Whiteness*. Through their examination of psychoanalysis and postcoloniality, the pioneering works of Frantz Fanon in *Black Skin, White Masks*; Anne McClintock in *Imperial Leather: Race, Gender and Sexuality in the Colonial Conquest*; Homi Bhabha in *The Location of Culture*; and Dina Al-Kassim in *On Pain of Speech* help us to understand the deep imprint of colonialism in the psychic life of the subjugator and the subjugated and the persistent framings of the dark interior as colonized by whiteness. White feminist scholars Teresa de Lauretis and Kaja Silverman in several field-defining books;[52] Jean Walton in *Fair Sex, Savage Dreams*; Jessica Benjamin in *The Bonds of Love*; Jane Gallop in *The Daughter's Seduction: Feminism and Psychoanalysis*; Elisabeth Young-Breuhl in *Mind and the Body Politic*; and Ann Pellegrini in *Performance Anxieties: Staging Psychoanalysis, Staging Race* have interrogated whiteness and the problematic rendering of race in psychoanalysis through their study of various objects in popular culture. I stand on their shoulders in expanding psychoanalytic inquiry to the sites of Asian American sexualized and bereaved childhoods.

Methodologically, I understand representations of childhood sexualities and grieving as cases, where subjects have histories and memories that inform their actions, which may be repetitive over time, in relation to the self and in its relations to others and to objects. I practice agentic attunement on films that contain arguments their authors make about how to interpret the protagonists' actions, whether they are informed by consciousness, unconsciousness, fantasy, and/or desire—within a life, a context, and a story. Spectators practicing agentic attunement, too, bring these to bear on their own experiences of childhood that inform their comprehension of and engagement with films. People relate to others and to objects shaping their self-perception and their attendant feelings. What happens to children whose ownership of their own bodies is undermined and organized by adults and authority should be a concern for all of us, as should the specificity of their racialized experiences.

As with my other work, here I maintain a consistent focus on the imbrication of Asia and America in Asian/American objects and subjects. With this book, I intend to make the wide range of subjectivities living under the label Asian American more visible and much more accounted for in critical inquiry, while identifying the continuing tensions between Asia and America that impact the subjects in these films. Finally, I turn to psychoanalysis not only for sexuality studies but also because trauma from death organizes the lives of most of the children in these films. The grief infusing all of these stories also necessitates it.

Trauma and Care: Race and Sexuality in Bereaved Childhoods

The body experiences and retains childhood trauma in ways that the adult may not know and in ways others are unable to see. Yet trauma is a compendium of what is both seen and unseen. Movies have shown us that trauma is visible on the body. Bessel van der Kolk tells us that in 1941, "The new technology of motion pictures made it possible to film . . . the physical, embodied expression of trauma," which he defines as "a memory that is inscribed simultaneously in the mind as interior images, and words, and on the body."[53] We must address the sight of trauma for the good of the person and for the good of society, he argues.[54] Individually, disassociation or dissociation with suffering and neglect or other abuses can lead adults to disconnect from their bodies, resulting in lives that are still perpetually alert to the danger and the damage of what they experienced. Dissociation is more commonly named as a response following trauma. Disassociation here would mean that the individual separates themselves/severs the association from suffering, neglect, and abuse, and that leads to disconnection. Dissociation is when one experiences suffering, neglect, and abuse that leads to disconnection. More recently, in *What My Bones*

Know, journalist Stephanie Foo explores how to emerge healthily from complex post-traumatic stress disorder by confronting one's experiences.

My concept of agentic attunement makes visible this disconnection of adult problems from childhood trauma so that we see how films can offer lessons on how to live, and live more healthily, with a stronger sense of self emerging from experiences of damage and abuse. For depleted and disparaged subjects, asserting a kind of grandiose self can be a step in the process of developing a lifesaving, healthy narcissism. Narcissism is not pathological, as discussed in earlier psychoanalysis, but can be critical to survival, according to psychoanalyst Heinz Kohut. Disconnected from oneself, the adult is fragmented and unable to feel and achieve happiness or peace unless the psyche and the body are addressed. Dissociating—a defense rendering one unable to remember traumas—can be harmful to self and society, too, because inequality cannot be addressed or changed if it is not acknowledged. When filmmakers take us to these sites, they can help us sense and approach trauma so that we, as viewers, practice agentic attunement to acknowledge, feel, and bear what we see and detect when someone is traumatized; in turn, we use film to attend to and understand our own questions about trauma.

The embodiment of grief and trauma lives in an ongoing manner. I birthed my younger son, whose life was extinguished: I recall his body as his life left him—that is what the monitors showed in the emergency room. Upon our arrival at the emergency room, there was a 10 percent chance of survival, said the doctor, then suddenly there was none. He was not sick; a common virus attacked his heart, and within twenty-four hours he died suddenly; the last twenty minutes were catastrophic. I can still hear his voice, telling me everything in his body hurts. It is the same voice I recall asking me about his double front teeth being rare; or having to wear a retainer; or to use crutches after an injury: it gave him pleasure to be special, like how he loved having solos in school musical performances. When his extra row of front teeth was found in X-rays, I was supposed to pay attention to it every day and alert the dentist if I noticed any coming in. We checked together every night before bed. No longer. Suddenly. I hear his voice now asking me if his death was rare, too. *A rare catastrophe*, I mouth. I recall his mole to the left of his left eye. The very muscular weight of his body when he sat on my lap after dinner every night. How he loved brown lentils and also egg whites, noting that when his dad cooked them, however, they were yellow. The way he controlled his body hanging upside down from the monkey bars in any playground to the concern of the caregivers all around. The robust, inventive dancing that inspired others to watch or join. The creative piano and drum playing that compelled his teacher to come up with new methods. The way he would challenge her with composition contests on either instrument. His last words in that sweet voice: "Everything hurts." How could it be? The body missing from mine is tied to my grief in a way that I feel as a severance of my own body from me, or of me. This is why we must address trauma through bodily experience, to surrender to the pain of his missing and to acknowledge the pain of his undergoing death. Trauma is embodied!

While such scenarios of trauma and sexuality—for both adults and children—are easily assumed to be private, quiet, and closed, they are still social and essentially open, public moments because they are intensely gendered, raced, and classed. I unify my life as a working woman of color who leads and serves at a high level in a prominent position and as a grieving mother, each life informing the other. Each identity is very present in the other, determines the other. The suffering I feel enables my empathy. These situations of mothering and of children growing up—thriving, and in the rare case of my younger child, the sudden death—make us conscious of being intensely alive in the world. Whether it is class or other social forces that organize the experience of life and the aftermath of death, in the grief too, the unconscious becomes aware of itself through the object of love in both the lost and living child. In agentic attunement, I aim for my attention to grief, sexuality, race, and class to make these experiences come to the fore to understand how childhood is situated in the social world. In this way, I write this book as a mother-author-spectator with the view of caring for children's lives through the movies.

From my perspective, spectatorship and critique are intertwined as a caring vision of agentic attunement; this includes feeling the impact of seeing harm and identifying how particular acts and interactions on-screen shape lives in the aftermath of the moment. In my reading and writing for the reader, I am a mother, not in the censorial and moralistic sense of policing responses, but in caring for the well-being of the filmmaker, the character, and the spectator. They are embodiments of how to live. Similarly, entanglements between individual desire and social context arise beyond infantile relations with the mother. Representations of adolescent sexuality—as a blooming and burgeoning awareness of desire in growing up, including all aspects of the psychic, social, and physical—make clear that it is an encounter between drives, instincts, and feelings as both individual and social. Thus, coming-of-age sexuality and racial identity in the movies show how individual experiences help us understand the power of the structural in whatever the sites may be. And the presence of death, whether of the parent or fear of one's own in the child, reveals the abundance of the social forces that determine lives every day.

The Cinematic Case Histories

The films I study span US and Asian cities and suburbs, rural and urban areas, including an unnamed rural town in Arkansas, San Diego, the Bay Area, Minneapolis, Chicago, Miami, and the provinces of the Philippines; Koreatown in Los Angeles and a town in upstate New York; the city of Manila in the Philippines; an unnamed town in rural Texas; Sherman Oaks, California; Portland, Oregon; the Hamptons in New York; Orlando, Florida; and a fictionalized rural area in the Pacific Northwest of the United States. This global set of movies representing the intimacies of childhood shows the centrality of context to the focus I place on intimate encounters in my book. These films also include a wide range of sexualities and grief as the subjects on-screen encounter social discipline and death. I employ Freud's case histories approach, in which he treats sexuality with an unflinching precision, whether in naming sex acts or exploring questions about desire. This is another method that I uniquely deploy in addressing childhood sexuality beyond sex acts—I do so to illuminate the wide range of their cinematic lives as we encounter them as spectators.

In chapter 1, "A Deluge of Delusions and Lies: Race, Sex, and Class in *American Crime Story: The Assassination of Gianni Versace*," I begin with the coming-of-age story of a young, mixed-race, Filipino-Italian American man who grew up to become the notorious "gay serial killer," as depicted in *American Crime Story: The Assassination of Gianni Versace* (2018). The popular episodic miniseries on Netflix by Ryan Murphy presents the life of Andrew Cunanan, one of very few Filipino Americans to be represented on American screens. He became infamous for a criminal killing spree that culminated in his murder of a famous gay icon, Italian American fashion designer Gianni Versace. In this opening chapter, I focus on the creative drive of lying that structures Andrew Cunanan's life—one that is tied to the experience of his disparagement by social forces judging race and sexuality. I explore the racial narrative of the miniseries that is primarily organized by sexual identity and the gay life, pressures, and problems gay men face due to the heteronormativity driving their lives.

This force is inseparable from Cunanan's mixed-race interpellation that shapes him. The film presents how we cannot ignore heritage, history, and racialization in the development of identity, aspirations, and delusions.

Cunanan's was a life of lying rooted in childhood sexual trauma deeply imbricated with race and class. I use these lenses to understand the representations of childhood sexuality in the film and the way these experiences haunt his brown mixed body, precarious adulthood, and gay sexuality. The theorizations of the false self by psychoanalyst D. W. Winnicott help me unpack the trauma of Cunanan's racialized life and the carnage he left in his wake. I use object relations theory to make sense of the relations and spaces in all the films I study in this book, especially the role of selfobjects from self psychology. I focus on selfobjects as part of my approach to emphasize psychological interdependence on others in the affirmation of self, and I practice agentic attunement in parsing out the life he could have led. In particular, the parent as caregiver is critical to the formation of self-esteem. Cunanan's experience of distrust and the distortion of that parental relation contributed to his exceedingly fragmented self, which ultimately killed others unwilling to cooperate with his lies.

Chapter 2, "The Inner Life of Cinema and Selfobjects: Queer Asian American Youth in *Spa Night* and *Driveways*," studies Korean American director Andrew Ahn's two feature films, both focused on queer Asian American youth and the dependence on others—peers and parents both—in defining and understanding a healthy self. Growing up in Koreatown in Los Angeles, a young Korean American man is disenfranchised from the narrative of the Asian American model-minority path of going to a selective college and pursuing upward mobility. In veering off this path, he experiences fragmentation with his body that he addresses by running in the neighborhood, endlessly working on his fitness, and tirelessly working for his family in the ethnic enclave of Koreatown. To resolve the disconnection that results from psychic fragmentation, he connects with his body anew in the sweaty physical release that he experiences in the streets and ultimately at the gay spa where he works. He explores his sexuality in an iconic site of queer representation, the gay bathhouse, which is owned and run by Koreans. This sexual search for the self is tied to his Korean heritage, showing the entanglement of race and queer sexuality.

I study Andrew Ahn's work as a rare and prominent queer Asian American author who focuses his first two feature films precisely on the parent-child relationship and the social world of the child in forming the young self. In both, loss and mourning inform their growing up, whether through the loss of a recognizable path of the model minority in class demise and the failure of the father due to alcoholism in *Spa Night* or mourning the fragmented family in *Driveways*. While *Spa Night* features a young adult, *Driveways*, Ahn's sophomore film, tells the story of an eight-year-old child, the same age as Lakas when he died. The young boy is nurtured by the various experiences with the self, the boy's mother, and the boy's new friend, an older Korean War veteran next door. Their unconditional love encourages an agentic attunement to the self and an achievement of equanimity for the queer child.

In chapter 3, "Adolescent Curiosity and Mourning: *The Blossoming of Maximo Oliveros*," a young genderqueer Filipinx youth named Maximo or Maxie may be a boy, a girl, or in between the polarities of the gender binary. Their father and brothers, known criminals in their neighborhood slum, love and protect Maxie, who takes on the feminized role of cooking and cleaning their home after their mother dies. But after aligning with a policeman who seeks to arrest their family, Maxie experiences the threat of fragmenting their family in pursuing their feelings and concretizing them through action. This film is extraordinary for privileging the child's perspective and their desire, and it avoids the way in which certain bodies are treated in American cinema—where violence befalls those who present as genderqueer. The film exposes what we can learn from global cinema in terms of children's sexual self-sovereignty.

Because this is not a film about coming out, sexuality is not the primary social category of queer experience in Maxie's development. What this allows me to do, then, is to situate sexuality as part of a larger set of formative feelings and experiences, specifically mourning and grief. Poverty is also part of the larger context, as the development of the child occurs on a path toward criminality, not as something to which they are intrinsically prone but as the direction available to them, as encouraged by the adults in their life. This limited choice is contextualized by the family's extreme lack of resources as poor people in the Global South. Maxie's pursuit of a different life may be seen as a sexual one, due to the primacy of sex in defining queerness. In this film, however, we see different kinds of queer desires. And while erotic attachment is not denied, it is the broader life path that includes sexual desire, mourning, and poverty in childhood development that influences our agentic attunement.

In looking at the film through the lens of object relations, particularly in the work of Melanie Klein, we can see how the child's feelings exceed sexual instincts and aim to include romance, loyalty, envy, and grief. Thus, the interpersonal relationships must be examined for how they construct the protagonist and how we construct them as spectators. Object relations theory helps us to understand the stakes and vulnerabilities Maxie faces. Even more stunning is how this rich film about the intersection of youth, sexuality, grief, and poverty has not yet received significant attention in academic scholarship. The film explodes the genre of the coming-out film, and it deserves more consideration.

Chapter 4, "The Courage to Compose Oneself: Healthy Narcissism and Self-Sovereignty in *Yellow Rose*," studies first-time feature filmmaker and Filipina American immigrant Diane Paragas's focus on the life of Rose, an undocumented Filipina American teen who dreams of pursuing a country music career while growing up in rural Texas. Her dreams are interrupted when her mother is arrested and deported by US Immigration and Customs Enforcement. The film was produced and released while former president Donald J. Trump was in office, a time when discourses and occurrences of anti-Asian hate were on the rise, as were raids and deportations. Featuring a stellar multigenerational cast of Filipina and Filipina American actors, including Broadway star Eva Noblezada as Rose, award-winning Philippine film and television actress Princess Punzalan, and iconic transnational film and theater star Lea Salonga, the film captures the trauma of being undocumented and the precarity of youth when parents are unable to care for them. We trace how the family—parents, extended relatives, and children—make their way within institutions such as the immigration system, undocumented work, poverty, and in the encounter with others—Chicanx and white people in Texas—across the racial divide. I dissect the relationship between Rose and her mom, who attempts to mother across the carceral divide; Rose and her mother's sister—who won't give her niece a safe place to stay out of loyalty to her white husband; Rose and her relationship with adults/strangers who attempt to help prevent her from being deported; and, finally, her relationship to music as an allegory for the wish to be free from constraint. The film's director, Diane Paragas, grew up in Lubbock, Texas, a town about five hours from a major airport, as the only Filipina American girl for miles around, after immigrating there from the Philippines at age four. She asks, how will country music enable the freedom of this Filipina American immigrant girl?

Self psychology situates my exploration of Rose's psychic life within social and structural relations. Through not only music but also the self-confidence that it requires, Rose is able to forge and maintain a healthy self in light of the powerful structural forces that situate and shape her life and her mother's. They live undocumented in a hostile state, within a nation that separates mother and child. Music functions as a selfobject for Rose and is pivotal in helping her form positive self-regard. We see that she may have no path to citizenship, but through music, she makes an argument about cultural citizenship and the importance of developing healthy narcissism and a powerful, individual self who asserts not only belonging but also authorship and creativity in an unwelcome place of potential incarceration and deportation.

The final chapter, "The Unexpected and the Unforeseen: Cultural Complexes in *The Half of It*," filmmaker Alice Wu's story about Ellie Chu, a young immigrant Chinese American girl and the sole Asian American in her school, is located in present-day rural Washington State. Living in an apartment above a train depot, she remains stuck at home with her non-English-speaking and grieving immigrant Chinese father, whom she must help navigate adult pressures such as paying the bills and with his job as a station master. She is grieving, too, the loss of her fun mother. Her world, however, is largely determined by her relationships with her peers. A classmate, Paul Munsky, a gentle, white jock, pays her to write love letters to a gorgeous though poor Latinx classmate, Aster Flores, with whom Ellie Chu is also in love. Letters and texts convey the psychic power of love, intimacy, and desire, while they also become a way to navigate the various cultural complexes of their worlds. When Ellie and Aster meet in person, the act of listening to music and feeling the sensations of sound while immersed in water depict the cerebral dimensions of intimacy and interconnectedness, expanding our definition of adolescent sexuality beyond the act of touching bodies, in a direct challenge to hookup culture that defines young people today. In this chapter, I conclude the book by engaging the psychoanalytic concept of cultural complexes to identify the cultural, social, and collective constraints in fashioning self-sovereignty in the life of youth. I also show how film in particular can intervene through agentic attunement and provide instructions for how to use culture to explode archetypes that bind.

How may we learn from movies to nurture Asian American young people who seek and deserve care? As filmmakers and spectators, how may we care for our inner child through our engagement with movies? *The Movies of Racial Childhoods: Screening Self-Sovereignty in Asian/America* asserts the importance of representations of childhood development in Asian/American independent film with particular attention to grief and loss within the contexts of race, gender, sexuality, and poverty. The films I study dramatize Asian/American children and young people's struggles in growing up within times and spaces of precarity and even impecunity. Within this context, the films focus on the child's achievement of self-sovereignty—their freedom, self-determination, self-ownership, and autonomy are nothing less than empowering.

I utilize psychoanalysis, in particular object relations and self psychology, to survey the vulnerabilities and alienations haunting the lives of children and young people in ways that exceed melancholia, devastation, and pessimism. Instead, I seek the ways independent filmmakers present traumatized subjects achieving peace in learnings, community-building, and even healthy narcissisms that serve as balms, salves, and inspirations for spectators. The films I study capture a world no longer hidden in plain sight in their focus on young subjects of color. We already live in a world where more than half the young people under age eighteen in the United States are people of color. These films project that future of a people of color majority in the United States. In this book, I hope for empathetic understanding of Asian/American childhoods that we too rarely experience in the movies and especially to feel them achieve self-cohesion and confidence in a world still committed to their perpetual management as racialized, sexualized, and classed subjects. Films harm us. They can also free us.

1   A Deluge of Delusions and Lies

RACE, SEX, AND CLASS IN *AMERICAN CRIME STORY:*
THE ASSASSINATION OF GIANNI VERSACE

When I immigrated in 1983 as a teenager from a privileged life, with a home and household staff in the Philippines, I became brown and poor in the United States. With my family, I lived in Rindge Towers, the brick high-rise projects in Cambridge, Massachusetts. The projects consisted of three tall, twenty-two-story buildings at the edge of town; mine overlooked the freeway. A hill from the parking lot led to the sidewalk of the freeway bridge, and starting at age fourteen, I walked along it by myself at 4:00 a.m. on weekends to my job at Dunkin' Donuts. I needed to work to help my family; otherwise there would be less food and nothing to serve it in. With their parents, my friends from high school would visit me at work to buy doughnuts later in the day after they had slept in, when I had already been awake for hours. Sometimes I would visit their homes after work or after school. The act of getting there on my own and spending time with my friends felt so American in its freedom, independence, and mobility, in contradistinction to my actual American living in financial and spatial constraint, in a reality I did not see in the movies. The setting of my teen life was a cramped, two-bedroom, one-bath apartment on the seventh floor crowded with my six siblings, two parents, one grandma, and several immigrant families who stayed with us for many months from time to time. This is a global mapping of race and class that I understand, where in the Philippines my own family had employed less privileged others and crammed them into a much smaller space within our larger space and paid them little.

Thirty years since I lived there, I took my Californian kids to see the building where I lived in Massachusetts as a teen. As I looked up at its twenty-two stories at age forty-three, my eyes poured out tears, even if my face was not crying. Something inside remembered the depth of the hardship. My body remembered the tension, the discomfort, and the cramping of life there. I recall doing laundry for my family by myself while a big old man stared at me the whole time, walking by the hallway repeatedly, a glass window between us. My friends' homes were modern, Cape Cod or Victorian mansions with big, bright windows on the swanky side of town or on the Harvard campus itself, or contemporary townhouses with their interior walls made of glass blocks (the latest thing!) on pretty, tree-lined streets, walkable to restaurants and cafés. In all these homes, they had their own rooms, some with skylights, their own bathrooms, or very high princess beds. I could not reciprocate gifts they gave me at Christmas. And I was perplexed, since I could not fathom how they had disposable funds for the extravagance of colorful cookies in a tin. The cookies were decorated in various ways with sprinkles that to me represented so much disposable income from kids who did not work and, thus, another life altogether. They gave me a glimpse into a future where I could perhaps afford those things; they were my friends who enjoyed spending time with me and visited our apartment without flinching.

Working hard at school was a way out of poverty for me, though not just for economic mobility. It was the analysis I learned to do, exploding my rigid Philippine school habits of orderly memorization and docile repetition, instead awakening to creative analysis and argumentation. The curriculum, the public library within the campus, the student groups and activities, and the teachers stimulated me with the bounty of learning, so many books and ideas and so much beauty in literature and art, in direct contrast to the scarcity in my life, the lack of food, and the perpetual absence of my parents, who each worked two jobs. My teachers and classmates were curious about the Philippines at the time of People Power, so I regaled them with stories of growing up under martial law and the lack of a free press. It was truly revelatory for me in the United States when I saw the *Nightline* cameras go behind the concrete facades of Imelda Marcos's projects in Manila to show the cardboard shacks propped up behind them.

In my actual life, though, I was embarrassed about my situation and mostly quiet. I needed coupons to buy lunch at school. Did my friends have homemade lunch from home? I don't recall them waiting in the line for the strange gray burgers. School, in its spaciousness and modern architecture of soaring ceilings, was a place of mind-expanding freedom-making and abundant possibility for me even if I may have been considered an undesirable friend by rich parents. I felt the dawning of a kind of freedom and mobility as I became competitive for college.

Eventually, too, my education taught me about structures of inequality that helped me understand my situation. I learned that I was immigrant low-wage labor and that my friends benefited from the wealth of not needing to work or, for those who had it, from white privilege itself. Eventually, as I scaled elite institutions, I learned the value of my struggles connecting me to others. As a teen, I enjoyed telling my community about my old life of privilege in the Philippines, which got more lavish with the distance of space and time. As I lived it, I wanted to unsee and unfeel my impecunity and meagerness. I am sure they smelled it. I had cockroaches crawling out of my bag in Advanced Placement English.

In this context, in this life where so few, if barely any, Filipinx are seen or our stories represented on-screen, I examine the life of the "gay serial killer," the mixed-race Filipino American Andrew Cunanan portrayed by the mixed-race television heartthrob Darren Criss in the miniseries. The representation of Cunanan's life in *The Assassination of Gianni Versace*, the celebrated television series, is structured by the lies he arrayed to impress others. I wonder if the difference in his life—the suffering, the trauma, and his enduring it, rather than the lies he deployed to hide the details of his struggle—would have led to empathy from others. He did not believe it. Learning to recognize the structural forces that act upon him rather than internalizing them as truths—racial inferiority, poverty as queer perversity—hurt him, rather than healed him. He then hurt others.

Podcast producer and *New York Times* best-selling writer Stephanie Foo identifies standing at the crossroads of choosing to unlearn her parents' abuse. She chose to follow a different path from her complex post-traumatic stress disorder as one where she recognizes in herself the "famous line about trauma: *Hurt people hurt people*. I didn't want to hurt people anymore."[1] Andrew Cunanan, who killed five people brutally, did not learn to or wish to undo the hurt and harm inflicted upon him in his childhood, choosing instead to continue what he knew and experienced: lying to oneself as flight from oneself. He turned toward repeating his parents' methods of destruction, validating their disregard of him, and as such, he turned away from a better, harder, and more redemptive path for himself and turned toward destroying others instead.

In this chapter, I explore how the television series shows Cunanan as choosing to lead a life of lies in order to create an alternative universe that regrettably others would find intolerable, most of all himself. That fabricated world was punctured and exploded by the traumatic memories his body held: the possibility of pedophilic incest, the shame of poverty, and the raging racialized inferiority internalized by his father who passed it on. While the episodic series, made primarily by white male filmmakers, presents sexuality as the primary category of Cunanan's social experience, it also looks through the lenses of race and class. I understand the representations of his childhood sexuality in the film to be intensely racialized, and I examine the way these experiences haunted Cunanan's psyche, brown mixed body, precarious adulthood, and gay sexuality. I use the two theorizations of the false self and the good mother by psychoanalyst D. W. Winnicott to help me unpack the trauma of Cunanan's racialized life, which included class and classed dynamics. Race and class are so tightly tied to his sexuality that identifying this intertwining helps us understand how lies and lying fabricated for him a world he wished for. The world he chose to live in needed witnesses and collaborators to validate him. Those he was intimate with refused to help him cultivate an unhealthy self, and so he brutally killed them. The episodic miniseries, based on journalist Maureen Orth's best-selling book *Vulgar Favors: Andrew Cunanan, Gianni Versace, and the Largest Failed Manhunt in U.S. History* (1999), tells the story of how Andrew Cunanan killed, most famously, the designer Gianni Versace, only after killing his closest friends and others who got in the way of his efforts to maintain a false self.

I begin with the pairing of the serial killer Cunanan and his final victim, Versace, a contrast in characters who possess a false self and a true self, respectively, which opens the series. The sexual formation and framing of these gay men—Cunanan and Versace—were racialized and classed from early childhood. The filmmakers emphasize this by starting from their adolescence to depict the beginning of their manhoods. As literary scholar

Karen Sánchez-Eppler argues, "National ideologies of class promise that in the United States, poverty, like childhood, is merely a stage to be out-grown." But, she says, class is "an identity to be grown into and childhood [is] a powerful site for such growth." She argues that children are usually seen as freed from the "constraints and abjection of labor."[2] In the case of Gianni Versace in relation to his killer, Andrew Cunanan, childhood was the training ground for the differing worlds of dignity and lowliness they came to inhabit as adults.

First, I will discuss this difference between the two men, particularly in terms of the valorization of two acts: lying (or the delusional yet imag-inative narrative framing of one's life) and work (the act of passionately devoting oneself to creativity versus the act of diminishing oneself to make money) that is established in childhood. The shame and the trauma of poverty and sexual subjection relate to and shape these practices of lying and work. I conclude the chapter with a meditation on sexual practices that reenact dynamics of race and class. I contend with D. W. Winnicott's psychoanalytic concepts of the true and false self and the good and not good enough mother, as well as his theories about why people lie and how that relates to creating a livable world for the marginalized.

The Abject and the Eminent: Context and Class in Shaping True and False Selves

In the opening of the Netflix miniseries *American Crime Story: The Assas-sination of Gianni Versace* (2018), by Ryan Murphy, the first episode, "The Man Who Would Be Vogue," shows Gianni Versace (Edgar Ramírez) waking up in his lavish and glamorous pink oceanfront mansion. He pur-posefully saunters through the ornate halls into a closet where he dons a sumptuous pink robe before standing on his opulent Juliet balcony over-looking Miami Beach's palm trees, white sands, and blue ocean. Versace is an international fashion icon, and the set is his actual mansion where he was shot. The series opens with the day of his murder. We recognize the iconic designs associated with him—the Medusa logo of his company, the maximalist layering of complex patterns, and the extravagance of gold and pink colors.

Nearby, on the beach directly in front of Versace's home, the infamous murderer Andrew Cunanan, who at the time was already on the FBI's Ten Most Wanted Fugitives list, wears a loose top, jean shorts, and baseball cap. He sits on the sand as he opens his backpack and pulls out a book about fashion, then a gun. As he looks up, we see the dark semicircles under his eyes that blaze worry and fear. The extent of his reach into the fashion world is his possession of a book that confirms both his aspirations for and his long distance from its center.

Just across from the mansion, Cunanan is physically close to Versace yet so far from him, so out of reach. Cunanan looks around to see that no one notices his gun. He then lifts up the lower edge of his shorts to reveal a large wound on his thigh. With the skin scraped off, his insides are visible. He walks into the water, leaving his backpack on the desolate public beach. We see his body that is falling apart and how there is no public/private distinction in the space he occupies. He is, essentially, of the outside—an outsider to property and an outsider in terms of his unaddressed health care needs. As the waves hit his chest, he cowers and screams with desperation and pain. The intercutting contrasts Cunanan's embodied abjection with Versace's eminence and peace.

Back in the bejeweled serenity of Gianni Versace's privately secured world, the scene cuts to two bottles of pills, from which he takes some pills before gazing into a gold mirror. Versace's HIV-positive status and the medications he takes because of it are presented in a matter-of-fact manner. This reveals a self without stigma for being infected by a virus that usually led to shame. As more of the mansion is shown, we see that he is not isolated but caringly propped up by employees. His various attendants anticipate his needs, orange juice on a silver tray ready for him to take as he glides by, and a healthy poolside breakfast of fresh fruit while reading the newspapers neatly folded on a plate readied for him. In his pampered life, he is supported by affectionate employees whom he treats with the intimacy of a mutually tender gaze and a passing, casual squeeze of an arm or caress of a cheek, all gestures met with affectionate gazes. He lives in a loving environment, in contrast to his murderer's hostile world.

Andrew Cunanan runs into a public restroom on the beach. On his knees and with his arms flanking the rim, he bows into a toilet bowl browned with fecal matter. The skinny, sickly, and dirty Cunanan vomits, unifying his body with the disgusting receptacle of excrement. Sitting spent on the dirty floor, he then leans against the wall and sees graffiti of the words "FILTHY FAGGOTS" scrawled on the stall at the same level as his face. He stares at the slur. What is shared between these two figures of Versace and Cunanan is queerness indeed, yet each occupies a different economic and racial rung in the hierarchy of valued subjectivity. Sexuality is what connects them, while race and class divide and distinguish them in the social world.

In the opening sequence of the television series, this class distinction is immediately apparent. Cunanan's racial identity remains ambiguous, but the show immediately makes clear that gay identity and the experience of homophobia are what make Cunanan abject, while they simultaneously frame Versace as truly eminent. The lack of separation between dirt and body is linked directly to the subjugation of homosexuality, which in this representation broadly refers to those cast to live under the moniker. However, the mixed-race Filipino and Italian American Cunanan is the one rendered abject, while the Italian/American international icon is exalted. The representations of enfranchisement in Versace and disenfranchisement in Cunanan are tied to racial and class contexts, as we will experience more fully in the series.

These opening shots establish Cunanan as an infamous yet disenfranchised and reprehensible criminal suspect while cutting away to another gay world, that of the coveted, iconic, and celebrated. Wealthy, white, and sun-kissed, Versace bids goodbye to his lover before nonchalantly and coolly walking alone in a pristine, expensive black T-shirt and luxurious tan shorts along the beachside Ocean Drive, as if he is not a god among men. The nauseating and abhorrent juxtapose with the desirable and pleasing in the opening shots before the two men come together in one moment when the disprized assassinates the prized. From this opening sequence, the episodic series explores the contexts that make up the two figures, and how one becomes infamous for killing the famous. The difference is racialized and classed.

Indeed, race and class figure powerfully in the sexual lives of these two gay men in ways that the series makes very apparent; Cunanan's visibility as an abject and repugnant figure is tied to the representations of these social categories of experience. Cunanan constantly lies about his ethnic heritage. While he is a mixed-race Filipino and Italian American man, he suffers from white supremacy's disparagement of his brownness. Aspiring to straightness, he prefers to lie about his gay sexuality even to his gay and ally friends, as well as lying about his low-wage work as a clerk in a chain drugstore and his education (pretending he is getting a PhD rather than being a college dropout). In disavowing queerness and brownness, he prioritizes access to whiteness and wealth.

Versace claims his ethnic heritage as an Italian (white) man, his gay sexuality, and his work. Cunanan's commitment to lying about these intensely racial and classed experiences is so strong that we cannot assume that homophobia is the primary social force, and sexuality the foremost lens of identity, that will help us most understand him as a cultural figure. The sexualities of both men are always and persistently racialized and classed. The sex scenes in the series, which centers homophobia, depict Andrew Cunanan's bodily disconnection, which drugs and violent sex are supposed to resolve for him, but instead reenact the racial, class, and sexual silences that traumatize him. Racial poverty impacts sexuality. More precisely, his racial poverty has a profound impact on his sexuality. Drugs, overspending, and sex perpetuate the alternate universe Cunanan creates through his lies, which are devices that move him away from experiencing his body and even his memory—and healing both. His lying prevents him from being present in his actual life in his persistence to create a false self and, ultimately, a false world.

Race, sex, class, and context are related to the concepts of true and false selves. D. W. Winnicott, psychoanalyst and pediatrician, defines the true self as one who lives in the world, ever present and attuned to one's experiences as they transpire, responding organically and authentically. That is, for Winnicott, "Only the True Self can be creative, and only the True Self can feel real. Whereas a True Self feels real the existence of a False Self results in a feeling unreal or a sense of futility."[3] This true self develops early in infancy through the mother or mother figure, who in her responses to the baby's needs makes the world safe and dependable so that the child can flourish. For Versace, his whiteness affords access to an authentic way of living as such, including his sexuality and his class. In the experiences of homophobia that Versace encounters, his mother makes sure he accepts the "woman's work" he wishes to pursue and what others classify as undesirable: his effeminacy. In this way, his parental inheritance is the ability to express a real or true self based on the assurance his mother provides.

The false self essentially is unable to live with authenticity and spontaneity and must live behind a facade of performance instead, so as to protect the true self.[4] In the case of Cunanan, the shame that he feels subjectively about being Filipino and brown leads him to deny his heritage and to disparage himself into creating a world that prevents him from feeling his abundance—as possessing mixed-race heritage, culture, and history. His father, Modesto "Pete" Cunanan (Jon Jon Briones), passes on to him a self-hatred of brownness as tied to poverty and an aspiration for whiteness as tied to wealth. Because Andrew is unable to accept what composes him—whether race or sexuality—he fabricates a world that is stagnant, where the voices of the past control his responses in the present. He remains unresponsive to lived experience and is therefore not growing, not changing, not developing, and not fulfilling his potential, which includes undoing the harms of white supremacy and homophobia.

This is different from the notion of performance of multiple selves; instead, it is about the impediments of knowing one's self and allowing its expression. As Winnicott explains, "Each person has a polite or socialized self, and also a personal private self that is not available except in intimacy. This is what is commonly found, and we call it normal."[5] That is, the true self and false self in Winnicott's view are notions to help the individual access self-understanding or healthiness. Andrew Cunanan exists alone, hiding his gun and his wounds. In contrast, Versace lives within an accepting community, his HIV status revealed; Versace divulges his wealth and his wounds. We see the abject as a false self, a lying and hiding figure, and the eminent as a prominent, truthful self and an open figure. Critical to the true self and the false self is the parental relationship to the child, what Winnicott calls the "good mother" regardless of gender, emphasizing the role of the caregiver in this process of self-formation for which we must attune in order to figure the self as an agent in one's own life.

Gianni Versace in an Idealized Childhood Home: Work and the Good Enough Mother

In "The Concept of a Healthy Individual," D. W. Winnicott argues that "inheritance and the environment are each external factors if we speak in terms of the emotional development of the individual person, that is to say, of psychomorphology."[6] As a psychoanalyst of object relations theory and a pediatrician both, Winnicott is best known for his theory of the "good enough mother," which was part of his foundational idea that the evolution of the self is tied to the relationship between parent and child, and that this relationship influences significantly relations and interactions with others, including those outside of the family. I use this framework of external relations as shaping the development of one's internal mind to capture how Gianni Versace inherited a legacy of confidence and self-acceptance from his mother as love and how Andrew Cunanan's legacy differed. It is death.

"Creator/Destroyer," the seventh of nine hour-long episodes in the miniseries, depicts Versace's and Cunanan's early years. The episode begins with a scene from Versace's lovely, idyllic, white-European childhood in

1957 Italy as a counterpoint to what we will learn of Cunanan's violently distorted brown American childhood in the United States twenty-three years later. Versace's is an ideal representation, replete with soft lighting and a set design that incorporates the calm and warm colors of his childhood village in Calabria, Italy. The young teen sits in the corner of his mom's shop. A customer gazes with pleasure at a mirror while trying on a new dress. Gianni admires his mother's work as a dressmaker whose creations enable self-affirmation for her customers. Though the scene is set in a village, the women, including Gianni's mother, look like supermodels: tall, statuesque, with unique features and a pride in their carriage. The boy looks to his mother—revealing his attachment to her person and her craft as he mimics her creativity, her way of being in the world as a craftsperson and artist, while he sketches in the corner. She asks her son to come out from the shadowed corner of the shop and encourages him to claim his passion for dressmaking, framing this invitation with an acknowledgment that it is a female-gendered path of work for which he must hold no shame. Immediately after this scene, young Versace is shown in the social world of school, where his choice is mocked and ridiculed.

The classroom scene begins with an establishing shot that shows the uniformity of the space, which contains twelve seats arranged in four rows, three deep. Although the small room's ceiling is quite tall, the space is narrow and confining—like a jail where little light seeps in from the windows high above. The arrangement of furniture is harmonious, but the lighting creates a regimented and imprisoning picture. The severe teacher's lecture is interrupted by her calling Gianni a pervert for drawing dresses, to which a classmate chuckles, "not a pervert, a pansy," a comment that is met with laughter from the rest of his class. While both terms suggest "woman impersonator," the gender-crossing classification also indicates a crossing of sexual norms that Gianni knows is tied to the craft he learned from his mother. At the same time, drawing dresses is a comfort that is internally pleasurable while also external in that it comes from his mother. The teasing impacts him; it creates a disillusionment with the external world in contrast to the comfort he receives from his mother at home. It affects him in terms of understanding the forces at work in the social world. Gianni's face shatters as the teacher tears up the paper illustrated with his design.

A lesson from Gianni's mother redirects this defining experience in the outside world to a cathartic one at home, strengthening his sense of self toward a healthier adulthood where his true self can emerge. He comes home bearing the torn-up pieces of his drawing with dejection on his face and in his countenance. His mother demands an explanation and then says, "I have no time for lies," when Gianni claims nothing had happened. She rejects his inability to tell her what hurt him. For her, the truth is her passing on to Gianni her craft, part of herself, to her son as a "good enough mother," to use Winnicott's term. The good enough mother presents the illusion of catering to him entirely and prepares him for the disillusion-ment that will occur with certainty—that is the impossibility of her being there for him always. In affirming his pleasure from working on clothes and embracing work purportedly belonging to women, she essentially teaches Gianni that he needs to rely on the comfort she provides in order to withstand a world that will be hostile to their family's gifts. In Winnicott's example, the mother's illusion is providing the breast (or its substitute) as "part of the infant" when really her "eventual task is to disillusion the in-fant" by weaning at the right time of child development, when frustra-tion can be overcome.[7] In this representation of Versace's childhood, her creativity is the thing she teaches him to own. She wants him to be able to take this from her as his mother. In affirming their attachment through shared work and passion, she prioritizes her bond with her child as what will protect him in an act of agentic attunement. She arms him with what will strengthen him for the rest of his life. He must not lie about the op-position he encounters and must instead confront those frustrations from the external world by prioritizing the world of their family. She is pre-paring him through agentic attunement to become strongly independent in the face of hostility. The family is thus made real as a source of self-fortification against condemnations by the external world, especially re-garding creativity as the wealth of family inheritance.

This film's first framing of lying, as a practice that deserves no time or space in their relationship or in their home, begins this episode, which then ends with Cunanan's deep and unrelenting commitment to lying as a way of life that he inherits from his father. Lying, thus, is tied to social forces of race, sex, and class that organize their contexts and self-perceptions. In Versace's context, he learns to not lie about his attachment to creativity and his creative practice. As I will show, in Cunanan's context, lying about his creativity and his inability to create is something he learns he must do. Both men learn these practices from within their families.

The second lesson in Gianni Versace's childhood story is that hard work makes one special, for what it produces and achieves: beauty, pleasure, and happiness not just for the self but also for others. Creativity itself becomes an antidote to the trauma of social denigration. One can undo harm by making a different world and deploying an alternative frame. As a way to undo the ridicule he experiences at school, Versace's mother invites Gianni to make the dress he fantasizes about, urging him, "We make it for real." Here, his act of creativity makes his family inheritance real. He begins to cut the large, brown draft paper with scissors but then stops, unable to continue because it is too hard to cross the border of gender that embracing the act signifies or undeniably "makes real." His mother combats this hesitation and instills in him that "hard work and practice . . . never easy" are what actually make something special. In this lesson, the politics of work directly addresses not only family but also gender and sex. In this statement, she makes his fear of homosexuality as tied to gendered work something that strengthens him. It is thus different, as an identity too, which is even more special. That is, work and the beauty created there can liberate one from social denigration and exclusion. The structure of the episode thus far shows the success Gianni Versace achieved through truthfulness and dignity in work; it affirms his existence. This world of Versace's is white—though it is certainly formed by gender and sexual discrimination. We will see this whiteness more clearly in the inescapable brownness of Cunanan's mixed-race world. In Versace's childhood, work is seen as a reprieve from social hierarchy, but for Cunanan, work is a confirmation of abjection and the need to flee it.

Andrew Cunanan: Living with Lies

In contrast to Versace, Andrew Cunanan inherits a legacy of racial self-hatred from his father, who diminishes his white mother, Mary Anne Schillaci, played by Joanna P. Adler. Thus, he inherits not only racism and adherence to white supremacy but also sexism and patriarchy. In doing so, Andrew's attachment to his mother is alienated and subsumed, rather than elevated and made real as in Versace's case. Although Winnicott addresses the parent-child relation, it is important to note that the caregiving within this family is assigned primarily to the stay-at-home mom; thus, I consider the father an external force that relentlessly contests the primary bond of the maternal for Andrew.

Significant for Cunanan is how the disillusionment, or weaning from his mother's attachment, happens violently and deliberately, and too soon. This is so that his father could abuse him. That is, the mother cares for Andrew's healthy growth while the father is invested in his own gain at the expense of his son's developing adulthood. For Winnicott, "Children who have suffered some too great or sudden access of disillusionment find themselves under a great compulsion to do things without knowing why, to make messes."[8] I examine first the racial insecurity from the father and assignation of the mother as "not good enough," leading to the sexual and other trauma Andrew carries—a violation that he must bury underneath the lies of his false self.

We meet Andrew Cunanan at around age thirteen, the same formative age as Gianni Versace in the previous scene that took place twenty-three years earlier. The family is moving within San Diego, California, from the poorer side of town to a richer one. The camera pans across an abandoned lot and a dumpy yard fronting the fleapit shack. His loud and overbearing dad, Pete Cunanan, commands Andrew's mother, brother, and two sisters to move their family's possessions. He shouts, "We don't need professional movers! We do it ourselves. We save $500 and turn it into $10,000 in one week," illustrating the grandstanding, self-important bullying that relegates the actual physical labor to the rest of his family. He refers to a future windfall that excuses him from the labor of his wife and children occurring in real time. Plus, he says to his sweating brood, "It's good exercise!" to dupe them further into thinking this work for the patriarch is really for the benefit of them as individuals. His wife and children work while he, directly benefiting from their labor, commands from a perch. The choreography of the scene, in which he appears kingly while they flank him like lowly laboring subjects, captures what patriarchy literally looks like in this family. As the breadwinner, he declares himself king so that as the distant, unaffected father he determines how the other family members experience the subjugation of their bodies. That is, he does not relate to his children and wife beyond commanding them to serve. He does not demonstrate care for anyone within their family other than Andrew.

Meanwhile, Andrew is the prince within the family order, where his father is king and his siblings and mother are laboring subjects. As the recipient of favor and privilege (including not laboring), Andrew reads a book by himself inside the old empty house. Effeminate, preppy, and almost stately, in contrast to his disheveled and sweaty siblings, he remains seated inside a barren room. He reads while seated in a small chair on a dirty, stained floor next to a wall with peeling paint. Clean, polished, and groomed, he looks like he does not belong in this house. The book in his hands shows its author's name in big, bold print on the cover: Evelyn Waugh, a British writer known for his satire and mask of indifference. This is not the teen fare of *The Hardy Boys* or graphic novels. We gather that he is already distinct from his peers, and not just his siblings, who indeed call him "Prince Andrew."

The setting and props establish Andrew as an abstruse youth. His father calls him to come outside, to say, literally, "This is not for you," as he gestures toward the dilapidated hovel of a house. They then drive away, with the youngest son, Andrew, in the passenger seat in the front of the moving truck, while his mom kneels behind him, perched like a child. The windowless, dark space behind her contains her beleaguered older children. Already, we see that Andrew occupies the privileged place, in the front passenger seat, while the mother kneels in a less desirable and more servile position. He is elevated to the adult seat, and she is infantilized on the floor in the back. The other children are tertiary. In these establishing shots, we see the mixed-race family with ongoing and insistent patriarchal dynamics. The white wife accommodates her brown husband, while their mixed-race children experience a hierarchy where the patriarch clearly favors the youngest child in how Andrew is exempt from the labor that is required of the others. His value is not determined by his ability to labor. His siblings accept this order of things, as does his acquiescent and accommodating servile mother, who cedes to this disordered hierarchy.

As a young child, Andrew is quite confused by the situation because of how patriarchy produces violence that destabilizes his home and how his place in it distorts the family to create a feeling of disorder. In the chapter "The Location of Cultural Experience" in his classic book *Playing and Reality*, D. W. Winnicott examines "the potential space between the subjective object and the object objectively perceived, between me-extensions and the not-me . . . at the interplay between there being nothing but me and there being objects and phenomena outside omnipotent control."[9] This space between the self and the other and the self and the environment is critical for forming confidence derived from the reliance on others' agentic attunement. This is what we see in the relationship between Gianni Versace and his mother: the affirmation of their child and parent bond, the reliance on work, and the importance of a creative life. In Andrew Cunanan's case, the "exploitation of this area leads to a pathological condition in which the individual is cluttered up with persecutory elements of which he has no means of ridding himself."[10] That is, his elevation to the role of son-wife perplexes him, particularly in how he counts on his mother as his primary caregiver, who is constantly and continually disparaged by the father. Andrew is unable to count on his parental figures as dependable in loving and protecting him with his future self in mind. The father abuses him, and the mother is unable to protect him—or herself.

Cultural context matters in the interpretation of an action: Andrew reads inside a poor home versus a rich home. Then Andrew lives in a home where the white mother is undermined by the brown father who privileges him. The class, race, and gender dynamics matter in how he perceives himself and the world. Winnicott makes sure to spotlight the cultural context that determines the meaning of an action: "A child goes into the larder to take a bun or two. . . . In a good home, no one calls the child who does this a thief. Yet the same child in an institution may be punished and branded."[11] In Cunanan's case, he is the child who benefits from patriarchy within a home where the parental relationship is distorted, especially in how it leads him to distrust his own attachment to his mother on whom he relies. He is unable to trust himself. Unlike Versace's mother, who trains her son to become confident, Cunanan is unable to achieve this same sense of self-confidence. This then leads to predation by the father as represented by the television series.

When the Cunanan family arrives at their big, new two-story tract house, with a large palm tree in the landscaped front yard, leaves billowing in the wind, the siblings and mom unload the furniture while the dad takes their brother Andrew inside. The camera frames the father's hand taking the boy up the stairs to the master bedroom, usually the purview of a mother and father. This is a continuation of the configuration of the family where Andrew's mom and siblings are workers while he and his dad are masters of the household. Andrew is put into a peculiar role: favored child or child bride? A gendered and sexual element to the dynamic between father and son is hinted at in the choreography of the family's move into their new home. Pete ceremoniously gives Andrew what he calls the biggest bedroom, explaining: "The master bedroom is your bedroom. You know why? Every morning when you wake up, I want you to remember, you are special. And when you feel special, success will follow." Here, the attunement that Pete practices to ready his son Andrew for the world is premised on an innate entitlement versus the hard work that Versace's mom cultivates in her son Gianni. It is not an agentic attunement, rather a disabling hazing. This directly contrasts with the adage that hard work is what makes something special, as Gianni Versace's mom espoused. It also has a sexual component, however, that asks us to think about the relationship between racism and heterosexism, especially as they occur in the development of a child.

Winnicott challenges us to think about the cultural location of our experiences. He asserts that "cultural experience has not found its true place in the theory used by analysts in their work and in their thinking."[12] He defines experience as the interplay of the contributions of one's inner reality (self-perception as subject) and external life (others and objects). Pete Cunanan anoints his son as special to combat Andrew's exclusion from whiteness and wealth in the external world, while providing his son with a distorted internal world of a disordered family, especially in the invalidation of Andrew's mother, his primary caregiver. Pete Cunanan is counting on an inner feeling of entitlement that he hopes will buoy his son in a world where he will experience racism. While he attempts to validate his son, the effort is dependent on an entitlement rather than on work. He aims to instill belief in an inherent specialness—his assessment of how white privilege must work—that he hopes will fuel success for his mixed-race son. The status comes not from work alone but from a quality that he believes will prepare Andrew for the racial exclusion ahead. Yet, this feeling of specialness is tinged with sexual predation that will occur in the master bedroom—the site of Andrew's privilege within the family and the site where his fortification against racism is formed—thus tying together the forces of sexuality, race, and class, social categories of experience as well as social forces that work together and against each other.

The American Dream Is a Lie:
Fortifying against Racism

While this fortification from the outside world is given to Andrew, his siblings are treated poorly and are dejected. While Andrew enjoys the air-conditioned master bedroom and his own bathroom, the other siblings sleep together, crammed in one small, very hot room. The girls share the bed while the boy lies on a mattress on the floor, uncomfortable and hot. Here, the other children represent what Viviana Zelizer calls "economic utility" for their labor and their cheaper keep, versus what Andrew provides, which is not only "emotional value" for the father but also sexual value.[13]

The father does not have an attraction to, sexual relations with, or tender emotional regard toward the mother. She sleeps on a single bed in a sparse room where we see her praying, as if she lives in an austere convent. Like her children other than Andrew, she accepts servant conditions in an otherwise massive house. She is also relegated by the father to a peripheral role in Andrew's life, following the patriarch's wishes for the child to favor her less. This is a confusing situation because the mother actually gives Andrew emotional support and unconditional love. The father considers this form of love undesirable and judges the need for it as an indication of weakness; Andrew should not want or need it, especially from the mother. We see this especially in how the father diminishes the mother's role when she helps Andrew enter elite spaces, like the private school near their new home. It is entry into a white world that Pete Cunanan himself craves, and one that Andrew finds uncomfortable as an adolescent.

Andrew's application for admission to the storied Bishop's School, with its Mediterranean-style buildings overlooking the ocean, requires an interview. Scenes of the interview are intercut with his dad's interview at the prestigious financial firm Merrill Lynch, both institutions of whiteness and wealth now and in the Reagan era, when the interviews take place. They dress up in the master bedroom together, each in a suit and with a handkerchief, too, and not just a tie. The father dictates this desire for entry into predominantly white spaces where they are racially different. As Andrew approaches the school with his mom, another suit-clad boy exits the building with his similarly dressed white mother. He waits among other boys and mothers who look like him and his mom: a thin, white woman and a (near-)white boy in a hallway decorated with trophies and plaques that tell of prized hegemonic male athleticism and white privilege. His attempt to enter this world dramatically occurs at the same time as his father's own interview, presenting Andrew's attempt not only as fulfill-ment of the father's desire but also as something he must enact for himself.

In the interview, the admissions officer asks Andrew what one wish he has, and he answers with at least five: a big house, Mercedes Benz cars, children, and so on. When pressed for just one answer, Andrew says, "To be special," repeating the narrative his father constantly imposes on him. For him, this lesson is not yet secured in his personality but remains a wish to be attained. In his childhood, the imposition of his father's dream is gargantuan and hard to navigate in terms of identifying his own wants and desires. Andrew actually conflates material and normative social success with the condition of being special, following his father's lessons about success. This is in direct contrast to Versace's lessons about creativity as grounded in the family bond and hard work.

At the father's interview, a large group of younger white men sit and wait in chairs lining the wall of a luxurious, large office. Pete Cunanan surveys the competition. He is the only one who is older and the only one who is not white. He encounters the barrier not only of whiteness but also of age as well as pedigree. This does not stop him but instead energizes him, as he rises to the occasion. He is here for the interview and is all in, as if elated for the opportunity, walking into the room with a swagger. The three stodgy white male interviewers immediately tell him they do not usually interview many candidates like him, making sure to emphasize his difference by defining him with words like *night-schooled* and *bootstraps*. Pete Cunanan provides a counternarrative of this scene to them: he asks the interviewees how many of the candidates who queue up for the interview come from the Ivy League but are nothing like him, who picked himself up from nothing. When the interviewers say they need "more business and not biography," Cunanan convinces them that business and biography are inextricably linked. For Pete Cunanan to assert that "business is biography" signifies an affirmation of the United States by this immigrant Filipino man; what he says is American nationalist, that is, his rise, is only possible thanks to American exceptionalism. In this, he traffics in the myth of the American Dream. Similarly, he promises to tell his clients, "I will cross oceans with their money," meaning that no obstacle would be too big for him in building his clients' wealth. This of course comes true in a different way; he does eventually get hired and then steals from his clients, taking their money across oceans when he flees both the firm and the FBI and escapes to the Philippines.

Although the financial industry is steeped in lying, the kind of lying the elder Cunanan does is linked to his racial nonbelonging in the United States. He is without a pedigreed education in a domain that is very white and elite in terms of background and training. As he enters the trading room on his first day, an older brown man among a sea of much younger white men, an upstart announces that Cunanan "beat out five hundred applicants!" Cunanan is thrilled by the acknowledgment and boasts: "Let me show you how it's done." But in his very first phone call, his bravado does not match his stride. He possesses no talent and no grit. The client hangs up. But instead of showing diligence by calling another, Cunanan pretends to make a sale. This ultimately leads to other fraudulent acts that get him fired from Merrill Lynch, a financial industry giant that would later be fined millions by the Securities and Exchange Commission for lying to its clients.

Pete Cunanan is not merely part of a larger culture that lies for profit, however. There is a racial dimension to his experience. Andrew's father lies to compensate for what he considers racial and class disadvantage. He feels entitled to steal from others and wishes he could steal more, even after he is caught. This lying, however, is linked to Andrew's upbringing not only in racial and class terms but also in terms of gender and sexuality.

Alongside his rampant lying, Pete Cunanan belittles Andrew's mother, whom his son relies on for support as a stay-at-home mom who is thoroughly devoted to and present in his life. When Andrew and Pete get home from their respective interviews, the dad "jokes" that he did not get the job, which the mom believes and for which she expresses her sympathy. Her response enrages Pete. In revealing his announcement to be a prank, Pete questions her sanity and gaslights her: "Your thoughts are confused. Did you take your meds?" In constructing the mother as inadequate, mentally unreliable, and just plain wrong in not believing what he can achieve, the father invites Andrew to identify with him and for the boy to see himself as different from her, not sharing his mother's "weak mind," for he needs to be stronger in a white world. The fortification against racism comes with the application of sexism. When Pete describes his wife in this exact way, he implies that if Andrew were smart, he would both escape from and turn against his mother. Indeed, there is an official record of Andrew Cunanan having shoved his mother and dislocated her shoulder, which is represented later in the series. Pete constantly tells Andrew they moved to their new house to be closer to the school, Andrew's entry to white acceptance and inclusion. But Andrew's mom wants to protect him from this pressure. The father anticipates the son needing his mother's support and protection, which to him signals weakness. He aims to separate son from mother and set the scene for his further predation.

What is a lie? So far, I have discussed lying as a multilayered practice for Andrew's dad, Pete Cunanan. His dad's lies provide Andrew his cultural context. Lying has so many different manifestations in his life, particularly in how he witnesses his father create an alternative reality through it. The American Dream is a type of lie in his father's life. In Pete's unreliable narration, we can see that there are lies that families tell. There are family legends and myths that are lies, while they also serve as the foundation of one's inheritance: the falsehood of family lore. Lying can also be the inheritance of a practice of being in and occupying the world. For example, Pete uses lies to cheat and manipulate others for personal gain. When a parent lies to a child, however, it creates distrust in how one understands the world and how it works. Lies from particular people for whom special regard is reserved, within a certain developmental moment in a child's life, create a profound mess. The lines between lying, delusion, unreality, fantasy, and fiction are blurred to distort Andrew's vision and relations. Truth, presented as known, enables Gianni Versace to understand his mother's reality, his creativity, and his family as the source of his strong self, as a way to forge success and fight homophobia. The lies lead Andrew Cunanan to distrust his sense of what is real about his parents, his work, and his family—himself essentially—and make him even more vulnerable to racism, sexism, sexual trauma, and more. He is far away from earned secure attachment—a healthy and present attitude in living that undoes trauma. In this way, Pete does not practice agentic attunement for Andrew, who is weakened by his upbringing. For Andrew, the trauma remains large in ways that shape his attitude toward others. Because he is unable to achieve true intimacy or to help others, his friends flee him for he dismisses reality that would be the basis for their relation.

The Sex of Racial Childhood: Inheriting Lies and Sexual Trauma from His Father

Sexual trauma informs the lying that becomes Andrew's way of life. He inherits both from his father, who bequeaths Andrew a passionate commitment to lying and causes him tremendous sexual trauma through what the series presents as incestuous pedophilia. This is what Andrew's father has been grooming him for. Lying becomes part of the sexual trauma Pete inflicts when telling Andrew he is the son he "loves more than my whole life." This love is linked to material success as an antidote to racism, which is a belief in the self as inherently deserving. This is a tenet he teaches Andrew as they sit together in bed, reading books on culture and manners to learn how to converse and perform in white America. The dad says to him, "It's not enough to be smart but to fit in." In matching pajamas, they are twinning again, yet the scene also relays how they sleep together in the main bed of the house. Andrew looks up at his father in this moment of closeness with a disclosure of his own dreams for himself, risking vulnerability. He shares how he wishes to become a writer. In response, the dad immediately relays that this dream is not good enough, quashing the boy's desire and rendering him as a not good enough child, an inadequate one who cannot trust himself. Unlike Versace's mom, who encourages her son to invest in himself and his organic desires and dreams as part of his true self, Cunanan's dad teaches him to prioritize the false self and distrust himself in order to cede to others.

Andrew was hoping to manage his frustrations with reality by homing in on the creativity that lying required, and to spin it away from destruction to something socially acceptable and not harmful. If he were to follow the path of lies, it would be to lie in the form of fiction as an act of imagination and creativity. This is the path his true self identifies as viable from his upbringing by a constantly lying father and from his own avid practice of reading. But Pete disapproves of his boy's wish and says Andrew should only pursue that career if someone offers him a million dollars. That is, Andrew must learn to value and trust his wishes only when an external societal judge gives them monetary significance. Thus, the patriarchal father devalues his son and creates doubt about Andrew's own self-perception. The dad reduces the dream to crass money. This is a turning point in Andrew's character, much like the lesson that Gianni internalizes from his mother, which is to trust in the self and in the work and the world will follow. Dupe the world is the lesson from Andrew's father.

This distrust of one's true self then permeates Andrew's life. His father shows him how to behave in an entitled manner, but Andrew hides a sense of inadequacy in not being the bearer of his own dreams and desires. He is told throughout his childhood that he must confront racial disadvantage with confidence. When Andrew gets accepted to Bishop's School, he weeps, stunning his mom with the power of his emotions as an adolescent child in the face of his infantilization—that is, he must get accepted to represent his family, while also feeling adultified in achieving success at a young age. The pressure on Andrew to succeed in limited terms is acute but hidden. His mother is attuned to his breaking down. She is further stunned when the father's response is to actually kiss his son's feet in an act that draws discomfort, captured in a close-up of Andrew's distressed and confused face that ends the scene.

Deep down, Andrew does not believe in the anointing of his specialness. He does not think he will be accepted. Lying becomes the method by which his false self emerges aggressively as an act of protecting his true self. The mother's empathy contrasts with the father's unfettered belief in the son's greatness; he does not see his son but, instead, sees who he wants him to be. Andrew sees his parents' differing regard for him: his mom's emotional support that he needs and his dad's projections of greatness that frighten him, evident in his face as he looks upon his father kneeling before him and kissing his feet. His mother's comforting proximity helps him as he looks at her with fear at that moment, his panicked eyes screaming for help. He recognizes the magnitude of his father's bowing as strange and inappropriate. Soon, his dad makes him choose between his two parents—after giving him a sports car, almost two years before Andrew can legally drive.

Pete silences the mother's protests when she insists that Andrew continue the homework they are doing together instead of going outside to see the gift. As Andrew and his dad sit in the brand-new gold sports car, Pete tells Andrew in one monologue: "Your brothers and sisters are . . . not special. You're the best friend I've ever had. Your mom was very sick when you were born . . . in the hospital with depression. A weak mind. It was me who looked after you. I was your mother and your father." As Andrew accommodates the dad's arguments, the dad aggressively asserts that she was not a good enough mother for Andrew and that he instead is the one who deserves that recognition of the good enough mother and father combined. Andrew listens intently to this campaign, and after a beat, we see his introspection and then the decision to reject his mother. He looks at his dad in the passenger seat of the sports car, which must smell brand new in a way that overwhelms the senses, then up to his mom as she stands next to the driver's door with her hands resting on the open window ledge. Andrew rolls up the car window, compelling her to move her hands away quickly, so they won't get smashed by the fast-closing automatic window. They are now separated by the closed glass, with father and son inside. This act also represents a threat to hurt her if she does not recede. Through the window, a barrier between them, we see the mother's reflection of dejection. When the dad forces Andrew to choose a parent, he distances a son from his supportive mother, revealing a distorted goal. His father aims to become the singular voice in Andrew's head now and when he is an adult.

Later that night, in the master bedroom together, Pete tucks Andrew into bed. He reminds Andrew of a moment when, as a child, Andrew burned his foot on a heater, and his dad "picked him up, kissed him to make him feel better." In recollecting this event, his father tells Andrew, "You did not make a sound. Not a sound." The dad then flicks off the lights as he descends upon Andrew face-to-face in bed. A fade to black seems to indicate an act of incestuous pedophilia for which Andrew's father has groomed him.[14] He enables this act by keeping Andrew away from labor, placing him on the pedestal of the main bedroom, distinguishing him from his siblings, and devaluing his mother to silence and disempower her and in declarations of ultimate love—all inappropriate behaviors toward a child in Andrew's situation. The boy is alienated from his siblings and his mother when his father puts him in the place of a wife sexually.

1.1 In the car with his dad, Andrew looks up at his mom outside the door with her hand resting on the open window ledge. *American Crime Story: The Assassination of Gianni Versace* (Ryan Murphy, 2018).

I isolate this original shot, as a horrible, horrendous, and confusing event that must have resonated throughout Andrew's life or, at least, as the film represents it. The scene concludes the film's representation of Andrew's childhood not as one defined by a singular trauma but as one that occurs in a larger context of parenting and childhood where the voice of his father dominates. Lying, distrust of the self, and blurred lines of sex and parenting are the structuring forces in Andrew's life.

That is, his life of lying comes from the inability to confront and live within a reality where the trauma of pedophilia occurred. Then there is the loss of his mother. The trauma of incestuous pedophilia, the infliction of a sexual encounter with an adult that is also your father, leads to a powerful trauma that D. W. Winnicott defines as the "breaking of the continuity of the line of the individual's existence."[15] For Andrew, it is aggravated by the loss of his primary caregiver on whom he has relied. Cunanan loses his mother when his father manipulates him with lies to convince him to abandon her, to classify her as deranged, weak, and thus unnecessary in a life that is ambitious and grand in its goal to overcome racism and attain capitalist success. The father gaslights the mother and the son, essentially separating them so they cannot protect each other.

Winnicott meditates on why people thieve and lie in order to help us understand how to reform those who steal and tell falsehoods. Winnicott explains that a child who lies, "instead of feeling almost unbearable guilt as a result of being misunderstood or blamed, will become . . . split into two parts, one terribly strict, and the other possessed by evil. . . . [T]he child then no longer feels guilty [and is] transformed into . . . a liar."[16] In Andrew Cunanan's case, the world of lying protects him from confronting the trauma of abuse by his predatory father. There is also the matter of his separation from his mother that he actively chose and for which he feels guilt, as a child manipulated by his father. Andrew Cunanan, the child who grows up to become a man who lies, who insists on living lies, is looking for a world that contained his mother before she was classified as not reliable and not worthy. He looked to her for guidance and counted on her devotion. She belonged to him, and his father cast her away. The web of lies cocoons him from their separation. Following this division and her devastation, he joins his father and his investment in lying. He does so deeply that all his subsequent relations require their cooperation in his lies, in the foregrounding of his false self, which makes for unreliable friendships unless they comply. If not, they must eventually be eliminated for his false world to persist.

For Andrew and his father, reality is perceived as traumatic, and their response is to insist on living in an alternate world. The father's world-making binds him and his son to lies. According to Maureen Orth, author of *Vulgar Favors: Andrew Cunanan, Gianni Versace, and the Largest Failed Manhunt in U.S. History*, on which the episodic series by Ryan Murphy is based, Pete Cunanan eventually returned to the United States after going to the Philippines and joining a cult to look for buried treasure that the Japanese supposedly left in World War II.[17] Here we see that Pete is not just a lying narcissist but is entirely committed to an alternate universe throughout his life. It is flabbergasting to see that his belief in a ridiculous story is so strong that he forsakes rationality for illusion. This confidence in falsehood is striking in Andrew as well.

Dancing with Abandon in the Red Suit: Relying on Others to Prop Up His Illusions

In the representation of Andrew's next four years, from around 1984 to 1988, he appears as a flamboyant, young gay teenager in a wealthy high school community. He does not quite have a rational understanding of the social world. His confidence is not grounded in the real world but in the one he wishes to inhabit. From home, he gets in a car with a much older man, who gives him a gift of perfume. As Andrew applies it on his neck and wrists, he tries to tell the man that this relationship means more to him than receiving gifts. The man tells him to lighten up. Even within the confined space of the car, the two perceive their relationship so differently in ways we shall soon recognize as terribly vast. Andrew instructs the man to go somewhere unknown, a surprise. The man is actually his forty-plus-year-old lover, and Andrew intends to take him as a date to a high school party, as if this is acceptable and normal within the community. When they arrive at the house party, the man is shocked that Andrew expects him to join the teenagers. Andrew is struck by the refusal, unable to understand how inappropriate and outside of the social norm it would be to insist their relationship come out into the open. The older man has to spell out that their relationship is secret (as well as illegal and criminal) and also why, for him, this is necessary: "This is strictly on the side, I'm married." Andrew does not understand his desire to display his older lover to his peers as socially unacceptable. The man commands him to get out of the car. Cunanan storms out and saunters down the driveway, at first with a look of glum dejection that becomes outright rage. The people packed along the driveway now gaze on him as he treats this as a runway walk while the song "Whip It" by the 1980s pop group Devo plays loudly. He strides faster into the house party, undoing and then throwing away his black trench coat to reveal a bright red leather jumpsuit. Readily readable on his body—its comportment and movements—is both sexual confidence and confusion, which we see in his shy, hesitant eyes. What is striking about seeing Andrew as a teenager and almost a man is observing the fullness and vitality of his life. He dares to promenade in, bearing a face of confidence while courageously moving his body like he is a work of art.

As he flounces into the party in his red suit, he goes straight to the dance floor, where he twirls and loops on his own with flair and abandon as he energetically fans his arms from side to side. A young man gushes that he has a crush on Andrew and intends to ask him out. Andrew's dance intensifies—his confidence bursting and his self-assurance overflowing in how he demands all eyes remain on him through his bodily performance. It makes sense that others desire him and admire the freedom his body expresses. Unsurprisingly, the confidence to defy gender norms by wearing a fiery red leather jumpsuit and dancing on his own, demanding to be seen, compels this interest. The red suit truly captures Andrew's need for others to see him and affirm him. As someone who secures attention through lying, he is volatile and dangerous through the powerful hunger for external validation he expresses.

The attendees at the house party are predominantly white and definitely wealthy. Athletes in varsity jackets look upon Andrew, who moves within this space, so different from his home, with a mix of caution and bravado. Indeed, he dances in a frenzy but begins to teeter on the edge of absolute fear when no one joins him. It feels as if the risk of exposing his true vulnerable self emerges in ways he wishes to contain. He depends on others to agree that he is desirable, not boring, but worthy of joining. They don't. He risks becoming a spectacle to be laughed at as his false self threatens to disappear and reveal the true self he deems unworthy. With increasing fear, he looks around the room as he dances more slowly—not knowing a young man is gearing up to ask him out. Only when Lizzie (Annaleigh Ashford), a wealthy white woman who is slightly older than the other partygoers, joins him and affirms him on the dance floor with her own energetic moves, does he resume his display. Her whiteness and wealth save him, and he is quite visibly and breathlessly relieved as his dancing resumes its flamboyance. Lizzie introduces herself, and they sit down to share the illusory world they agree upon—bonding over their favorite celebrities, colors, and fashions. With her wealthy whiteness, she essentially rescues him just as his swagger threatens to become shame. She lifts him up from the threat of exposing his lie: his false self's flimsy confidence.

However, Cunanan's racial background enters the picture inconveniently again when, after dropping out of college and working a dead-end job as a pharmacy clerk, he comes face-to-face with his lack of money and his lack of cultural capital. He perceives his race and class as part of his true self that is inadequate, even in the face of the cultural capital of his false self. As a gay Asian college dropout, he seeks work with an escort service, where his physical assets rather than his ability to entertain with his wit are what matter. His Filipino heritage, however, does not help him present as a cultured companion; there is no registry in popular culture for a person like him. The woman assessing him for the job explicitly says that even if the size of his penis counts, his race, sexuality, and class limit his opportunities. She tells him that "a Filipino even with a big dick" does not fit gay white male fantasies of who to take home. Running out of money makes these disadvantages even more traumatic; he is undeniably situated in what is to him a horrific condition of poverty and lacking racial value, not just in the queer world. This is a confrontation with the external world that classifies him as unworthy. This experience irrefutably renders the reality of his true self undesirable, and lying through his false self becomes a way out of it. At this juncture, he makes an even deeper investment in lying. And thus, his reliance on others to believe him so that he does not have to accept his racial and classed reality becomes even more urgent and necessary.

The Illusion of the False Self: Even against the Reality of Evidence

Returning to the "Creator/Destroyer" episode that anchors this chapter, we see similar struggles with accepting reality that flood Andrew's life as a young man. Now a senior in high school and presumably seventeen or eighteen, Andrew drives his sports car onto campus and saunters over to a bench where his friends sit. He flings his school jacket onto the back of the bench and sits down like a prince. Flamboyantly gay, he claims prominent space, loudly voicing his critique of the long line to take yearbook pictures. He loudly declares, "Are we sheep?" as he critiques having to stand in line. A jock refers to him using a gay slur, which Andrew dismisses, motivating him to cut the line ahead of the typically heteronormative cis white male classmate. Andrew rips open his white oxford button-up shirt and takes a photo with a smug face and a pose of open-shirt abs-exposed bravado. Using this photo, the high school yearbook names him "Most Likely to Be Remembered," which he prides himself on. Underneath his senior picture, he chooses the dictum "Apres moi, le deluge" because it sounds "kinda cool." Yet, its declaration of "after me, the storm" becomes fulfilled in the heinous acts he commits and the devastating damage he does to many families. His subsequent lack of remorse is consistent with the characteristics of a sociopath.

Pete Cunanan similarly acts like a sociopath in a scene that occurs concurrent to Andrew's performance in the yearbook line at Bishop's School. We see that Pete, four years since his Merrill Lynch interview, is now working for a much humbler company. It is a real downfall. His body and face tense, he enters a dodgy establishment in a downtrodden strip mall that looks worlds away from Merrill Lynch. We soon learn from a phone conversation at his desk that Pete is cheating an elderly woman out of her savings. The woman's grandson catches him and threatens him on the phone, which scares Pete. In an interrogation by his bosses, he becomes even more tense as he continues to lie, denying that he is selling fake stocks to the woman. His bosses confront Pete in a framing that looks like the interview at Merrill Lynch, but here they are disclosing how the FBI is investigating him, with the firm's cooperation. He somehow makes it back to his desk. His tension is most palpable in his cubicle when he stretches his arms taut as he grips the desk. He begins to shred incriminating documents and then calls his travel agent to activate existing reservation details. He scrambles to exit as the FBI agents almost catch him. At home, he grabs a wad of money in a ziplock bag hidden beneath the floor of the master bedroom closet and violently pushes away his wife, who frantically chases after him shouting questions. As the agents bang on the door, Pete escapes out the back and encounters Andrew approaching the house; he had parked his car down the street after glimpsing the FBI cars.

The lies coming to a head, Pete now commands Andrew to remain in the bubble, telling him, "Don't believe a word they say" before fleeing in Andrew's car. Soon, his mom reveals the new discovery that the "credit cards are maxed out. He's transferred all the money. This house, he sold it weeks ago. He knew they were coming. We have nowhere to live. We have nothing." As Andrew struggles to accept the facts of their abandonment, we begin to see how deeply he is entrenched within his father's version and narrative of the world. His mom continues to try to intervene: "He's gone. He left us. He left the country. He fled to Manila like a sorry rat. He is a thief and liar." This assertion acts like a knife that threatens to puncture Andrew's self-perception and his understanding of the world itself.

However, Andrew remains committed to the delusion, asking his mom to quiet down, holding up a piece of paper on which he's written that the FBI "are listening" and "Dad has money hidden." Andrew's mom, clearly not weak-minded, says, "Dad does not have money. He's dangerous." We see Andrew almost hit her, much like his dad casually shoved her to the ground to quell her complaints about buying Andrew the car. Andrew simply tells her, "You are wrong about him." Soon after, he flies to Manila to follow his father, who is living in a kind of squalor Andrew did not expect. At this point, Andrew has come to a crossroads, with the lie and lying as a way of life, and with the truth of his experience at the precipice of becoming an unsettled, precarious person. Within his unstable, dysfunctional family, his source of support—his mother—is constantly attacked by his father, who perversely worships and sexually victimizes him. Now the reality of the lie is before him. At age eighteen, Andrew now can choose whether to accept the truth about his father, whose hold on him remains strong. Since Andrew won't believe his mother, we now see that the commitment to lying is an inseparable part of him. He chooses to remain in the lie.

Following Winnicott's "reality principle," which states that the "world exists whether the child creates it or not," we can anticipate a "potential breakdown" looming in Andrew's future.[18] He insists on propping up his "false self to cope with the world, this false front being a defense designed to protect the true self. (The true self has been traumatized and it must never be found and wounded again.)"[19] So in the scene in which his mom outright states the unquestionable truth—based on the evidence of Pete's actions—Andrew still refuses to believe her. Clearly, Pete's gaslighting of her worked. Andrew's trip to confront his dad is revelatory; nevertheless, the reality of his father's lies won't destroy the false self to which Andrew has so strongly committed.

Lying becomes part of his character in his way of engaging the world. It is not the same kind of creativity that Winnicott describes as the ability "to create the world" in a "life worth living."[20] A creative life would indicate a continually growing and developing self, interacting with others and objects. However, Andrew's fabricated stories are deployed to present a version of the self that is unchanging and not developing—one that is based on a lie. His creativity is based on adhering to social definition in propping up the false self and not to the social redefinition that his self-acceptance of socially disparaged identities would entail. He lies about his sexuality when he is unable to come out as gay to straight people; he changes his very Filipino-sounding name of Cunanan to the more Spanish-sounding Da Silva; and he represents his father not as an embezzler but as the owner of pineapple plantations in the Philippines whose fantasy character somehow is entangled with Imelda Marcos, herself known as a world-class liar. The question then emerges: What is his ethical relation to the real and the lie, when there is a physical reality and a psychic condition of dejection that must be overcome by any means necessary, including fantasy, delusion, and mythmaking? The response to this audacity of falsifying reality is key, too: when those listening to his lies refuse to participate and instead begin to laugh at him, fear him, pity him, and abandon him, he kills them. He literally murders them; he does not just silence them or run away from them. To him, they must die if they are no longer willing to support his lying and his illusions.

Trauma: An Encounter with Lying (Where the True Self Loses to the False Self)

In the Philippines, Andrew finds his father in a sorry compound of homes that embody what he described in his Merrill Lynch interview as "houses you can buy with the money in your wallet." The production design of the miniseries is minimal here, but the point is to convey through sheaths of white veiling and haphazardly strewn mosquito nets that these are poor houses. Andrew's white polo shirt is drenched with sweat and stuck on his chest while his dad's linen whites look light, loose, and cool. The confrontation between father and son explores the trauma that tethers them. They are mirrored, as they had been when they put on their suits and ties for the interviews at Bishop's School and Merrill Lynch, or when they slept in matching pajamas. Here, Andrew is at the cusp of adulthood, and Pete has fled to Manila after taking a shot at American life through his lies. Pete clearly likes living in the lie and escaping reality. We can see this represented in the question Andrew asks: Is there money, or is there no money? The question identifies the heart of the matter, and Andrew really needs to hear from his dad what he already knows. The version of the world the father had narrated for the son is about to explode, and Andrew has to choose which life to cultivate going forward. Winnicott says the choice of undoing "the basic patterns . . . laid down in the process of emotional growth . . . near the beginning (when) the factors . . . have the greatest influence" is an "opportunity for us to affect our own patterns."[21] For Andrew, this confrontation with his father becomes the moment when he comes face-to-face with his trauma, which he can either undo or repeat.

"I knew you'd come," Pete says as he serves his son pork rind that "does not look pretty." Confrontation ensues, however, when they must speak truthfully. Pete cuts to the chase: "You have questions." Andrew replies, "Mom says there is no money." Pete resorts to the lie that has become truth through repetition: "Your mother has a weak mind." With these words he reverts to the narrative of Andrew's childhood, in which the son had to choose between parents: the one who is attuned to him yet is powerless in the face of patriarchy or the one who abuses him and teaches him how to lie. The search for truth is not mutual, as each of Andrew's demands for it is met with another lie from his dad. "You sold the house" is a statement of fact that Pete meets with a prescription for how to perceive it: "I needed to move everything out of reach." Andrew's face lights up as he says, "There's money, then." "Millions, I would say," his dad responds. Andrew's face expresses doubt, but hope rises, even if the assertion of "millions" is qualified by the phrase "I would say." "Where?" Andrew asks, to which his father answers, "Out of reach." Andrew's face now shows confusion and hesitation. His dad tells him, "So happy you are here," to maintain the hold of delusion. But Andrew decides to confront him. Later that night, while his dad is sleeping, Andrew stands ready behind the white veil. He turns on the light.

His father suggests that the heat is what's keeping Andrew awake. "It's the heat. Me, I'm used to it. Grew up in it. Played in it, worked in it. It's been a while since I've been back, but the body remembers. You can pretend you belong somewhere else. The body knows." Similarly, Andrew knows in a psychic and bodily way that he does not belong here. And after hearing how the body knows its truths, Andrew then speaks most directly to his father. Moreover, in realizing it, he asserts a factual statement that ends in a question. "There's no money, is there?" Finally, the dad plainly speaks the truth: "No." And Andrew confirms, "There is no plan. No millions." The dad warns, "Watch your tone with me, young man. I am still your father." Andrew asserts the factual truth like a litany: "My father. He's a liar. He's a thief." But Pete will not give up his authority, even as he finally admits to lying and stealing. He even blames Andrew for it—saying it is fatherhood that made him do it.

Pete presents another narrative, attempting to change Andrew's perception. "Don't judge me, boy. You want to know what my crime was? I stole too small. Thousand dollars here. I admit it. I stole. Only what I needed to be a father. To be American. You can't go to America and start from nothing, so I stole. If I stole a hundred million, they would have promoted me." Here is the framing of race and racialization that has prevented his rise. If Merrill Lynch thrives on lying, this practice is permitted not for him but for those who are pedigreed and for others who belong because of their race and class. Andrew responds, "I can't be this. I can't be you." With incredulity, Pete retorts, "I'm not good enough for you now." He is neither the good enough father nor the good enough mother. Andrew explains how he organizes his reality, with his father performing a particular role: "I brag to my friends about your success. You were everything to me, Dad. It's a lie. If you are a lie, I am a lie. I can't be a lie, I can't." This moment of framing the lie as an undesirable identity, even if he has embraced it so fully, is a description of trauma—the understanding that one's life is shattered and broken from its continuous line. Wrecking one's narrative is damaging, confusing, and debilitating.

Pete then asks, "Are you crying? Weak. Just like your mother." This homophobic and patriarchal macho claim also withdraws from Andrew the princely stature previously assigned by his father. Pete implicates Andrew and his mother for knowing about the theft. "She never cared about stealing as soon as there was money. You are upset because I stopped. You have to work. You, sissy kid with a sissy mind. I judge you. I spit on you," and he does. "My special sissy boy. Be a man for once." Here, the father's lie is now acknowledged and is framed within homophobia and effeminization within the hierarchies of patriarchy. Andrew cannot be a man, even if he finally calls his dad out for lying, because his dad deems him to be gay and effeminized. Here, the sex of racial childhood becomes apparent where the parent and adult child interact without speaking of what transpired when the adult child was much younger. In this case, Pete calls his son whom he sexually molested a gay slur. Andrew's sexuality—both his victimization as a child and his adult sexuality—is blamed on the instilling of confidence as protection from racism and poverty.

This scene is striking. Andrew is crying and holding a knife with which he has threatened his father. In the face of his dad's homophobia and machismo, he makes his own palm bleed instead as he grips the blade. Cinematically, he confirms that his father is the one who can hurt him most. The object that Andrew had originally intended to use to hurt his dad ends up hurting himself instead. In his dad's judgment, Andrew lacks worth: "You don't have it in you." By "it" his father means the ability to hurt as constituting manhood. This moment makes a link between killing, harming, and heterosexual manhood, and not just adulthood, especially for the son who becomes a serial killer.

Andrew does not possess the masculinity it takes to kill, according to Pete, but manhood is not what makes him kill. Andrew recognizes the homophobia in his dad's perception of him. So, lying, which he learned from his dad, is ultimately what he invests in even after this confrontation that reveals his father's lies. And when others don't want to participate in that world, "the drive to maintain the false self" emerges to kill five people violently. But in this scene, Andrew refuses the judgment of manhood and instead declares he will no longer lie, telling his father, "I'll never be like you." Only as the episode concludes and Andrew returns to San Diego, stuck in a menial job, does he make the choice to continue a life of lies when faced with the reality of poverty. He is unable to choose humility and reality, which would include going back to school and working, and instead chooses to falsify his world just like his father.

The Destruction of Self and the Loss of Community

When Andrew returns to the United States, he tears up his books in a rage. Books are creations: their myths and their fictions must be relinquished. He wishes to destroy them and also that part of himself. This is a destruction of the self, too—a thoughtful, quiet, and well-read child is now thrown away, strewn across the room. The true self, the traumatized and abandoned child, dies in the destruction of the books. He now has to get a job at a neighborhood pharmacy run by an older Filipino man whom Andrew deems ordinary or simply too real. When asked about his father, Andrew reverts to lying. "He lives in Manila now. I've just come back." And when the pharmacist asks, "What is he up to there?" Andrew answers, "He owns multiple pineapple plantations." The older Filipino man clearly hears the lie but responds, "Is that so?"—which in Andrew's judgment indicates the pharmacist is simply too ordinary. "As far as the eye can see," Andrew replies, doubling down. So, it is embedded fully now, lying for a seductively fantastic and ultimately disastrously damaging life that others in his community and society have to pay for. He chooses to lie as his path for adulthood.

When Andrew lands a sugar daddy or two, from his performance as an educated and entertaining intellectual of sorts, he lavishes his friends and hangers-on with extravagant restaurant meals. He encounters a young man from the Midwest named David Madson (Cody Fern), wholesomely blond and white, earnest and gentle, and impressively ambitious. Andrew's lies to him, even when articulated in fancy hotel rooms and restaurants, lead to David's dissatisfaction with their blossoming relationship, and he loses interest. Essentially, their intimacy becomes limited in the face of Andrew's false self.

Another friend, Jeffrey Trail (Finn Wittrock), similarly loses his respect for and trust in Andrew. Jeff, a military officer suffering from the "Don't Ask, Don't Tell" policy of the Clinton era, seeks sincerity and honesty in friendship, which Andrew is simply unable to provide. Instead, Andrew insists they share in an illusion of success and wealth that is not his own. Andrew forces Jeff to pretend to give him an expensive pair of shoes as a birthday present. He demands that Jeff fake his own wealth to present to others the kind of friends Andrew pretends to have. At first Jeff plays along, until his own struggles with coming out in the military make it impossible for him to participate any longer in these efforts to create and maintain a false self.

At the same time, Andrew's older lover Norman Blachford (Michael Nouri), who supports him with a luxurious home, fancy car, and large allowance that allows him to shop and take friends out, tells him to his face that he is lying. Norman offers to help Andrew adjust to reality, instead of trafficking in unbelievable stories about wealth, travel, jobs, and real estate. It is too late. In the face of his trauma, Andrew is unable to destroy the facade and his false self. When Andrew loses his older lover due to his own persistent lying, he descends into poverty.

The series shows how this act of rampant lying is a way of life that worsens over time as Andrew becomes older. He lies to his best friend, Lizzie, whom he lives with in Berkeley after dropping out of college, about being gay—calling the gay club where he supposedly met Versace a private, members-only club. Lizzie's husband indicates his awareness of and frustration with Andrew's lying by rolling his eyes when Andrew turns away. Lizzie acknowledges the lying to her husband yet indulges her friend. Andrew's other friends are less patient. The boy who had a crush on Andrew and wanted to make a move on him at the high school house party is now a student at UC Berkeley. When Andrew shares the same Versace story, his friend cannot believe it is real. He challenges Andrew over his incessant lying about matters as serious as his coming out, his religion, and even his experiences with sexual abuse that he presumably heard about from him. Andrew steadfastly maintains his false self in the confrontation.

When his friend offers love for Andrew's true self—a traumatized boy—asking him not to lie and instead to recognize the goodness of the ordinary, Andrew refuses. He says he wants big things: fame, wealth, and the sublime. The friend confronts him, asking what kind of relationship they can have if he has to follow Andrew's lead and lie? He asks: "How am I supposed to behave? Do I pretend to know the person you're pretending to be? I can't keep up. Every time I feel like I'm getting close to you, you say you're someone else." This is the first we see of Andrew's close friends' terrible discomfort with having to pretend and keep up with his many imagined personas, his false self as presented to many. It is accompanied by the frustration of encountering his false self as a real obstacle when trying to make a connection and achieve intimacy.

And then there is the representation of Versace himself as someone Andrew had early encounters with in the Bay Area. When Cunanan goes to the San Francisco Opera, purportedly at the invitation of Versace, who was working as its costume designer, Andrew dons a suit and a gold watch, both owned by Lizzie's husband. He is in costume himself, a disguise, an embodied lie. In conversing with Versace after the opera, he reveals his youthful fantasies of fabricating a persona—including how he is considering changing his name to Da Silva. Versace presents a different path: "You should be proud of your name." Cunanan is very Filipino, so his wish to change it is part of a larger narrative of fleeing a denigrated and devalued identity. He wishes to become a "Da Silva"—a more racially ambiguous name—that can be European rather than Asian, white rather than brown, colonizer rather than colonized. Indeed, when he is profiled after killing Versace, he is described as "Latino, a security guard, parking attendant." The specter of racial judgment follows him even in death; during his life, he resisted this hailing by way of lying and fantasy-making.

The first two men he kills are his closest and most intimate friends who he most wishes would invest in his lies: David Madson and Jeffrey Trail. Thus, in the end, those who try to help him stop lying are those he destroys. He kills them for refusing to continue in the illusory world he inhabits. Lying is the refusal to live not only under poverty and homophobia, and to flee his trauma, but to do otherwise no matter what. He refuses the world he does not want, to be subjected to sexual predation by his father as well as a world of homophobia, racism, and poverty, by taking the lives of others who won't allow him to lie. Unfortunately, his white victims struggle with these forces as well: like him, they are gay men who experience denigration, deprivation from privilege, and falling short of the norm. The one exception to this is the simple and presumably heterosexual working man—William Reese, the caretaker of a New Jersey cemetery—who gets caught up in Andrew's spree and his need for escape by stealing a car.

American Crime Story: The Assassination of Gianni Versace portrays the world-making deployment of an illusory false self performed by the gay, mixed-race Filipino American serial killer Andrew Cunanan. As a young man, he says "what people want to hear" when he plays straight to straight people and only comes out as gay to gay people. His friends find it frustrating, not knowing what is true and what is fabricated. His full-blown and energetic attempt to embody lies about wealth and his wishes for whiteness are presented as a flight from his marginalized, not-rich, not-white, and not-straight self.

Rather than resign himself to an ordinary life that offers no pleasures, Cunanan chooses to work relentlessly on lying, cultivating deceit as a talent. The lies, however, also function as hopeful and painful attempts to connect and form a lineage with his father. Thus, the lying and erasure of the past are complex. They index the pain, shame, and embarrassment of the realities of denigrated brown lives that are rooted in childhood—one that is not white and not innocent—which extends to his poor, brown, queer adulthood. It does not justify his acts.

Racialized Childhoods: White Innocence and Brown Pathology in Adulthood

In her book *Racial Innocence: Performing American Childhood from Slavery to Civil Rights* (2011), Robin Bernstein returns repeatedly to the book *Uncle Tom's Cabin* by Harriet Beecher Stowe, paying attention to the installation of a "black-white logic in American visions of childhood," particularly in the white angel child who is susceptible to pain and the black ruined child who is not, naturalizing the latter to labor and slavery. Stowe created a character who is "an essentially innocent child who has been brutalized—hardened and made 'wicked' by slavery."[22] Stowe uses this as a device to regain what African American children were deprived of: sinlessness and worthiness. I am intrigued by the notion of how racism similarly makes Cunanan corrupted and perverted, first as a child, and then as an adult.

The young men that Cunanan kills also have childhood stories in the television series. His former lover David Madson, whom he calls the love of his life, is a kindhearted and ambitious architect in Minnesota—where a predominantly white Germanic population lives. Blond and blue-eyed, he looks like the cis all-American white boy. Successful, he lives in a modern loft with a devoted dog to which he is attached, while rising up in his career through his focused and impassioned work ethic. His death at the hands of Cunanan is intercut with a depiction of his childhood aversion to guns and killing. A young David's father takes him to a cabin and demonstrates compassion to his son, who does not share his own passion for hunting. David's gentleness as a boy extends to his coming out to his father as a young man. They have a calm relationship even in the face of a fundamental difference that could cause a schism between them but does not, indicating their deep bond. Unconditional love, recognition, and compassion infuse the Madson father-son relationship in an inversion of Andrew's relationship with his father.

During the 1997 manhunt for Andrew Cunanan, Filipinx Americans paid attention. Their responses included horror and shame, as well as lamenting the young man's good looks and perceived intelligence at avoiding capture. Invested in Filipinx American representation, they mourned how a member of the community possessing these seeming advantages could go toward a terribly wrong way instead. Indeed, he lived near or around me—we are the same age—we graduated from high school around the same time. Later, friends would say he was in our vicinity at UC Berkeley during our time there. I partied and clubbed in the city too, likely traveling in parallel across the Bay Bridge. According to what I heard in 1997, the summer I got married and was spending time around Filipinx family and friends, Cunanan was both a waste of representation and a baffling source of awe. Hardly any Filipinx were depicted on-screen and in popular culture at the time (or now), and here was a serial killer with good looks and a prominently Filipino name. *Sayang* (What a waste)! Yet there was also the perverse thrill in complimenting him: How smart was he not to get caught? *Galing naman* (So skilled—his excellence)! Such is the plight of a community with rare representative figures in popular culture. We are made perverse spectators to a killer. Responses of waste and excellence result from the same Filipinx American spectators who, because of a lack of representation, found pleasure in identifying something redeeming in the image of another in popular culture. In this sense, Cunanan is the waste (*sayang*) of excellence (*galing*) and the demise of possibility that his choices represent.

Perhaps it is a new day. When Darren Criss, a mixed-race Filipino American actor, won a Golden Globe in 2019 for his portrayal of the serial killer in the television series, the community exclaimed enthusiasm ecstatically—especially when he dedicated the award to his mother and essentially came out as Filipino on television, after having been reticent to do so previously. The next day, Criss posted on social media how he celebrated: brunch with his mom at a Filipinx restaurant in LA, one that my sisters and I also frequented.

In Closing: Killing Self and Others

The rare representation of Filipinx Americans occurs in the form of a serial killer. As such, Andrew Cunanan's representation in *American Crime Story* can help us better understand racialized and sexualized childhoods as differentiated from white ones, when the wound of race and poverty is drilled through sexuality, and lying becomes a strategy to alleviate pain and create doomed opportunity. Cunanan's racialized sexuality purportedly emerges from incestuous pedophilia, and this trauma is unresolved when the child is buried so that a false self can emerge. The representation of this trauma is compared to the opposite experiences of his white counterparts, Gianni Versace and David Madson, whose childhoods were innocent and nurtured as sinless. Andrew Cunanan's is corrupted by sexual predation that is then worsened by lying and associated with race and class through his father. Andrew is unable to establish a healthy self or gain self-sovereignty and self-governance at a young age due to a father who models a life of lying assuming racial inferiority and aversion to poverty.

The narrative of Andrew Cunanan's life is rooted in this wound of race-sex and the threat of poverty, so that his instinct is to survive no matter what, and his drive is toward a pleasure that distances him from trauma. At the end of the film, moments before he kills himself by placing a gun into his mouth and shooting, eliminating his face and recognizability, the filmmakers compose a frame that illustrates this unresolved trauma. At age twenty-seven, Andrew Cunanan looks upon his younger self at the age represented in the episode "Creator/Destroyer." The younger boy at about thirteen was moving to the bigger house where he occupied the master bedroom, the site of his wish to become a writer and the site of his supposed pedophilic victimization by his father. In a two-shot, the younger Andrew Cunanan is shown in profile and directly next to the older Andrew Cunanan. The boy dons a half smile, possessing a kind of beatific serenity and glowing peace. The older Andrew looks tortured, wearing a face of longing and regret for not choosing the path of taking care of his inner child and thus losing the opportunity to redirect his future away from death, destruction, and demise. In "Ego Distortion in Terms of True and False Self," Winnicott discusses how the false self aims to "make it possible for the True Self to come to its own, and if there be doubt then the clinical result is suicide. Suicide in this context is the destruction of the total self in avoidance of annihilation of the True Self . . . eliminat[ing] the need for its continued existence, since its function is the protection of the True Self from insult."[23] The boy, the reader who wants to be a writer, represents his true self whom he, who fully embodies the false self, must kill now because of the world of destruction that he has created.

Instead of confronting and addressing his trauma, Andrew cultivated entitlement to superficial and easy pleasures—whether from wealth or

1.2 Before killing himself, an older Andrew looks upon his younger self. *American Crime Story: The Assassination of Gianni Versace* (Ryan Murphy, 2018).

beauty—accompanied by the lack of a work ethic that could ensure the attainment of those things. He does not put in the work that would provide him with money or resources to fulfill his desires or achieve the analytic power that comes from confronting the structures and obstacles that create barriers in our lives. Meanwhile, his body retains childhood trauma that makes him want to or need to escape it as an adult. *American Crime Story: The Assassination of Gianni Versace* clearly shows that Cunanan kills the people who want to help him or whom he randomly comes across along his way to self-destruction. The construction of childhood trauma in relation to race, class, sex, and gender shows him as thoroughly wicked and sociopathic. The series makes this apparent in ways that encourage audiences to acknowledge, feel, and bear his pain. Yet, there is no affirming, productive, or creative resolution because he won't confront his trauma. He finds no dignity in work, nor any value in exploring his experience of poverty and addressing the trauma of his predation. It is precisely in arresting the trauma and undoing the lies that prop up the false self that a life can form. But it is that confrontation with trauma that he unfortunately fears, leading him to persistently build a false self that his reality cannot support.

I begin the book with this chapter because it presents a method for how to read racialized childhoods through the lens of agentic attunement. This film is a fiction built around Andrew Cunanan that shows how filmmakers can understand racialized childhoods as shaped by race, sex, and trauma. What was he seeking, and how? Andrew was not afraid of the world; he used all his talent to not confront his wounds—in fear of himself—and he lived until he could no longer do so, destroying others in his wake. He did not practice empathy; he aggressively claimed other people's worldviews to prop up his own illusions. He saw his relationships as objects for his own destructive use, what he considered a kind of play to build another reality that would give him pleasure.

In presenting how racialized childhood is imbricated with sexuality in this chapter, and later throughout this book, I am not trying to instill an unexpected empathy for the wicked or condone the death Cunanan dealt to innocence. I hope to open up questions about an underrepresented life: When particular racialized children are denied innocence, what happens in their lives? I answer by showing how we can come to understand them as resulting from the entanglement of the social, structural, emotional, and psychic forces of race, sexuality, gender, and class. And in the cross-hairs of these structures that limit and organize experience, I hope we can imagine other paths where he would hold worth, in order to be loved if he were to have received agentic attunement—even if only from himself. The rest of the book will contend with subjects who are judged for what they do and show the importance of where they come from and what they endure in their bodies, which don't come to the fore of our archive of images very often. Their racial, class, and gendered sexual woundings are frequently unseen. How can we make sure we see their wounding by recognizing how different childhoods are valued not only in the movies but also in the world? And to center the perspective of the child and the young so that they can become the healthy and creative versus destructive agents of their own and others' lives? To center the child is to recognize their perspectives and their path toward a healthy adulthood that begins with accepting the self, and identifying one's life projects and goals that do not result in harming the self and others.

2 The Inner Life of Cinema and Selfobjects

QUEER ASIAN AMERICAN YOUTH IN
SPA NIGHT AND *DRIVEWAYS*

My son Lakas, up until his death at age eight, was my appendage. We developed a physical attunement through ages zero to three that endured through his lifetime, so strong it still haunts me and will for the rest of my life. When he was alive from infancy to middle childhood, friends and family would comment on how I held him so much—as if this was too much. I loved holding him, carrying him, and his crawling onto my lap after every meal even in the years just before his death. The week Lakas died, his brother and classmates returned to school, and I saw his best friend emotional with tears. A big love that revealed the depth of their connection, simply leaving me in veneration, whatever word captures my awe, at the bigness of their relationship and Lakas's life that I did not fully know. One day, months after Lakas died, his other best friend was playing handball at school, a dispute ensued, and the boy ran to the classroom looking for Lakas, who was elected judge to resolve such fights. He forgot Lakas had died and stood in the room with tears like mine now.

In hearing about the attunement of other children with my son, I recognized their positive and affirming bond as an established part of his friends' lives. It was also present in my son's. My son Lakas, who was so popular at school and at the summer camps he went to, where kids fought to sit next to him, had a life bigger than I ever knew, a life beyond me where he found affirmation in others and vice versa. The practice of agentic attunement is designed to stay with the child when the caregiver is not around, providing the illusion of omnipotence and even a kind of grandiosity necessary for the child (and appropriate for the age) so as to hold in himself as a young person an ever-flowing source of confidence and strength. And this intense bond of agentic attunement stays with me now, fueling these pages, and informing my search to understand that bond further with the awareness of the preciousness of that childhood time. Movies, in representing a child's inner life, enable us all to analyze ourselves and our relations. This potentiality reveals the cinema as a historically persistent site of harm and a particular source of self-affirmation as well so we may *become the agents of our own lives and the center of our own narratives*. Thus, the need exists for more authors and critics of color and women to helm and frame them.

This chapter studies Korean American director Andrew Ahn's first two feature films, both focused on queer Asian American youth. *Spa Night* (2016) features a young adult or older teen freshly graduated from high school, and *Driveways* (2019) tells the story of an eight-year-old child, the same age as Lakas when he died. In using object relations psychoanalytic theory that builds on Freudian drive theories to emphasize our dependence on relations with others in our self-formation, key terms inform my inquiry. Fragmentation describes the process of growing up and figuring out who one will be. Along the way, feelings of confusion and distress regarding good and bad objects can lead to feeling discombobulated and not (yet) oneself. Furthermore, the fragmentation of queer Asian American characters occurs within a social context, hence the importance of agentic attunement in studying the scenes of their lives: where the child lives, whom they meet, and the events they undergo to gain a sense of self—knowing they deserve attention, value, and worth. Fragmentation essentially requires our agentic attunement, our empathetic observation, in order to understand children and to work toward their well-being. Lakas was not fragmented, or perhaps he was in a state of prefragmentation. Working through the stories of racialized childhoods helps me continue mothering him and celebrating that time of helping him grow into self-sovereignty.

Spa Night portrays the world of a young Korean American man named David (Joe Seo) who forgos college to work with his parents at their Korean restaurant in contemporary Los Angeles, specifically Koreatown. It is an atypical choice for his demographic, according to responses he receives from members of his Korean American church community, who question why he is not in school. Even his parents wish for another life for him, one involving independence, higher education, socioeconomic mobility, living on his own, and having a girlfriend. Aggravating the fragmented situation, his working-class family experiences further financial downfall due to the closure of their restaurant and his father's alcoholism. The loss here is of class privilege and a sense of safety as David's father deteriorates, unable to serve as a masculine model when dwindling to a shell of a man. Due to consuming debilitating amounts of alcohol, he is unable to walk to his bedroom and instead falls asleep on the floor of the living room, where David sleeps. His mother takes on a full-time job as a waitress at the restaurant of a more successful friend while he and his father take jobs as day laborers. David is obsessed with his bodily fitness, single-mindedly running the streets, where we see the predominantly Korean-language signage. He also relentlessly works out at home, and then even more intensely takes selfies in the bathroom mirror not only of his chest and abs but also of his penis. Living with his parents, he straddles loyalty to them and his own burgeoning sexual desires as a gay man. He finds a job in a Korean spa, where he welcomes the discovery of a diverse group of naked men acting out their queer desires.

The drama between children and parents that is such a centerpiece of Asian American films expands to explore the character's relationship with other youth and his own sexuality. To see Koreatown in films by young filmmakers, working some thirty years since images of its burning signs and buildings were broadcast during the LA Uprising of 1992, is to track the role of the environment in the subjective and introspective experience of their characters. Historian Shelley Sang-hee Lee, in her book *Koreatown, Los Angeles*, argues for the emotional significance of Koreatown for the Korean Americans who built the region in order to meet their community's needs. To set *Spa Night*, which depicts a Korean American learning to accept his gay identity through enacting his sexual desires, in Koreatown expands this notion of carving out not only economic but also social and sexual belonging within this space.[1] For David, who spends time at the mirror evoking idealized bodies and making his own real, what it means to represent race, sexuality, and Asian Americans in the American imagination comes to the fore in the private space of home. By looking in the mirror, David projects a self that belongs to a particular social world, or a public that he imagines gazing upon him, to build on Michael Warner's formulation.[2] Moreover, in the public space of the mirror located in the Korean spa where David finds work, he discovers sex between men as the ideal site of his own investments and desires, revealing the terrain he needs to climb to challenge the limited futures for youth constrained by sex, gender, class, race, and culture.

The film depicts these constraints through its representational language of the face and the body as they express the character's inner life, not only as feeling subjects but also as thinking subjects. David's expressions and gestures challenge the opacity attributed to the Asian American face in the history of popular culture.[3] Cultural studies scholar Sunny Xiang's book *Tonal Intelligence* indeed challenges us to consider how the "inscrutable Oriental offers a unique opportunity to explore how racial perception informed the parameters of credible intelligence and the benchmarks for reliable friends."[4] After working on notions of race and representations for the past twenty-plus years, I continue to be struck by the ways in which critics negate the discursive context of racialized images in films like *Spa Night*. In one example, film critic Kate Erbland, in her review in *IndieWire*, admires the "beautifully lensed film," yet she bemoans how David "remains woefully opaque to the film's very last shot," which for her maintains him at an "unreachable distance, one even the most artfully lensed body can't quite touch."[5] She essentially reads the Asian guy as inscrutable, even as he blatantly expresses pain on his face—the very instrument of his acting. Detailed observation shows his psychic agony in the tightly shut eyes and the sharp grimace of his mouth—three differently sized and shaped slivers that harden parts of his face to exhibit suffering and other emotions. And it is physical torture manifest on his face, tears flowing from his eyes, when he vigorously rubs his own skin to the point of bursting blood vessels. Erbland's words "woefully opaque" discount the expression of the wide range of feelings he emotes and demonstrates.

According to Asian American cultural studies scholars Robert G. Lee and David Palumbo-Liu, Asian Americans have been deemed inscrutable since the earliest forms of mass culture. Not only does Erbland not situate the film in the context of this racial and sexual cultural specificity, but she appears to repeat a common racist trope in reading Asian American faces as opaque. Asserting particular faces as unreadable, historically read as inscrutable, is thus especially important—especially when applied to actors whose jobs include using their faces to express emotion. Furthermore, Erbland does not situate the film within its genre—whether of Asian American cinema, to read the family dynamic beyond one that is "universal," or of queer cinema, in David's attention to the body as queer, an identification that could lead to a falling-out with his family.[6] These contexts are critical to understanding the Asian American face when making such assertions about the few representations of Asian Americans in movies.

The second film, Andrew Ahn's *Driveways*, portrays Cody (Lucas Jaye), a young, mixed-race Asian American boy who travels with his mom, Kathy (Hong Chau), from Michigan to an unnamed small town in upstate New York in a drama about a fragmented Asian American family. They make the trip because his aunt (her sister) has died suddenly, leaving a house overflowing with "a ton of shit," including a dead cat in the bathtub. Despite the masks they wear at different times in the film to protect their lungs from the detritus of the dead, their world predates the COVID-19 pandemic. Their environment—including living at the aunt's house in a makeshift space on the front porch—allows us to examine his mother's relationship with her estranged sibling as well as the mother-son dynamic. Reviews and the film's publicity call Cody a "lonesome" boy, and the film is indeed concerned about his inner life, in a form of agentic attunement in its concerns about his welfare and future, depicted through his interactions with others and the new space he now navigates, including his relations with his neighbors, an old, white Korean War veteran named Del, a white racist grandmother, and a few white and Latinx children who live nearby.[7]

In this chapter, I follow two queer, male-presenting Asian Americans—one adolescent and one young adult—using object relations theory as I emphasize their relations with their parents, community, and environment. Their experiences with these relations lead me to the field of self psychology and the study of selfobjects. According to Heinz Kohut, a psychoanalyst of self psychology, *a selfobject refers to a set of relations and experiences—including animate and inanimate objects—that inform one's identity, or subject formation.* Selfobjects thus are people and objects that compose significant experiences in forming oneself. Both David and Cody are fragmented personalities in that their experiences with selfobjects do not give them the sense of cohesion and assuredness that would help them forge strong, happy, and confident lives, especially as marginalized members of their societies. As in object relations theory, their experiences with their parents lead them to question whether they are worthy of the resources, time, and attention that would give them confidence and self-assurance. In the case of David and the emergence of his sexual desires, he finds the heterosexual pressure of family suffocating, and he fights for himself by working on his physical fitness and speaking his sexuality through his fit body as he partakes in the culture of gay male desire. For Cody, his travel with his mother and the resulting lack of home, father, stability, and continuity prevent him from feeling whole and coherent; his body manifests this in frequent vomiting when he experiences fear and anxiety. He establishes a bond with an unexpected ally, the old white male veteran Del, who enables him, through their agentic attunement that nurtures him in conjunction with the support of his mother, to forge a stronger self.

The Fragmented Self: Environment and Selfobjects in Self Psychology

In the previous chapter, I discussed how Andrew Cunanan's bond with his caring mother was curtailed by a sadistic father who preyed on and traumatized him in a different kind of disempowering and disorienting attunement, resulting in the development of a distorted self. The two main characters here, David in *Spa Night* and Cody in *Driveways*, are at the cusp of what psychoanalyst Heinz Kohut has called "the development arrest," wherein "specific environmental factors (the personality of the parents, for example; certain traumatic external events" can launch personality disorders.[8] As I touched on in the introduction, self psychology is a theory of psychoanalysis that developed after Sigmund Freud. Freud, in the early twentieth and late nineteenth centuries, focused on sexual drives—biological and innate—in ways that differ from Kohut's focus on the self as a subject that "needs certain sustaining psychological responses from its surroundings in order to remain cohesive and vigorous."[9] In this way, working in the later twentieth century, Kohut expanded the purview of psychoanalysis beyond internal drives and instincts to emphasize the significance of the environmental context especially for children, who may not express themselves at a higher developmental stage. He aimed to include responses to others as well as objects, places, and events—as the building blocks of a life that compose films too. The ramifications of one's experiences with these agents—animate and inanimate—that

Kohut calls "selfobjects" matters in the formation of the subject, beyond innate drives to include their relations and changes over time.

Selfobjects, according to Ernest Wolf, "are those experiences that evoke, maintain and give cohesion to the self."[10] That is, one can become fragmented due to insufficient or insignificant responses or experiences with selfobjects. Such experiences show how selfobjects have particular effects on each individual: constant and reliable affirmation can lead to strength and confidence so that obstacles are brushed off. Conversely, the lack of affirmation can lead to a fracturing response and devastation at encountering the smallest slight. For Kohut, according to Wolf, his close collaborator, the "psychology of self-object experiences is concerned with those vicissitudes of the experience of selfhood."[11] Our experiences with others, events, and places challenge the construction of the self—whether in how we experience obstacles to our sexuality, our education, our friendships, our employment, and/or our intimate relationships.

The move toward Kohutian self psychology's emphasis on the selfobject—the context and environment that shape the self—in building from the Freudian concepts of ego, drives, and instincts as innate and biological forces within oneself is significant because of the importance of accounting for the external forces that shape the self, even from before one's birth and throughout one's development into adulthood. We inhabit our roles within the established ideas of our times. The emphasis on the outer world matters in the growth of these young people in the films; the parents' empathy shapes how the child can learn to regulate their self-esteem. Rather than simply engage with what feels like one's innate desires, the reflection of those desires in others shapes how one sees the self. Therefore, relationships with others and the location where one lives and interacts matter significantly in acknowledging how subjects remain in process.

This attention to the outside world is what psychoanalytic film theorist Kaja Silverman discusses in her seminal work, which uses psychoanalytic frameworks to understand racial and other representations. Speaking about her book *The Threshold of the Visible World* (1996), she argues that we are not outside of our relationship structures, whether in "language, kinship structures, [or] a given set of historical, social, economic and geographical circumstances, and . . . we have absolutely no agency until we have acknowledged these forms of finitude and determination."[12] So to become an agent in one's own life that is the goal of my agentic attunement requires inventory of and engagement with our relations—structural, interpersonal, and cultural. The context in which we live so thoroughly shapes what we believe are our own independent actions. Yet, all of our actions are touched by our place and those around us—our outer world. To understand the self, we must see how the mirror reflects the outer world of the subject. And in interacting with others in particular places, we process and revise their meanings.

We alone do not make up who we are but are shaped by those around us. This definition of the self combines self-interpretation as dependent on others in ways that inform our "cohesion," which Kohutian scholar Ernest Wolf defines as a "state of well-being derived from the cohesion of myself [where] the self is a structure; that is, it endures over time and changes comparatively slowly. Therefore, the self has a history—a past, a present and a future."[13] Our experiences of self include interactions that confirm us, deny us, and play with our acts of self-interpretation. We compare and analyze our experiences in relation to others. Wolf describes how "self psychology strikes deeply at a politico-religious value system in which the self-made individual is the ideal. We now have a deeper appreciation of our inescapable embeddedness in our environment."[14] For Wolf, following Kohut, to study the self in a vacuum, as primarily internal, is not possible, for the environment shapes the individual and these experiences of interacting, living, and engaging with the world that compose the person in an ongoing manner.

Cinema as Selfobject: Autonomy and Equanimity

In particular, Kohut's work helps me to frame how the young people represented in Andrew Ahn's films attempt to unify their fragmented selves: by seeking sexual autonomy in David's case and equanimity in Cody's. David's confinement in his family home and Koreatown becomes the basis for forging sexual subjection that won't leave his community behind. For Cody, the chaos of moving and the ensuing feeling of instability become the ground for seeking peace and stability. Kohutian fragmentation can be captured in what Wolf describes as the "occasional self-experience of being apprehensive, without energy, moody, ill-focused and disorganized. I might describe this feeling informally as the sense that I am falling apart . . . aspects of one's self-experience no longer coordinated or fitting together . . . in response to something going on in the surround[ings]."[15]

This fragmentation is precisely described as occasional; one's sense of self-disassemblage can be fleeting depending on the environment in which the self is situated.

The method I encourage for studying these characters' enduring and confronting fragmentation is what I advocate for in agentic attunement, which I identify as a process of caretaking for the child for their future self-sovereignty and the special way cinema arrests that process so we can see how the detailed observation of others we care for works. As in my previous study in *The Proximity of Other Skins* (2020), I encourage us to learn from the spectatorship of ethical intimacy as a form of empathetic observation, not judging the characters in global cinema but choosing to regard their different experiences as worth studying in order to learn from them, fueled by open-ended questions and attunement to the historical and discursive contexts of their appearances on-screen so that we may see them and ourselves within the context of difference.[16] I use "difference" in the sense of Cornel West in "The New Cultural Politics of Difference," which he defines as "diversity, multiplicity, and heterogeneity to reject the abstract, general, and universal in light of the concrete, specific, and particular, and to historicize, contextualize and pluralize, by highlighting the contingent, provisional, variable, tentative, shifting and changing."[17] In utilizing this understanding, cinema can then be a productive force to decenter the self, which we must do to learn from others in a decolonizing project. Doing so shows us what film is capable of beyond the way it injures colonized subjects, further aggravating their subjugation. In my previous work I also argue how the medium of cinema can show us worlds we don't necessarily want to see, but bear them we must. Here, I show how the medium of cinema focuses on the inner life vis-à-vis outer expression to argue that agentic attunement *provides an opportunity to understand not only film characters but also ourselves through the experience of cinema as a selfobject* that forms us and even transforms us.

Films document inner life as inseparable from its context. In this way, they offer psychoanalytic data as observable in different ways of acting—whether in speech or gesture—and setting, whether in various places or times and the choreography of bodies and gestures in space. That is, we move away from reading internal life as self-standing to recognizing it as always occurring in the context of relational experience. Through the cinema, which externalizes the internal through physical expressions of performance, space, and more, we see how the self develops through interactions that shape the character's psyche, including self-perceptions and self-regard. And in these films, facing unpleasant and unwelcome circumstances forces the self to apprehend and comprehend its current condition as fragmented, and thus needing change to become stronger and more whole. To apply agentic attunement to cinematic narratives encourages introspected experiences for the spectator as a selfobject, providing experiences with others, objects, places, and events that shape us and help us to achieve our own autonomy and equanimity.

Moreover, in both these films, mirroring relations with selfobjects helps in the growth of the young self's worth. Kohut states that objects "may suffice as other people, animals, pets, interests in things one pursues, such as art, music or whatever it may be. And generally, health has been measured by the degree to which people are capable of an unencumbered, rich, variegated, profound, intense interest in objects."[18] The key idea in such a definition is that one's experience with animate and inanimate objects contributes to the organization of one's self in key stages of development, such as those represented in the films—middle childhood, adolescence, and young adulthood—in terms of their aspirations for becoming strong and healthy people. For example, David works on his body as a love and/or sex object, while Cody reads manga comics and learns about genderqueer people as a way to make infinite identity.

According to Wolf, "The selfobject relationship refers to an intrapsychic experience and does not describe the interpersonal relationship between the self and other objects. It denotes the subjective experience of images that are needed for the sustenance of the self."[19] So the self is inherently social and dependent on selfobjects; it is forged and formed through the act of reflection, usually represented in moments when the character expresses emotion not only through the voice, face, and actions but also within space itself—and not necessarily only through the body. The intensity of the self-reflection that emerges from responding to experiences is communicated in the duration and expansion, temporal and spatial, of a filmic representation. Thus, if we were to understand the film as a selfobject, we are essentially bringing together psychoanalysis and phenomenology as Kohut does. I follow suit in my own work by attending to the phenomenology of cinema in agentic attunement that attends to our experience of spectatorship and the film itself as a subject whose project is made complete by our interaction. That is, we should always be careful in how we reflect on our physical and affective responses and how we process and interpret them.

Spa Night's Penis in the Mirror: Self-Sovereignty

In *Spa Night*, spectators get a view of archetypal Koreatown spaces—the family home; Korean restaurants; and the Koreatown streets and spas in which David lives, runs, and works. The space of his community and family encroaches on his expression of sexual desire and sexual being. Indeed, there is a tension between the racialized ethnic spaces and his racialized sexuality. At home, especially, is where he uses the mirror to aspire to a different self. At the spa, also a racialized ethnic space where sexuality is illicit, he achieves it not only in his interactions but also in looking at the mirror there—and in the form of a Korean lover. In the mirror, whether at home in its cold reflection or in the warm body of his sex partner at the spa, he confronts his fragmented self: Am I real? Am I falling apart and dissipating? The mirror becomes an agent of self-approval that he must take outside to other relations with other looks and other interactions beyond himself. In his experiences with his peers, his self—the one with same-sex desire—is not affirmed but instead is diminished by their homophobia and heterosexism. The spa—an ethnic, commercial, familial, and traditional space on the one hand, and interracial, young, queer, and illicit on the other—comes to be a place of much-needed affirmation, of seeing other men who look at and long for penises (literally) like David does. The coming expression of this self—one who looks at and desires other men—makes him whole. And only when he faces the truth of his desire after it is fulfilled with another young Korean man—which his disapproving homophobic boss sees—does he achieve strength to express rage over others' lack of acceptance.

April 29, 1992, is known to Koreans and Korean Americans as Sa-I-Gu, a day when the community of Koreatown in Los Angeles came into national prominence with indelible images of Korean American men with machine guns protecting their property during a time of racial reckoning for African Americans against police brutality. The following year, the acquittal of the policemen caught on videotape for the beating of Rodney King in 1991 led to the LA Uprising. With the murder by gunshot of African American teenager Latasha Harlins by fifty-one-year-old grocery store owner Soon Ja Du in Harlem thirteen days after Rodney King's videotaped beating, Korean American anti-Blackness also came to public consciousness. Almost twenty-five years later, Koreatown—as represented in the 2016 film *Spa Night*—is a bustling ethnic enclave full of establishments advertised by signage in the Korean language. David is part of this community, working in a restaurant and interacting in a familiar manner with a Latinx supplier to whom he speaks Spanish as an Angeleno. Another such business in Koreatown is the spa, represented as a cultural site for the propagation of Korean American and US state-sanctioned homophobia as well as a site for gay sexual connection among Koreans and non-Koreans.[20] It is also a site for culturally specific family and community practices that show the intersection of race, gender, and sexuality as the context for David's individual formation within a system.[21]

Spa Night opens at the spa with the main character, David, with a towel over his head in profile. Naked with his dad, they take turns scrubbing each other's backs. The physical intimacy between father and son mimics homoerotic intimacy, with their naked torsos touching each other with chest against back. Taking turns, and changing positions, they see and touch each other, either scrubbing or slapping each other's backs. The intimacy at the spa is familiar to Korean culture—the mom lies down comfortably with her feet up the back of a bench in the public gathering area as her husband and son join her. The gender segregation of the spa means she is alone while father and son bathe together. "It gets boring," she says, wishing they had a daughter or a daughter-in-law in their family and telling David, "When you get married, I will come to the spa with your wife." She communicates the family's racially heterosexual expectations in this casual declaration. A daughter or daughter-in-law would scrub her back because these are the gendered segregations reflected within the spatial arrangement of the Korean spa, which is also an extension of gendered expectations within the family. This opening scene immediately establishes David's worry that his assumed partner must be Korean in order to fit in his family. He asks, "What if I marry a white girl?" His mom answers that this has ramifications: How will they communicate with his wife? He should have a Korean wife (so she can have Korean grandkids). The next shot, away from this public area, announces a different agenda for David: in the locker room, he peers at a nearby man's nakedness.

At home, David defies his parents and their gendered and sexual expectations by working on his body's fitness. The mother questions his interest in exercise and sees it as excessive—and a waste of his cleanliness from the spa because he gets himself dirty again from sweating and working out on the floor. The father, with his habitual drunkenness and his physical weakness at his day jobs, is the opposite of David, a strapping and chiseled youth. In this way, David's youthful, vigorous body exposes difference from his older, unhealthy dad. For his cis straight peers, his fit body makes him more masculine, which hides his gay identity among them—while it also makes him more visible to other gay men. Against all these investments in his body, his fitness regimen may be a way for him to reclaim his time to serve himself and his interests. Not only does the visibility of his fit body communicate a different physical agenda, one that should announce a preference for a different culture, but the sweat that pours onto the floor as he performs sit-ups and boat pose side crunches asserts his undeniable physical autonomy. His mom complains, "You're sweating all over the floor. Stop sweating!" She does not command him to stop working out or stop doing sit-ups but to stop speaking with his body: its liquid excretions and heavy exhaling. David's fitness is an assertion of self against the constraining pressures of living in his family's common space. He works to achieve an adulthood that departs from the expectations of heteronormativity toward a queer future, one attuned to male fitness and beauty. He "suffers" physically to achieve a homonormative body in resistance to heteronormativity. His body seeks legibility to escape the illegibility of his experience with racial ethnic *selfobjects* that push him toward heterosexual and gendered normativity. His body endures this self-discipline to match dominant gay body culture, which perhaps also brings him joy as a reclamation of the body outside of his home and his family.

Fitness, thus, is an assertion of self within the confines of his space organized by his family. David's only private space in their small apartment is the bathroom, because he sleeps on the floor of the living room. This keeps him in an infantilized situation, close to the ground and unable to relax. He is literally on the floor with blankets, without a delineated space from the common area of the family. In a casual domination, his poor parents deny him the privacy typical of the US middle-class experience to which his family purports to belong. So, when he looks in the mirror to take detailed pictures of his abs, in a fragmented framing of his body, it is a way not only to see but also to experience his body alone so he can patch himself together. In photographing his body, his fragmentation continues in the framing we see on-screen: first his chest, then his flat stomach in profile. Each of these close-ups shows details of a fit body that imagines being seen in another setting, perhaps a more public one. Then the camera lowers to his penis, creating a shock when further zooming in because we usually do not see full-frontal male genital shots in US narrative fiction film.[22] Here, the shot indicates how others looking at his body may desire his genitalia. Through this shot of his penis, we see the need to shift away from his experience of fragmentation. The sight of his penis makes his desire real. His fitness is sexually motivated, as its appearance in the mirror indicates.

In "Building Psychic Structures that Regulate Self Esteem," Heinz Kohut describes the process of cognitive self-recognition: "When the small child cognitively begins to see that there are objects other than himself, they still serve a narcissistic dimension. They have names; they are selves. They have significance to him as libidinal objects for whom he longs and to whom he wants to give something."[23] He refers to this process as "mirror transference," which, he explains, "in its various phases of development is an expression of the fact that others are experienced and needed in the sense of being agents for self-confirmation, for self-approval."[24] The mirror becomes an agent of self-approval when used to create a different environment than the reality in which one lives. For David, this is especially important within the context of imagining another encounter, one that is more affirming than the one with his disapproving and disciplining family. What he gets from the mirror, however, is insufficient still.

The mirror, according to Kohut, is "cold," in contrast to an encounter with a selfobject that is not imagined but more real, actually warm and living, more intrapsychic and intraphysical. The sight of a penis within the context of another's presence looking back and the potentiality of a sexual encounter as an actual selfobject experience versus a projection matter. Kohut says, "One needs to experience oneself as having an effect, of receiving a response, of being important. . . . But a mirror is cold; it is only a mirror visually. The mother is not just such a mirror. She is a responding mirror, which is a very different kind of mirror for she is not his target for sexual aims."[25] David's own gaze upon his penis is not enough to satisfy; he looks upon the mirror with the aim of a future encounter of satisfaction. Moreover, the mirror cannot properly counter the father, who lies and hides how their restaurant is in financial distress and who responds not by getting a steady job but by drinking, saying it's "too hard. Much too hard." He distresses David, who asks, "Will we be OK?" as an indication of the anxiety instantiated by loss and precarity. In these instances, his mother and his father are each very strong mirrors that speak and reflect upon him their projection of normative heterosexual failure (mother) in his queerness and gendered failure (father) in not being able to succeed financially and fulfill his gendered role. Their mirror reflections help to compose him.

The mirror in the bathroom, with its promise of object status beyond his family, indeed feels good when he looks at it to see future possibility.

When David looks into the mirror, his fragmented parts come together in a pleasurable vision of queer wholeness. The mirror that evidences his bodily fitness speaks happily to his sense of self. In an interview, film theorist Kaja Silverman discusses the resonance of Lacan's conceptual use of the mirror as a "threshold of the visible world," which she uses as the title of one of her books. Referring to the mirror stage as primary for the development of the ego, Lacan identifies how the "child can already recognize his own image" in the mirror as a key process in "identification" or the "transformation that takes place in the subject when he assumes an image."[26] This moment of identification is one Silverman theorizes to better understand how we can identify with others unlike ourselves, and others who are degraded in society—even from the distance of movies.[27] She says the mirror stage possesses "the mortal danger inherent in the aspiration to approximate the ideal [in a] loop leading inexorably from the aspiration to ideality, to the experience of insufficiency and disintegration, and back again to the aspiration to ideality."[28] But, for David, this is not what is taking place.

David's idealization of the body leads not to incompleteness but to a projection of its wholeness elsewhere, making his home bearable. He is not shattered but made whole by the close-ups of his fragmented, chiseled abdomen—a testimony to an incompleteness that will be filled when taken outside in the future, where he really belongs, where he could be seen, embraced, desired, and touched. These feelings inspire him to take his pursuit of fitness outside in the form of running. When we see him run through the streets of Koreatown, we are grounded in his environment, and he brings his good feelings outside to cohere himself. David runs the streets of Koreatown looking for space to express his body's fitness and the desire for freedom and mobility it represents. Characters move from fragmentation and cohesion throughout life, yet quite intensely in youth and in the experience of the body.

The fitness of his body speaks to hegemonic masculine beauty in ways that resonate in heterosexual circles that privilege David yet torture him too. When his mother encounters her more successful friend, a restaurant owner who hires her for a wait staff position, she encourages David to visit her friend's son Eddie at the University of Southern California (USC). Promoting a normative path of success via college, the mom's friend pushes David to do a sleepover at USC with Eddie as his host. This visit offers the potential for a different experience with selfobjects, where a varying reflection can occur beyond the heteronormativity imposed by David's mother and gendered male expectations by his father.

As soon as he arrives at USC, David learns that Eddie's roommate is gay and sleeps at his "boyfriend's." David responds with a questioning, "Boyfriend?" to which Eddie responds with a tolerant though not accepting, "Yeah, right." David sees the disapproval of gayness in Eddie's face. Eddie takes him to a business class in a large lecture hall, which David does not find inviting either. His first selfobject experiences with Eddie repeat the reflection of his mother and father: homophobic heteronormativity and patriarchal masculinity via capitalism—which his dad fails at and to which David is not amenable. Meanwhile, his need to express sexual desire for the male body keeps rising. At the gym, he cannot stop staring at Eddie's hand while he holds on tightly to the treadmill. The selfobject encounter with Eddie thus unleashes David's desire at a site that is revealing itself to be unwelcoming and potentially dangerous for his gay male desire.

The experience at USC worsens for David. Later that night, at a house party, he is stiff, taller than all the others and standing rigidly against a wall while throngs of primarily Asian American partygoers wriggle past him, touching each other and squeezing through the small hallway space. His pent-up discomfort is apparent in how he tenses his jaw as the sea of fun-loving people ebb and flow around him. Young women flirt with him, touching his fit body and admiring his good looks. Another young man enters the scene, clearly less attractive and conventionally less masculine than David but also more talkative and more relaxed. In contrast, David is completely tense and absolutely silent. His physical behavior makes him odd, though his good looks compensate and make his unknowability, stiffness, and discomfort not yet an uncomfortable or unknowable presence; perhaps he reads as shy in the new and primarily cis and heterosexual space. He may not yet belong and may not yet achieve familiarity. That is, his queerness in the straight space may not be readable (yet). The contrast with the other young man who is readable as straight—entitled, comfortable, casual, and loud, someone who belongs—becomes significant in the next scene.

The party extends to a car ride headed to Koreatown. In the car, David stares intently at Eddie's hand holding that of his girlfriend, Esther, on the console between the passenger and the driver's seats. The position of the mother and father is replicated in this heterosexual hand-holding as David sits, childlike and silent, in the back seat, even as the girls from the party continue to include him. At the karaoke club, the singing and dancing contrast with his increasing stiffness. The young women are more daring in flirting with him, getting close to him, sitting next to him, then dancing, sandwiching him. He forces himself to dance, further revealing his discomfort. The fluidity of the bodies around him underscores his rigidity. Eddie starts looking at him with suspicion.

The experience becomes frightening when David and the others play spin the bottle drunkenly. The young women play a game of kissing each other, with the first one who retreats having to drink a shot. It is both a sexually titillating and homophobic game that makes same-sex kissing perverse and repulsive. The game is played for fun, accompanied by raucous laughter. The women demand that the men play the game, too, daring them to kiss each other. Paired to play against each other, Eddie's relaxed friend tells David, "I'm going to win. I have no fear." David, meanwhile, is bottled up with fear. The party music defies his heavy feeling. The young men slowly move toward each other's face as the others look on. David cringes. Both men close their eyes, one to avoid contact and one to hide from the proximity of desire to fear. The approach is long, with his pulsating desire surfacing alongside the fear of social death. David pulls back abruptly. The moment is so intense because of the difficulty, apparent in the hardness of his body, in stifling his energies and containing his desire. It is an unbearable experience that threatens to unravel him, to make him finally fall apart after holding himself together and containing his sexuality for so long throughout that day and the length of his adulthood thus far. Laughter descends upon a completely terrified David, who must combat his wish to release and express his sexual desire for men with his full yet waning strength. He is weakening from having to bear the weight of heterosexual normativity's demand to hide himself.

Later in the night, they all end up at the Korean spa, where the group of three men and three women must segregate by gender. At this point, other young adults provide David with a selfobject experience that is not satisfying—it deprives him of air. It is like being around his parents and makes indubitably clear the heteronormativity of his home and the community of his generation outside of his family. It recalls how David first speaks in the opening scene of the film, with a towel over his head, saying, "I can't breathe." It is not at all like the death of Black people such as George Floyd, who uttered these very words within our white-supremacist world, but a suffocating in having to contain himself constantly. Without sustaining and supporting selfobject experiences even with his peers, who represent a new world away from his parents, David becomes even more plagued with loneliness and suffering. The good feeling that he extracts from his fit body, which leads him to express the need for others to participate in the happiness and aspiration that fitness represents, finds no release or resonance here.

Weakened by the struggle to hold himself together, David can no longer avert his gaze. He no longer shyly lowers his head; instead, he succumbs to the sight of the naked young men with him while they are in the sauna. He openly studies the other young man's thigh and hip as an aperture for him to catch sight of the penis. "What are you looking at?" says Eddie, with a violent stare, an evil eye emanating homophobia and a threatening policing. The film cuts away from the menacing look to another scene in which we see David vomit, likely a result of the volatile confrontation. As he pukes into the toilet, the other young man pushes David away so he can urinate. Sitting on the floor next to the toilet, David cannot help himself again and peers at the genitals near his face. The young man accuses him with a rhetorical question that is a hostile command, "Can you stop looking at my dick?" Eddie and his friend begin to call David "penis-looker," in a representation of these Korean American youths as intensely homophobic, and indicating that the group now perceives something wrong with him, which is so precisely articulated in this term that indicates "gay equals pervert." Among his peers, and the homophobic world they occupy, David cannot release his pent-up self even when he is away from his family, even as he needs to as a normal part of his development.

The spa as a workplace, however, becomes a site for him to explore his desire and defragmentation. His going there, likely for the first time away from his family and any friends, makes the space one that he can independently explore both in his search for freedom away from family expectations and to express his sexual desire for men. He returns to get a job there, stopping the expensive SAT lessons his parents pay off one at a time. Although they cannot afford it, his parents arrange for a payment plan for the exorbitant fees, fueled by their unified dream for David to become independent through higher education. This vision, however, occurs in their terms of cis heterosexual normativity and gendered patriarchy. It does not match David's own definition of freedom and autonomy outside of school and perhaps the world of work instead, especially one where his sexuality can find expression. While his parents wish for him independence in the form of thinking about his agency, they are not attuned to his desire as a gay man or to his talents and ability apart from the normative path of college. Despite his best efforts, he is a colossal six hundred points away on the SAT exam from being considered a competitive applicant to USC. In recognition of his limits as a student, he instead pursues an under-the-table cash-paying job at the spa—where he cleans the facilities by scrubbing the tiles, mopping the floor, and tidying up the bathrooms. Inadvertently, the job grants him proximity to gay life in the comforts of a familiar homespace that brings together usually illicit gay identity with an ethnic enclave in Koreatown, or what bell hooks calls "homeplace" in another setting—a site of comfort and resistance to the hostility of the outside world for Black women.[29] Happy to be making money, David places the cash in his mother's wallet even as he lies about going to his SAT classes—an act of filial devotion and betrayal both. "I did a lot better" on the practice test, he tells her.

Meanwhile, he finally forges space for his sexual desires as he discovers the practice of gay sex by other men in special locations within the spa. A man looks at another with open sexual longing, in ways David reads and recognizes through study. He closely reviews their dynamic as he scrubs the same spot over and over again. The men get up, and he watches them go into a private sauna. From somewhere else, a third man follows them in. David gets up, in an act of recognition, to give the three men safe space for sex and to protect them from unwelcome others by putting up a sign that reads "Closed for Cleaning." He also instructs another man to go elsewhere by saying, "I have to clean the sauna, it will take a few minutes." His is an act of gay allegiance, when utilizing his power as a worker or gatekeeper in the spa, which is also an act he uses as an entry into a group identity as gay. He even explores his own desires. In another sauna, he sits as an older white man attempts to fondle him. He refuses, saying "no touching," as he strokes himself instead. Respectfully, the other man caresses himself, and together, they share the feel-good joy of their bodies in public, masturbating together.

David discovers more areas of gay sexual activity upstairs in a room meant for individual relaxation where, instead, the men drape their legs over each other and even have sex. He notices the towel covering the light to dim the room. Aroused by what he sees, he masturbates in the bathroom downstairs, only to be stopped by the sound of trouble outside. The spa manager is tempering the rage of an irate client who complains about the gay sex in the spa. "It's dirty, it's filthy. I want this guy arrested. He . . . bad things. I've tried to ignore it but it has gotten worse . . . better give me my money back." The Latinx man accused of gay sex speaks in Spanish only, pleading "ayúda me" (help me) to David, who finds himself stuck and silent. We know from David's earlier interactions with the food delivery worker to their restaurant that he speaks Spanish fluently. Yet at this moment, he won't translate so as to help the Latinx gay man defend himself. It is his first encounter that demands a kind of coming out to join the community by defending gay men and gay sex.

Subsequently, the spa manager asks David to police the space, telling him, "If you see anything strange, you have to tell me." The naming of the sex acts that arouse him as forbidden and disallowed alerts him to the danger of his own situation. He decides to follow his boss's instructions, taking down the towel that dims the lights in the room where sex transpires. He even puts up a sign that reads, "If you are caught engaging in inappropriate activity, we will call the authorities." This sign marks the policing of gay sex that he himself wishes to partake in more fully, but not yet. David attempts to curb his desire in the face of this discipline and surveillance at the Koreatown business enterprise. While gay sex and its expression through practices with others promise a wholeness away from fragmentation, the path of repression is one that he is familiar with as we learn more about his family.

At a traditional party for a Korean baby, the father is ashamed by what the community would perceive as an embarrassingly small amount of money in their gift. His wife accuses him of bringing shame by being unable to contribute financially to their family. The parents and the guests all witness together the Korean cultural tradition of the baby's choosing from a selection of objects that represent various paths to his future, such as money for wealth or a book for wisdom. When David asks his parents what he chose, they cannot remember, leading him to ask himself if they truly know him at all. He recognizes their lack of attunement even as they emphasize his need for agency. Their impositions of filial expectations are tied to the American Dream, similar to my discussion in chapter 1, of making money, having a job, and marrying a Korean woman. These are all exposed as heterosexual and patriarchal dreams that are not his. In this scene, he zooms in to another message that his parents relay to him instead. His dad says, "Don't worry about us. You've already done so much. You are such a good kid. That's why you'll make it. You're winning to find success for us." Here, David redefines success as his actual self-defined independence, which includes his sexual desires, expressions, and choices.

In another scene, his mother communicates a similar message when she reveals her own fragmentation. She tells him, as they stand before the house where she and her husband first lived in Los Angeles, that they were so young when they came to the United States, and she does not know what happened to them, exposing their dashed dreams. To see his parents' fragmentation ignites a new understanding in David about the stakes of his own life. Here, a path forges toward what Mary Main, Nancy Kaplan, and Jude Cassidy have called "earned secure attachment"—where he created assurance and belief in himself where there was none in his selfobjects—in the ambivalence he felt toward his parents becoming something less anxious, less preoccupied, and more assured and present.[30] We see this when he next returns to the spa with confidence about his desires.

Actually, David returns to the spa with his drunk dad in tow, whom he drops off on a recliner to sleep. It is fascinating that his father must be there for David to finally feel at home in the spa—in terms of expressing himself more fully sexually. He must bring home (through the father) to the spa or unify the racial ethnic and cultural self that is tied to his father with the public expression of his gay male gendered queer sexuality. Anthropologist Nancy Chodorow's influential work on the mother-daughter bond and the framing of female and male child development can help us understand this dynamic. In her review of Chodorow's body of work, including *The Reproduction of Mothering: Psychoanalysis and the Sociology of Gender* (1979), Marilyn Newman Metzi captures the different processes of development for boys: "Masculinity is defined as much negatively as positively." Chodorow theorizes that feminine identification processes are relational, whereas male identification processes tend to be counterrelational, defined more by rejection than by acceptance.[31] If the drunken father is unable to provide financially, classified as a failure who is unable to do anything, and proclaims life as just too hard, David differentiates from him by emerging with his own gay manhood.

David, accepting his manhood as different from his father in terms of both making money and heterosexuality, relishes the beauty of independence he finds at the spa: with his hand in its flowing waters and then in the full-body immersion the tubs enable. It is at this moment that he sees another young Korean American man enter the sauna. He follows him. They look at each other intently and he begins touching his own penis. The young man considers this an invitation and kneels before David to suck his penis. Before they have sex, David asks, "Are you Korean?" in a Kohutian act of mirror transference where he reestablishes at this moment the family need for acceptance—a Korean American partner—as a "confirmation of himself."[32] The shot repeats the fragmented shots of the father and son that open the film as they wash each other's backs. But now, in a sexual version of that familial bodily choreography, we see extreme close-ups of the skin of their chests, in parallel, as arms reach around torsos. David penetrates from behind the other young man, who sits on his lap while they fuck. David comes and afterward attempts to kiss the man—who runs away as the spa manager witnesses the aftermath of their sexual experience. Seeing the spa manager, David remains seated but looks away with his eyes down, his pose frozen with alert intensity. He refuses shame and instead expresses a kind of stoicism. I do not mean being expressionless or lacking feeling but a steely and determined refusal of homophobic judgment that entails his courage, reflection, and self-inventory. After the moment passes between him and the spa manager, he showers while rubbing his skin so hard that he begins to bleed. His face grimaces in agony as he reflects on his selfobject encounter with the Korean man, and then the spa manager immediately after—the affirming act followed so closely by the condemning judgment. A tear rolls down his cheek. The physical gesture of rubbing his skin to the point of bleeding is the same as the scrubbing of the walls that he performed when he first discovered gay sex at the spa. It is an act that reveals the cost of pent-up rage while also illustrating that the work at the spa also helps him recover his feeling and collect himself.

Along with his father, David checks out of the spa and directly faces the spa manager, who silently judges him with a frown. Staring proudly at the manager, David throws the locker keys at his face in response to the disapproval. His forceful act is a rejection of the man's homophobia and the assertion of David's emergence as a cis masculine gay man. It is a full embrace of himself and the admixture of his racial ethnic gendered queer qualities. In facing the unpleasant truth of the spa manager's rejection, David

2.1 In the film's conclusion, David reflects on his selfobject encounter of the affirming sex act followed so closely by a condemning judgment. A tear rolls down his cheek. *Spa Night* (Andrew Ahn, 2016).

rises up with strength and anger. Armed with his father's acceptance, he achieves his own Korean American cis gay manhood through a collective of selfobject experiences that he wishes to be affirmative and sustaining. He refuses the unsatisfying and unsustaining response. He thus mobilizes the strength from finally fully experiencing his sexual autonomy to achieve independence. The selfobjects, or the experiences that he organizes to structure himself in a form of agentic attunement, come to fruition, are now chosen, interpreted, and felt as he moves toward a happier existence.

I read this moment of coming to anger not as a heteronormative, cis male rage. David's development does not fit into a homonormative patriarchal mode, for it is anchored within the context of the spa. At this site of illicit gay sex known to its customers—both those who wish to close it down and those who wish to keep it alive—he finally harnesses anger to express a stake in that struggle for queer space. His own coming out requires the presence of his family too; he needs the space of the Korean spa to become a *sexual homeplace* where he will not be caught, not straitjacketed in his sexuality, as where he can explore sex within his ethnic community. He is not seeking a coupling but an expression of gay sexual desire and practices within Koreatown—what I am calling his claiming of a cultural homespace, recalling hooks's racial homeplace of belonging and Lauren Berlant and Michael Warner's theorization of sex in public. They define this as "queer zones and other worlds estranged from heterosexual culture, but also more tacit scenes of sexuality like official national culture," which the Korean spa encapsulates.[33] David is allied with the sanctity of the gay sexual community space of the Korean spa as he continues to process his coming into being as a gay Korean American man. He wishes to develop as a proper gay man within a public sphere contending with the legibility and illegibility of his identity and actions within a racialized and sexualized space.

In connecting with his body anew in the sweaty physical release that he experiences in the pursuit of fitness and ultimately through satisfying sex at the gay spa where he works, David truly gets more connected with his body and his psyche in terms of his racial and sexual identity and his feeling of belonging within his community. He does so even more as he explores his sexuality in an iconic site of racial queer representation, the gay bathhouse owned and run by Koreans in Koreatown. And in needing a partner to be Korean as a prerequisite for the act to continue, his search for the self in sex acts ties to his heritage, showing the entanglement of race with sexuality. His sexual assertion of racial freedom is also an undoing of his parental expectations tied to a particularly constricted gender role.

When the truth of David's sexuality comes out, and the fragmentation dissipates, his assertion of himself is unapologetic, for it bares not only himself but also his family, through the physical presence of his father, the cultural ethnic space of the spa, and the Korean identity of his sexual encounter. His individual self contains a collective identity dependent on others. He needs his heritage to establish an autonomy defined as reliant on sustaining selfobject experiences, which now include his defiance of homophobic judgment. The absurdity of the world is exposed; the spa enables David to see others like himself and learn to sense that the cohesion he seeks through his family is more arbitrary and senseless. His parents don't remember what symbolic gift he chose as a baby, yet his choices now of how to act, interpret, and respond to others are what concretely matter in his developing life. Through an attunement to his own desires and priorities, David becomes an agent in his own life, the center of his own narrative. In this way, the film offers a class critique too—in how this racial sexual affirmation lends him self-sovereignty against normative definitions of success.

Queer Childhood, Selfobjects, and Equanimity in *Driveways*

Like David in *Spa Night*, young Cody in *Driveways* needs to gain a stronger sense of self, including his feeling of worthiness, self-regard, and esteem in agentic attunement. Selfobject relations are less reliable and sustained for Cody, whose environment is new and whose family is broken. Unlike David, who is situated within Koreatown, Cody is a newcomer to Upstate New York. Navigating a new space with his mom shows the importance of environment, and one's acceptance within it, in helping to determine the "total unity of self."[34] As visitors, Cody and his mom familiarize themselves with an unknown town, meeting and measuring the trustworthiness of neighbors, going to the hardware store, finding a real estate agent, and even celebrating Cody's ninth birthday at the local skating rink. Cody befriends the neighbor Del (Brian Dennehy in his final film role), an old white male Korean War veteran and widower who lives alone. Del spends his days at the VFW hall, where he plays bingo with his community of other old white men. At this juncture of his life, as a close friend begins to lose his memory, Del measures his generation's collective nearness to death as he takes stock of his own regret in working too much and parenting too little.

Del and Cody's friendship is one of mutual recognition of their in-progress and in-process selves in relation to queerness. Del attempts to undo his mistakes, such as making life hard for his queer daughter, through an unconditional love that quickly becomes apparent to Cody, whom he recognizes as queer—whether through his race, his sexuality, or both (in the sense of Stuart Gaffney's "my race is queer").[35] And Cody seeks a more coherent sense of himself in the company of this old Korean War veteran, whose agentic attunement to the boy is the scaffolding that supports Cody's mom, Kathy, who lacks resources, even as she loves him like a lioness. As Kathy clears the belongings from her dead sister's house, and the friendship develops between Del and Cody, the mother and child decide not to sell the house and move in there instead. When Cody shares this news with Del, he discloses that his daughter is moving him away to Seattle. The film concludes with a monologue by Del about the importance of equanimity in order to live a full life, which Cody hears and uses to establish a confident self in his new town, even as Del moves away.

The film begins with Kathy and Cody driving their car at night, with Kathy frequently looking over at Cody to check on his well-being (much like the other young Asian American mother, Monica, does with her son, David, in the opening scenes of *Minari*). Cody calmly enjoys his iPad. The mom is entirely attuned to him when she looks at him in the car in frequent attempts to read his body and face so as to assess his disposition. She speaks with him gently. They move from the car to a house with no power to a motel, then back to a house with borrowed power and piles of garbage they must throw away in a dumpster or dispose of in a garage sale. This move is destabilizing for Cody, who asks when they will go home so he can return to camp, which was interrupted by this trip. Their financial precarity becomes apparent when we learn that Kathy is relying on receiving the camp refund. Cody also has a missing parent to whom his access is questionable in a form of parental loss that links him to other characters in this movie. His father reaches out to his mom, revealing their palpable resentment toward and frustration with each other.

These three selfobjects—unknown environment, missing father, financially precarious yet caring mother—are external relations that contribute to Cody's sense of self, or what Kohut calls "feeling real about" himself, which can be determined by how one holds oneself together.[36] Within this context, Cody's interactions with his mom reveal an agentic attunement that the film marvelously displays. Yet, as a single mother who has few resources, the mother, through her status, also exposes the unmet needs of Cody's childhood.

At eight years of age, Cody is in middle childhood, beginning to emerge from the space his mom provides—of affirmation and nurturing care. As he enters a new space that he explores—in direct relation to the development of himself—he receives the added support of the magnifying mirror he finds in Del as a second mother, following the primacy of maternal care in self psychology, where the mother is not necessarily female.[37] The magnifying mirror is an "asset" to the developing child who encounters obstacles that he "is trying to absorb the blow" of—trying challenges such as a move or encounters with bullies. And in the process of "helping him with that effort . . . he is beginning to display strength."[38] Through his mother's and Del's support in agentic attunement, Cody is able to develop equanimity, holding steady in the face of struggles he will certainly encounter.

The experiences of selfobjects Cody has with his mother, Kathy, are sustaining ones in their agentic attunement to each other, where they recognize the need to support each other through struggle that comes from the context of their limited resources. As they drive into town, Kathy and Cody stop to get gas and eat. Kathy smokes while waiting for Cody to use the bathroom. When he comes out, she drops her lit cigarette on the ground, which Cody stubs out in a choreography that speaks of their bond. While their attunement is physical, in how she watches him as she drives or eats his leftovers at the restaurant, their conversations reveal a deep, open, honest, and truthful relationship that reveals their attention to their individual agency—the ability to act within their constraints as defined by Saba Mahmood[39]—and bodes well for their future relations as mother and, one day, adult child. She is straightforward with him about their finances (their family's intent is to sell and get money from the house) and in her open acknowledgment of death, as Cody can ask her any question, including about the circumstances of her sister's death. When he accidentally wets his pants when he discovers a dead cat in the bath, he matter-of-factly discloses it to her as a sign of their trust, in contrast to the bedwetting that David hides from his parents in *Minari*. As his mother, Kathy encourages him to overcome obstacles. Hers is not a premature adultification; because she is aware of his developmental stage, instead of discussing the cost of a hotel, she presents staying on the porch as a fun thing to do—like camping—so as not to cause undue anxiety. And when he asks about her relationship with his aunt—her sister—she does not flinch in helping him to understand the nuances of important relationships. She explains that siblings can drift apart, and emotions can get carried away. Kathy tells Cody she was "pissed" at her sister: "Remember when you and me moved in with grandma? I thought she should have offered to take care of her. She had a house, a real adult. I didn't know . . ." as she gestures toward the house overflowing with garbage as an acknowledgment of her sister's struggles that she may not have been fully aware of until now. In these ways, Cody counts on his mom for an interpretation of the world that is realistic, which brings him to an equally real self-understanding that is the aim of agentic attunement in child-rearing.

According to Kohutian self psychology, the "key person for needed selfobject responsiveness is the mother (or the mother figure)," but this does not account for contemporary situations wherein the mother must work, leading to "gradual impoverishment of the self-sustaining aspects of the selfobject experiences that the child has."[40] There is indeed an instability to Cody, who frequently vomits. His mother explains this occurrence without judgment or resentment but with understanding and empathy about his relationship to selfobjects—spaces, events, and people. His mom says the reason is that "he gets overwhelmed . . . with lessons, birthday parties, camp." Perhaps, at these sites, Cody experiences selfobject responses tied to his marginal identity, leading to traumatic threats to self.

We don't know if Cody, an eight-year-old child, is queer, though Andrew Ahn is a queer filmmaker who makes queer films or films related to queerness. While Cody may not yet be fully aware of his queerness, and without my trying to identify his sexuality prematurely, he can still be queer if we understand queer sexuality beyond the primacy of sex acts. In *The Queer Child*, Kathryn Bond Stockton discusses the process of "growing sideways," which is distinct from the normative form of development that consists of "vertical movement" or is knowably linear and heteronormative in its progress.[41] The concept of "sideways" or a more expansive movement to the future, feared by adults observing the child and the child observing their queer self, is similar to queer and gender studies philosopher Sara Ahmed's formulation of an oblique perspective—one that disorients straight spaces with a nonconforming perspective based on queer life experience.[42] "Sideways" and the "oblique" can both help describe how the usually straight progression of growing up is actually composed of unruly, wayward, and meandering paths, including driveways between homes that don't actually divide property but bridge them as they do in this film.

In the case of Cody and his helpful and nurturing neighbor, Del, there is not a hierarchical development of self through gender roles and normative sexuality; different kinds of affiliations can be cultivated, even across generations. Cody and Del have a nonnormative relationship that helps fuel a nonnormative queer childhood. Even though Del eventually leaves the state, Cody has learned from their relationship to continue cultivating relations with those who are similarly outcast and do not fit normative space. He chooses the like-minded Latinx kids versus the antagonistic white kids who are constantly terrorizing him. After one tries to beat him up, they set off fireworks in front of his house in the middle of the night in an act that must be read as racial terror. His bond with Del is queer, as is his friendship with the manga-reading Latinx kids who are cast in a racist light by the white grandma next door. Cody comes to himself as a queer selfobject from his initial shattering and fragmentation, which then becomes a completeness that is nonnormative in the sense that he does not have a rigid definition of family and friendship. Various forms of alternative belonging occur other than what one might expect.

In response to the question of whether *Driveways* is a queer film, director Ahn explained, "I don't know if *Driveways* fits into that conversation, but I think it poses a question within the conversation. It's this question of how do we talk about queerness? How do we talk about queer characters, queer culture, outside of defining sexual desire?"[43] Sexuality is not represented in Cody's eight-year-old realm, although it lingers as a fear that the adults on-screen impose on him. Indeed, it occurs when Cody encounters strangers. When he first meets Del, who from a distance on his porch helps Cody turn on the faucet to get a drink, even Cody's mother suspects foul play. She confronts Del, asking him, "Is my son bothering you? Did you spray water on him? He shouldn't talk to strangers." Del didn't spray Cody, and Del affirms her rule not to talk to strangers. Another example is when Kathy leaves Cody alone on the porch by himself, asleep in the middle of the night, and his safety is a concern. Another neighbor, a white grandma, claims to Kathy, "I'm not racist or anything," while making racist observations. When this woman tries to talk to him, Cody suspects her of being dangerous too. This is the context that informs our viewing, even if the only sexual representation in the film is a man propositioning Cody's mom at a bar.

Nevertheless, critics like Michael Cuby deem Cody queer when discussing how the film exemplifies a fresh new queer cinema that does not center the act of coming out for its characters. In describing popular representations of queer youth such as in *Love, Simon* (2019), Cuby points out how coming out feels like a tired and "outdated trope." His review focuses on how "a number of films are taking a more clued-in approach to what queer sexuality actually looks and feels like in 2019, and they're telling more interesting stories about their protagonists as a result."[44] The trope of coming out, according to Cuby, does not capture the ways in which young people today are more fluid in their understanding of gender and sexuality, including the emergence of age-old trans identities and genderqueer self-presentations. As Cuby writes about Cody in *Driveways*, which he considers the best representation of the phenomenon of liberating today's queer youth from the narrative representation of coming out, to expand their stories for a more fluid, contemporary understanding of sexual life: "When two even-mannered kids from down the block share some of their Japanese manga comics with him, he reads one and his eyes perk up after stumbling across one of the more overtly sexualized queer pairings on the page. Cody doesn't say anything when he finds out that his elderly veteran neighbor has a lesbian daughter that he loves, but it's clear that seeing it was possible was eye-opening."[45] As a child, Cody gravitates toward the Latinx children whom critic Cuby calls "even-mannered" versus the white bullying kids next door. I agree that the orchestration of both the prop of same-sex characters within intimate representations of manga in the film and the narration of Del's queer daughter's challenges contributes to rendering queerness as an option for Cody's future that appeases, pleases, and comforts him. This queer reading as affirmation also appears when Del tells Kathy that her son reminds him of his daughter, who we find out is queer. He identifies Cody's boyhood as resonant with a particular queer development.

Among his peers, Cody occupies a position outside the norm of what gender theorist R. W. Connell calls hegemonic masculinity, which is embodied in the white, burly, adolescent neighborhood boys who wrestle in the yard and also in their house while watching a World Wrestling Federation–like show.[46] Cody grimaces with distaste as he witnesses the other boys swear at and hurt each other on the grass. He even runs away from the sight. When he is at these boys' house, he shows no interest in the wrestling show on television. The boys set their sights on him, saying with laughter that his "aunt was so fat" in a condemning and cruel man-ner. When they assess that Cody does not like wrestling, they force him to participate in it with a commanding "I said, get up!" Cody resignedly rises. They wield a particular kind of masculinity that he finds repugnant. He vomits his cherry-red fruit drink before running away, deterring the boys from further bullying or its escalation.

Clearing a dead hoarder's house is not appropriate work for a child, and Kathy struggles to accommodate Cody's needs as well as fulfilling her own responsibilities. Because she has to work to make money, and the house has no internet access that would allow her to do her usual job as a medical transcriber, she has to seek online access elsewhere. This is how Cody ends up at the house of the racist grandma neighbor, where the grandchildren behave in monstrous masculine ways that make him vomit. Kathy's work is also the reason she can't be at home with Cody; such restriction on a working parent often puts the child in an unsafe position, vulnerable to bullies and predators.

While Cody's experience appears to be gendered marginality, it is re-lated to sexualization. The boys see difference in him when they challenge him for wearing a turquoise blue necklace. They judge it as an emblem of his nonnormative identity that may include a queerness they deem weak enough to dominate or repulsive enough to expel. In an interview with Tre'vell Anderson, filmmaker Andrew Ahn comments on the signification of the necklace, linking it to queerness itself: "Whether he grows up to be queer or not . . . that's his choice. And for me, that perspective of 'it's a per-son's choice' feels queer to me in philosophy, if not in actual definition."[47] Ahn keeps open the definition of Cody's sexuality as the child's choice and precisely aligns with Stockton's theorization of the inherent queerness in all childhoods, echoing Freud's "polymorphous perversity" that narrows in adulthood through social norms that limit the legibility of the infini-tude of genders and sexualities.

Another critic, David Fear, describes Cody similarly, writing that "Cody doesn't really want to be anywhere—he's the kind of shy, reces-sive kid who's happy to keep to himself."[48] I disagree with the assessment of Cody as happy, for he moves with hesitation, trepidation, and uncer-tainty. While Ahn resists compulsory heterosexuality in his understand-ing of Cody, and Fear describes Cody's lonesomeness as a happy one, I find that the boy's marginality indicates fragmentation, a self-questioning of his worth that is about his precarity and feeling unstable in this place, which means something for his sense of belonging in the world. This is why Kathy's agentic attunement to him is important. Perhaps his ability to throw up to express his distaste for the toxic masculinity wielded by the wrestling boys comes from that confidence she instills in him through the strong sense of self that the illusion of attunement provides.

The neighbor Del's entry into their life comes as a welcome support to both Kathy and Cody. When Kathy was able to help Del by driving him to his VFW bingo game, he reciprocated by taking care of Cody when Kathy was not home. Due to her circumstances as a single mother in a financially precarious situation, she was unable to be at home and needed Del's support. In this way, Del functions as a "magnifying mirror" that serves both mother and child. In *Spa Night*, the mirror for David became an act of self-acceptance. For Kathy and Cody, Del offers a sustaining and supportive selfobject experience. The magnifying mirror helps the struggling subject by offering affirmation as one interprets obstacles. In an act of agentic attunement, Del bonds with Cody over the act of vomiting by sharing stories of his own puking during his military days. It enables Cody to identify how his vomiting is less frequent, that he is getting better. In effect, Del provides a mirroring selfobject experience for Cody as validating and confidence-building in teaching him how to interpret his own development and progression in growing up.

A "mirroring selfobject experience" essentially shows how "a person's sense of self is enhanced by the knowledge that another person understands his inner experience—that is, is aware of that inner experience and is responding to it with warmly colored positive effects."[49] This is key to an agentic attunement approach in validating the child with a larger knowledge he can translate as part of well development. Similarly, when Kathy returns home, she proposes going to the bullying boys' house. Del tells her not to, that it's a pointless exercise, saying, "I would not waste time talking to that lady," which affirms Kathy's own instincts. "Yeah, fuck it!" she agrees in another mirroring selfobject experience for both of them as they share and affirm each other's worldview in the practice of parenting. This shared assessment of who is trustworthy and worthwhile bonds them. This is a physical bond, too, as Del places a long, orange extension cord across the driveway between their homes to power Kathy and Cody's house from his.

This sharing of power enables Kathy to clean the house thoroughly, including kneeling to scrub the toilet. They gather the "gooey" body of the cat from the tub, which Cody buries in the back yard while Del, nearby, watches in support. Kathy meets the real estate agent, a Black woman who also feels displaced in the town, who helps her prepare the house—acknowledging that the overwhelming mass of stuff is "too much for one person." The recognition by the other woman of color makes Kathy weep, for someone has recognized how she is struggling with the meaning of so many things, too many objects. The real estate agent proposes that the objects may have given comfort to Kathy's sister. In her selfobject experience with the real estate agent, Kathy is affirmed in the loss of her estranged sister, mended through the purging of her sister's things and the recognition of the selfobjects in her life. Agentic attunement, thus, can also occur within the same generation in the form of an alliance between these women of color who recognize each other's struggles.

This simple act of empathetic observation from selfobjects in agentic attunement emerges most clearly when Cody begins spending time with Del as they read. Whether it is on Del's porch reading issues of *National Geographic* or at the library, where they donate books before they sit together to confer on genderqueer representations in manga that are affirming and nonjudgmental and Del asks, "Are those two girls?" Cody responds, "Two boys—they just look like that." There is no homophobic glare but simple acceptance and matter-of-fact understanding. Cody basks in the pride Del feels when reviewing newspaper articles about his lesbian daughter, a judge in Seattle. Cody recognizes the love and recognition Del feels for his queer daughter. The acceptance of genderqueer identities and lesbian existence affirms and expands Cody's choices, in a more infinite understanding of a world with more varied sexual futures. These discussions are in tune with what Cody needs to affirm his sense of self, whatever his orientation may be.

The agentic attunement Cody receives occurs at a crucial time in his development of self within middle childhood—at age eight, turning nine. His life makes clear that the selfobject experience is not simply about others or objects but the "function" of both in the development of the self and its potential.[50] Even his mom is aware that this is a time to ensure Cody's understanding of sexuality. At the garage sale where Del discloses that his daughter is "engaged to her lady friend," Cody shares that his mom already prepared him to understand sex in society. He says, "My mom had to tell me about sex and how babies are made. Do you know what a blow job is? They laugh at you if you don't know." The acknowledgment of sex and sexual identities helps Cody fashion a cohesive version of himself—whether or not he is or yet knows he is queer in a world where sexual acts and identities are judged and hierarchized. Indeed, this sense of wholeness achieved does not follow a normative development of growing up, but instead Stockton's "sideways" development or Ahmed's "oblique" perspective. By providing sexual knowledge to her child as a no-nonsense part of life, Cody's mom helps structure and organize his understanding of himself and the world. Kohut calls this the "emerging self" at work. As explained by Ernest Wolf, "This emerging self, when it achieves a degree of cohesion, is experienced by the child as a sense of selfhood and is accompanied by self-esteem and an experience of wellbeing."[51] So, the self is an age-appropriate structuring of information that is evoked and maintained toward a healthy psychological development in agentic attunement.

Kohut asserts that the "most mature people have strong ideals which are more important to them than external approval."[52] As Del and Cody's friendship strengthens, especially during Cody's birthday, where Del recognizes Cody as suited to the quiet of the VFW versus the circus of the loud skating rink, Cody speaks more freely about his sense of self in monologues like this: "I have not [sic] religion. I have strong beliefs." In this way, the search for equanimity in a strong sense of self sees results in his confident speech. We can see that he is moving toward managing himself—such as when he makes controversial assertions without being significantly swayed by external forces—through the power of selfobject experiences that are affirming, sustaining, and supportive, to generating a form of inner strength in the self. Kohut recognizes the importance of this stage of early childhood in the formation of self-esteem when he expresses that he "realize[s] what an enormous role disturbance in this area plays in human behavior."[53] Thus, when Cody discovers that Del is moving away right when he and his mom have decided not to sell the house but to stay, the event does not wreck him, though he has to run it off after screaming "No!" Del slowly follows him up the hill and hugs him.

The film's concluding scenes feature the two of them on the porch as Del shares a lesson in agentic attunement that resonates for Cody: "People say things, but it does not matter. You're a good kid. Fuck them." He teaches Cody that he will encounter people who will try to convince him to doubt himself. The boy must hold on to the good and the pleasurable in his self-identity as a way to protect himself from those who do not care about his future. In response to this act of care, Cody reaches out to Del and puts an arm around his shoulder. The shot is from the back while the two face the deep green foliage of their environs. Adults typically hug kids while kids are typically told, commanded, or requested by parents or adults to do so. Here, Cody enacts the hug as an expression of trust in the care by Del for his well-being now and in the future. While we cannot

2.2 Cody hugs Del on the front stoop of Del's home, where they spent much time reading together. *Driveways* (Andrew Ahn, 2019).

know if Cody achieves an earned secure attachment, he is clearly on his way, buoyed by the confidence he learns from both Del and his mother. The last shot of the film is of Cody with his friends Miguel and Anna, the levelheaded no-drama kids of color from up the street. They are dancing and mimicking moves from the popular video game *Fortnight*. Del is gone to Seattle with his daughter. And Cody has chosen the room that overlooks Del's porch, where they spent so much time reading together, as a homespace of affirming memory, to evoke the selfobject experiences of love and acceptance he learned from the agentic attunement he received.

Agentic Attunement: Selfobjects in the Formation of Strong Subjects

The platonic, nonsexual relationship between the young boy Cody and the older man Del in *Driveways* mirrors the seminal moment when David interacts in a consensual encounter with the older white man in *Spa Night*. The rapport between Cody and Del shows a mutual recognition between someone starting his life and someone close to the end of life; an unconditional love emerges. David has his first sexual rapport with an elderly white man whose sexual desirability is close to expiring in a culture that prizes youth. Here, sex is a site of agentic attunement as well, where David's first foray into partnered gay sexuality is one where he encounters respect for his own sexual boundaries. Through their interaction, David learns to assert his needs and desires by speaking through his body. It is an odd and jarring connection to imagine these two dissimilar figures of a young Korean American teen and one in middle childhood both connecting with old white men. Yet their encounters show powerful cross-generational and cross-racial bonds that resist the ostracism that they encounter from others—whether USC Korean American male students or brash white children in the neighborhood. David and Cody are able to find nonexploitative, nonpathological, and nontoxic intergenerational friendship or queer kinship in the unexpected bonds they each establish through agentic attunement from the older other.

As a filmmaker, Andrew Ahn is conscious of the rampant representations within queer cinema of "hatred," and he wishes instead for "stories where the drama is fueled . . . by love."[54] In making films about queer characters who are also racialized subjects, Ahn presents them as the best recipients of love. The death of queer people and the lack of visibility of stories that center their representations in US fiction films are violent experiences. To suffuse queer-of-color stories with love follows the late filmmaker Marlon Riggs's manifesto/statement that "black men loving black men is THE revolutionary act," which closes his film *Tongues Untied* (1989). Close, or nearby, is the love for self that Andrew Ahn cultivates for his characters. He constructs his films with selfobjects—essentially the building blocks of film in the form of props, characters, lines, and scenes— to create affirming experiences for characters who struggle with their fragmentation. His films are composed of scenes in which older people can practice agentic attunement to care for the futures of young, queer Asian/ Americans.

Unfortunately, not all of us are here to see queer subjects of color, even if they are presented to us as the main protagonists of a film. In yet another moment when critics should be more aware of a film's history, what struck me about Jeannette Catsoulis's *New York Times* review of the film *Driveways* is her not granting the central role of the film to the mixed-race child, as the bearer of the story; instead, she focuses on the white character Del, who is actually the one in a supporting role. Catsoulis renders the child, mother, and neighbor Del as an ensemble cast, even if Hong Chau was nominated by the Independent Spirit Awards for Lead Actress. She essentially equalizes their roles when writing that the arrival of mom and child "doesn't so much disrupt Del's long-held routine as expand it in ways that will offer unexpected gifts to all three."[55] I, in contrast, consider the role of the late, great Brian Dennehy and his character as a supporting one to the development of the brown future of our country, populated by mixed-race kids of color like Cody who are also queer and independent, self-supporting single moms like Kathy. These subjects are most in need of affirmation in a world where they are rendered unseen. We need to give them their due as bearers of the story, especially as the majority of the US population is to consist of people of color by 2045. Films that center characters like Cody and his mom need to be in place, and recognized as such: that they are the agents of their own stories, centers of their own narratives, who are worth occupying the role of storyteller in the time, space, energies, and resources provided by a feature film.

The selfobject mirroring experience that these characters undergo— whether Kathy in the face of the real estate agent or Cody in the face of Del—also helps us as spectators, for through them we see how the characters pay attention to each other with agentic attunement. They not only recognize the effects of experiences like disenfranchisement and marginalization but also see the power of interpretation to cast one's inner life in a more affirming and supportive way. The phenomenon essentially captures how spectatorship in cinema works similarly to how we, as viewers, must tune in to focus, hear, see, and feel the inner lives of the characters for whom we must cultivate empathy through our observations. This agentic attunement should be a lesson for learning how to recognize others, especially those who are not usually accorded empathy. They may be the ones with whom we form alternative attachments that provide affirming and sustaining selfobject relations.

3 Adolescent Curiosity and Mourning

THE BLOSSOMING OF MAXIMO OLIVEROS

Within Philippine cinema, *The Blossoming of Maximo Oliveros* (2005) is significant for launching a new movement, what notable Filipino film scholar Rolando Tolentino calls "Pinoy indie digi cinema," or Philippine-style independent digital cinema, which takes up the legacy of filmmakers like Marilou Diaz Abaya, Ishmael Bernal, Mike De Leon, and Lino Brocka, whose careers include an "aestheticization of poverty" that remains imprinted in the country's new cinematic traditions.[1] As such, "Pinoy indie digi cinema" is a third golden age, the first having taken place in the 1950s and the second in the 1970s. By the early aughts, the quantity of 35mm films produced in the country had dropped significantly. More recently, in 2016, Amy Qin, in the *New York Times*, observed, "It's been a remarkable turnaround for an industry that just 15 years ago was nearly moribund."[2]

Premier Philippine actor and director Laurice Guillen, who ran the Film Development Council of the Philippines, worried about the quality of films during that time in the early aughts. She approached Antonio Co-juangco, a business leader who heads a major private corporation that includes communications and television, to support a new film foundation committed to developing filmmakers and creating new content that comes directly from young Filipinos to ignite the industry anew. Cine Malaya was born, what eminent Philippine cinema scholar J. B. Capino calls "a private sector–government partnership to aid Philippine cinema that has led to the explosive growth of the indie digital scene in the country."[3] Cine Malaya gave seed money to young filmmakers and premiered their films at a major annual independent film festival. It has since galvanized new filmmakers and, as an organization, won accolades for bringing new life to the Philippine film industry. Auraeus Solito's *The Blossoming of Maximo Oliveros* was one of its early funded projects and an early independent film shot in digital video, capturing the rising tide of digital film as the industry's new standard.[4] As a product of independent film, versus the commercial Philippine industry, the film cast virtually unknown (although now globally celebrated) actors such as Soliman Cruz in lead roles as well as lead actor Nathan Lopez, who has played gay roles but identifies as straight. The director, Auraeus Solito, began his career in theater before venturing into the independent film scene. After its screening at the Philippine Cultural Center, the film has reached more than one hundred film festival audiences; won several prestigious awards, including at the Berlin International Film Festival in 2006; represented the Philippines at the Oscars; was selected to open New Directors/New Films, a prestigious film festival at the Museum of Modern Art and Lincoln Center in New York City; was screened at New York University in December 2022, almost twenty years after its release; and is widely available online today.[5] Auraeus Solito has since launched a celebrated career as a director.[6]

The English title of the film, *The Blossoming of Maximo Oliveros*, is quite beautiful yet imprecise in its translation of the original Tagalog *Ang Pagdadalaga ni Maximo Oliveros*, which literally translates as "The Blossoming Young Womanhood of Maximo Oliveros." To be clear, the original Tagalog title is gendered: young womanhood signals the path of a male-named character who may actually be trans or nonbinary in gender. In Filipino, the word *dalaga* means young woman, and the conjugation of *pagdadalaga* indicates becoming. To translate "growing womanhood" as "blossoming" in the sense of "flowering" goes beyond developing and growing as an adult woman in the community. Flowering can also be read as a vaginal reference in the sense of an enlarged labia.[7] The film is thus much richer than its English title suggests in its representation of the child's sexuality and how it is situated in a larger constellation of identities. The gendered meaning, omitted in the official title of the film in English, may be an indication of that complexity that I will parse.

In *The Blossoming of Maximo Oliveros*, a young genderqueer Filipinx youth named Maximo, or Maxie (Nathan Lopez), may be an effeminate boy, a boyish girl, or somewhere in between on the expansive spectrum of gender. At twelve years old, the adolescent may merely express themself in an aggressive effeminacy, troubling the spectator's categories; but in their neighborhood slums of Manila, no one is confused or discomforted by their defiance of gender boundaries. Because there are other children like Maxie, their gender expression is normalized as just one available option among many. They are not alone as genderqueer in this film, so they do not represent a singular anomaly or an individual perversity. That is, there are many other youths like Maxie in the film.

While their gendered femininity or blurring of gendered boundaries makes them vulnerable to harassment outside the home, especially after dark, Maxie's own family is composed of a kind and doting father named Paco (Soliman Cruz) and two protective older brothers, the quietly intense Boy (Neil Ryan Sese) and the lighthearted and flirtatious Bogs (Ping Medina). All are locally known criminals—petty thieves working in the underground economy—selling stolen cell phones or running numbers. Even Maxie's future aspiration to sell pirated DVDs is unlawful. The Oliveros clan, in all its cisgender straight macho comportment, loves and protects Maxie, who has taken on the gendered female role of cooking, cleaning, and maintaining the household since the death of their mother, whose hospitalization plunged them into deep debt and subsequent criminality. When Maxie develops a crush on or a curious and affectionate interest in the rookie policeman Victor Perez (J. R. Valentin), who eventually seeks to arrest their family members after a local murder, their affection and care for this man of the law threaten to fragment the family. This film is extraordinary for the way it privileges the child's perspective, including the full-blown vulnerability in their desirous curiosity for another, but it is not a depiction of a sexual relationship or a coming-out narrative. Maxie's queer gender and sexuality remain ambiguous and in progress.

Because this is not a film about coming out, Maxie's sexuality is not the primary social category of experience in their development. Indeed, Maxie's sexuality is situated within a larger set of formative feelings and experiences, specifically mourning, grief, and poverty that arises for their family from the death of their mother and wife. Maxie seems to be heading in the direction of criminality as they lose the familiarity and steadiness of having both parents. This path is not presented as something to which they are intrinsically prone, but as the most viable path exemplified and encouraged by the adults in their life. This limited choice is contextualized by their extreme lack of resources as poor people in the Global South. The family is bound by grief and poverty as criminalized urban dwellers whose disposability in global capitalism is what postcolonial theorist Neferti X. Tadiar calls "remaindered life"—subjects whose lives and living conditions we must pay attention to in order to address the inequalities of our present day.[8] The Oliveros home, filmed in darkness and confinement, renders them as a unit enshrouded in the lack of a promising future and as bound to their entrenched economic disenfranchisement. A calendar looms over the family, indicating the passing of time without reprieve from problems. They sit around the dinner table together; however, they do not connect with each other. The father turns away, slightly vexed and agitated. Long-haired and shirtless Bogs is troubled, with his hand on his forehead also looking elsewhere with worry. Boy, preoccupied, looks askance. Maxie looks down with their hands on the table as if praying nervously. They are unified in grief over the missing wife and mother while living with no reprieve from their debt.

So, while Maxie's pursuit of a different life may be seen as a sexual one, due to the primacy of sex in defining queerness, this film presents different kinds of queer desire that, while not denying erotic attachment, provide a broader map for this quest that is situated within the multipronged forces of deep inequality. In looking at the film through the lens of object relations, focusing on dealings and interactions with others and their representative inanimate objects, we can see how the child's feelings exceed sexual instincts and include romance, loyalty, and grief. This allows us to examine the interpersonal relationship for how it constructs the protagonist and how we interpret them as both spectator and actor. Object relations theory helps us to understand the stakes and vulnerabilities Maxie faces when expressing what I consider their preoedipal love for Victor.

In this chapter, I analyze the act of affection toward an external love object that Maxie asserts within the context of a loving, accepting, and caring family—where every member is grieving the loss of a wife or mother. I argue that Maxie's creative confidence is not only an expression of their sexuality but also a direct result of fully mourning their mother and of being accepted as genderqueer within their family and community in a form of agentic attunement. Their adolescent expression of love for the police officer, though nongenital in its developmental stage, and perhaps the seeking of a replacement for the mother, could be dangerous if met by a predator. Its adult recipient, however, is kind, loving, and affirming, like their family. This allows for a relationship composed of agentic attunement where the adult ensures the child is not harmed as they develop into adulthood, expanding their connection beyond sexuality to the mentoring search for different forms of adulthood not immersed in criminality and grief. Yet, the relationship between Maxie and Victor does not preclude the possibility of eroticism and sensuousness that, as I will explore through psychoanalysis, is both like and not like the maternal. The method of agentic attunement pays attention to the developmental stage of the child as the organizing structure of the relationship, which renders sex as inappropriate.

The film, set outside the United States, thus counters the moralism in Hollywood cinema and its myopic understanding of representations of childhood sexuality as to be feared, rather than assuming the innocence of the child outside the adult's imposition of genital sexuality. In this way, Maxie's differently queer sexuality transgresses the imperial boundaries of the Philippines and the United States, questioning how the concept of queerness travels across borders. Moreover, situating Maxie's sexual self-sovereignty within poverty, grief, and mourning illuminates the richness of contextual relationships that shape us as we grow up, and those we experience in movies. This film meaningfully engages queer childhood enmeshed in playful creativity directly linked within the mourning for a mother and in the development of self-sovereignty through a love object that cannot be limited to sexual desire.

The Taboo of Adolescent Expressions of Romance

In eliding sexual categorization, this film reveals the limits of how we understand queerness. Queerness is not simply about same-sex attraction, or trans identity that does not conform to the gender binary. Queerness, as pointed out in the previous chapter in connection with the work of Sara Ahmed and Kathryn Bond Stockton, is a critique that centrally lambastes the constrictions of compulsory heterosexuality, explodes the gender binary, and frames the world askew, at an angle that expands to infinitude our existing structures of sexual existence, including race and class privilege and denigration. *The Blossoming of Maximo Oliveros* explores sexuality beyond an instinct that needs to be fed and aims that need to be expressed, viewing it instead as a simmering, percolating, blooming, and existing desire for bodily pleasure as well as intrapsychic connections with another. It includes the erotics of the visual in evaluating the beauty and desirability of the self and another. As this film illustrates, this does not always emanate from or result in genital sex but could instead involve filling in the beautiful contours of the missing mother with a motherlike figure with whom the child has a sensuous relation.

Sex—in all its allurement—can detract from this multipronged, multifaceted view of queerness. And this film certainly presents twists and turns of queer youth—sexual desire, erotic attachment, mourning the mother, navigating poverty—moving in multiple directions to show how multiple factors upend the life of a character in flux. The queerness of the film is not about being confined to a certain kind of desire—even prohibitive desire—but about the gaps that exist in the developing child's life that the film form attempts to represent. The film may be about a child on the preoedipal cusp of coming into their own sexuality. The desire for an adult significantly older than themself exists, but it is not the end goal of the film. It is not to make prohibitive desire materialize in a sexual or conjugal way, but about what kind of life one forges ideally as one embarks on adolescence and young adulthood through object relations. Through this film's performances, production design, and structure, the genderqueer child asks: Can I be the woman or person I want to be? This question is part of a larger quest to materialize one's queerness and establish a different sense of belonging as one who lives within and fashions the self as critical and nonnormative.

Maxie's personality is established in the film by their hips, which move from side to side with energy as if Maxie is modeling on a runway or competing in a beauty pageant on a stage. Maxie's physical expression is accompanied by a ferocious confidence that we see immediately, along with the poverty of their situation. The film opens with a montage of the environs—a small, white mass in green water is revealed to be part of a monstrous pile of colorful floating garbage collecting against the concrete barrier flanking the homes of the urban slums. The garbage piles so high it almost reaches the street, whose bustle of people is reflected in the water. A hand picks an orchid from the wretched, wet pile of muck. We hear the dense sounds of urbanity—crowds of people, transportation, and children playing with old bottles in the gutter. The song "I Love My Country the

Philippines" plays as jeepneys—World War II vehicles repurposed as community buses—drive by. A girl's pink dress hangs among tattered, brown men's clothes above the street. A shot of Maxie with the orchid tucked behind their ear is murky on-screen, serving as our first glimpse of the titular character. Immediately, the film establishes gender play within the situation of extreme poverty in the Global South.

The next shot of Maxie shows them passing through the narrow walkways of their neighborhood and past clusters of men. The men tease them by sexualizing their femininity, asking, "Who are you flirting with today?" In effect, their dressing up in feminine clothes of a young girl, a gendered act, is sexualized. In response, Maxie throws back the men's laughter with a growl. In a close-up shot, Maxie cackles and lunges toward the men without care, without fear. To behold little Maxie on the street is to recognize their gendered and sexed self-centeredness and their self-confidence in the face of recurring hostility. Their presentation in pastel tank tops and shorts with a ribbon, headband, or fresh flower in their hair while swaying their hips goes well with the unleashing of their ferocity. Maxie expresses joy and possesses rage simultaneously in their gender-nonbinary expression.

The earliest reviewers fearfully anticipated a hostile reception of the film, with its matter-of-fact representation of childhood sexuality. As film critic Keith Uhlich noted, "It is one of the great taboos, particularly in Western culture, to seriously consider the developing sexual feelings of children, a subject most easily infantilized, sensationalized, or brushed under the carpet, lest one become an unwitting Megan's Law pariah. What's often lost in this swirl of knee-jerk 'adult' protectiveness are the feelings of the child, which—raw though they may be—deserve to be included in the discussion rather than subsumed by argumentation."[9] The critic Uhlich captures well that moral panic logic can flee from the centrality of the child as entirely innocent in a world of adult sexuality. Freeing ourselves from the constraints of moral panic enables us to learn more about the existence of childhood sexuality as theirs, which condemnation prevents. Indeed, to avert our eyes from childhood sexuality in representation treats it as deviant, rather than a part of everyday development. One problem with the way childhood sexuality is commonly approached in the movies is the cultural and critical imposition by viewers and critics of a definition of physical genital sexuality versus understanding adolescent sexuality within a wider range, including a more emotional understanding or a psychic perspective on desire that does not involve sex itself.

In another early review in *Variety*, at the time of the film's premiere in the World Cinema Dramatic competition at Sundance, Dennis Harvey predicts that it will "prove a difficult sell offshore, where the twelve-year-old protagonist's cross-dressing precocity and his relationship with a hunky policeman may cause more discomfort than amusement," echoing some of Uhlich's observations.[10] I would add that perhaps the discomfort also comes from the imperial relationship between the United States and the Philippines as a historically sexualized one as well. Seeing a particular agency in the Filipinx child brings up this dynamic. Indeed, the child is truly agentic in their cross-dressing as a creative act, putting together a clever ensemble in a background of dreariness. Yet Harvey's use of the word *precocity* here seems to indicate maturity rather than brightness or intelligence. To then relate the maturity of the child to their desire for a "hunky" adult prematurely sexualizes the relationship—one that I will argue is much more complex than the adultification bestowed on brown youth. This complexity may have something to do with the fact that these critics' early predictions were proved wrong. The subsequent universal critical celebration of the film indicates the need to theorize the wider range of childhood sexuality the film manages to capture beyond a primitive expression of desire by a purportedly sexually precocious child.

As the film circulated the globe, the tone of the reviews changed from fear of pedophilia to something else, a kind of queer positivity. A review in the *New York Times* captures how "'Maximo' has charmed film festival audiences from Sundance to Jerusalem with its refreshingly blasé handling of homosexuality, its amiable actors and its delicacy of milieu."[11] Film critic Nathan Lee essentially concurs that there is a nonchalant matter-of-factness to the representation of child queerness. For him, whether the "homosexuality" is located in the adolescent's bodily performances of queerness, such as their undulating hips, or in the relationship with others is unclear, however. He mentions the performances, so homosexuality may be at the site of queer relationality, or perhaps it is the cultural context where homosexuality and its expression may be felt and thus seen in a different light. Nonetheless, the review captures the worldwide phenomenon of the film's glowing reception, proving earlier trepidation wrong.

Nathan Lopez, who plays Maxie, is globally celebrated and given credit for a performance that is crucial to defying the taboo of child sexuality in cinema. The BBC reviewer lauds how "Lopez is wholly convincing in the lead role, and throughout the film is appealingly non-judgmental in how it treats the taboo issue of pre-teen sexuality."[12] The presentation of queer childhood as matter-of-fact is once again noted in this review but within the context of a nonmoralistic frame that is key to its success. Notably, it is the fact of childhood sexuality that makes the film likable rather than abominable.

An Asian critic, Anomalilly, in a more recent review, almost fifteen years after the film was first released, echoes the British reviewer's identification of the "non-judgmental" aspect as key to the film. Anomalilly, however, goes even further, toward a desexualization of queerness. In their review, Anomalilly asserts that "Lopez doesn't turn [Maxie] into a caricature" of gay, effeminate, or genderqueer youth. Referencing a Doris Day song in comparison, the critic asserts that the child's "puppy love" is recognized by their love object, who is "a beautiful man . . . a wonderful counterpart. His realization that Maxi might not only be looking for a big friend and a role model is subtle and clear."[13] Here, Anomalilly expands the representation of childhood sexuality into a nongenital expression of desire, that perhaps what Maxie wants is a model in the developmental process of growing up. Indeed, the policeman Victor behaves like a parent who cares for the future development of the child, including teaching them about proper partners in love as well as proper careers outside the criminal. I claim that it is an agentic attunement to the child that imagines a future life, a future relationship, and a future adulthood that does not exist now.

To Anomalilly, the representation going beyond sex and sexuality is definite, though understated or indeed delicate, echoing Nathan Lee's review in the *New York Times*, whose discussion of "milieu" may not refer to environment but precisely to the relational matter between the child and the man. For Anomalilly, the environment of the film serves as a background for flamboyant Maxie to stand out colorfully. The film "portrays the world of its main protagonist with a great sense for details, leaving his queerness as a mere one of them. Quite unlike what we could have seen in western films, being gay is a character trait, but not the character issue."[14] While I agree that queerness is merely part of a larger world of so many social forces (poverty and crime) and internal forces (sexuality, loneliness, and grief), queerness is even more obscure and varied to me. Maxie's genderqueerness speaks to me through the inanimate objects of their fashion, too. That is, their relationship with the inanimate objects they adorn themself with is made queer too, along with the individual relations they cultivate with their family and many of their neighbors.

Indeed, in a pregenital world of desire, Maxie may be on a much wider spectrum of queer sexuality, recalling Freud's argument about preoedipal polymorphous perversity in his *Three Essays on the Theory of Sexuality*.[15] In his discussion of a "polymorphously perverse disposition," Freud states, "It is an instructive fact that under the influence of seduction children can become polymorphously perverse, and can be led into all possible kinds of sexual irregularities."[16] In this description, Freud asserts that the seduction of children by adults can shape their innate path—the expression and form of their instincts, essentially, especially when they are not yet formed by the external forces of "shame, disgust and morality" in the classification of their sexual aims.[17]

Critics frequently comment on Maxie's confident expressions of self, which include sexuality. Keith Uhlich, for example, characterizes Maxie as "defiantly true to himself."[18] Queerness here is identified as an internal force within an external context where its expression is certainly not easy. Ben Walters, writing in *Time Out*, echoes the observation of Maxie's assertive femme strength: "Maxi is an unapologetically effeminate Manila lad who gets on surprisingly well with his gangster pa and street-thug brothers . . . in the modest home that Maxi keeps with pride when not swishing fabulously around the slum streets."[19] The review captures Maxie's home life, where they are aware of their family's criminality, and points to the different world occupied by their crush, a law-abiding man living outside of the underground economy. Maxie, like David in *Minari*, absorbs the information of their family's hidden and frowned-upon activities while noting the dignity and respect of Victor's job. They are making sense of the world in the process of making choices about how to grow up. Here, Maxie's relationships with adults follow Anomalilly's observation that theirs is not only a quandary of sexuality and queerness alone, but of how to become a sexually healthy and strong queer adult in a precarious economy, especially in terms of their family's established status as respected members of the community. The *Time Out* review by Ben Walters certainly agrees. It identifies how Victor, the policeman, "presents Maxi with an appealingly robust model of manhood by determining to overcome the laissez-faire corruption that, problematically, allows his family to thrive."[20] To see the film beyond the formula of the dangers of expressing childhood sexuality, as these critics do and as I elaborate on, is to expand our understanding of childhood development and the role of relations with others as critical in a particular cultural, social, and economic context.

We can point to the sexual desire that comes from children—whether erotic or not, premature or not. However, we also need to see the larger picture of self-sovereignty that is crucial to their adult development. That is, we need to measure what is happening in childhood. Are children learning how to be strong, how to be free, how to represent their organic sexuality, or are they becoming distorted due to adult impositions, seizure, and deprivation of that self-sovereignty? Thus, I read this film, first, to understand Maxie's creativity and sexuality as a form of grief, and for the larger concern of how they are forging their adult life in the context of poverty. I understand the expression of child development as preoedipal, a nongenital desire that is part of a larger constellation of relationships forged on the path to adulthood—one of health and strength that unquestionably maintains queerness. To be clear, however, I do not disavow the nascent homoerotic stirrings that must be acknowledged, even in the search for a lost mother, or in what the critic Michael D. Klemm identifies as Victor's paternal treatment of Maxie.[21]

Despite the earlier predictions, why is this film so celebrated when its premise is a love story between a child and a man? Is Klemm right when he writes, "*The Blossoming of Maximo Oliveros* is a unique film that really isn't about homosexuality at all; it is but one component in a rich tapestry."[22] For the spectator, the film enables a larger view of childhood development, of which sexuality is one part. The child forges a gender performance and play as part of their normal development that only becomes sexual with the adult imposition of genital sex. My approach to this film fleshes out this claim of child development that exceeds sexual drives of pleasure fulfillment or genital love without disavowing the thing that is feared by queer sexuality—genital sex that is configured differently. The film does not disavow sex but expands our understanding of sexuality and queerness in situating Maxie's quest for identity in mourning and poverty. Object relations theory, which moves away from biological drives and instincts of aggression and sexuality to an emphasis on relationships that address life's crises of the self—whether loneliness, family, death, love, or growing up—can illuminate how Maxie pursues the opportunity to construct themself in a world with limited options.

Object Relations Theory: Moving Away from Sex to Relationality

To assert how cinema can help us live better and stronger lives, I turn to psychoanalysis and its theorizing of not only sexuality but also the broader expanse of life's struggles in order to support and guide each patient through their vulnerabilities. Object relations theory enables me to expand our understanding of child sexuality beyond innate biological desires determined by the pleasure principle, and to focus instead on the importance of relationality and the reality principle in the development of the self.[23] The psychoanalyst Nancy McWilliams helps me to map out the progression of psychoanalysis from Freudian drive theory to object relations theory that I find most useful in analyzing the film.

McWilliams describes how Freud essentially created "a biologically derived model that stressed the centrality of instinctual processes" toward gratification as an end point.[24] A person's development proceeded in an orderly way through bodily phases focused on the oral, anal, and phallic in the periods from infancy throughout their youth. The object relations model in psychoanalysis moved away from the biological basis of seeking fulfillment of drives to the search for relationships as well as a repetitive attachment to the events that compose those relationships. According to McWilliams: "A baby is not so much focused on getting mother's milk, as it is on having the experience of being nursed, with the sense of warmth and attachment that goes with that experience."[25] While both drive theory and object relations focus on the sensuousness of the experience between parent and child, each explains it differently.

Drive theory describes the baby as seeking fulfillment of their instincts through sensuous touch, and object relations theory focuses instead on the attunement to the sensations of the child's sensuous relationship with the caregiver. In this way, object relations theory asserts that "love, loneliness, creativity and integrity of the self . . . do not fit neatly within the confines of Freud's structural theory."[26] Rather than focusing on usurped or unmet drives that lead to frustrations that determine personality or fix character, object relations theory attends to the nature of relationships for the child: what they "had been like, how they had been experienced, how they felt aspects of them had been internalized, and how internal images and representations of them live on in the unconscious lives of adults."[27] Rather than a focus on innate instincts, these relational interactions shape the formation of the child's self significantly. In the development of the child, what is liberating about object relations theory is the movement away from the biological, instinctual focus that usually centers sex and aggression toward a larger scope of human relationality that can be evaluated.

Of particular significance to the case of Maxie, in terms of object relations, is that "oedipal issues loom less large than themes of safety and agency, and separation and individuation."[28] The oedipal phase occurs when the child turns to sexuality and fantasies related to their parents. There is an element of competition with the father for the desire of the mother, following the Greek tragedy of Oedipus. Interestingly, in Freudian drive theory the oedipal phase indicates a sense of independence in the child. As McWilliams explains it, "The oedipal phase was seen as a critical time for developing a sense of basic efficacy . . . and a sense of pleasure in identification with one's love objects."[29] In object relations theory, the oedipal phase is also considered a "cognitive milestone, not just a psychosexual one, in that it represents a victory over infantile egocentrism for a child to understand that two other people . . . may relate to each other in ways that do not involve the child."[30] In the psychoanalyses of drives and egos and then object relations and self psychology, the oedipal phase is the beginning of independence whether in one's internal drives or in recognizing others as separate from oneself. However, these issues of sexual fantasy involving parents, and competition for sex, focus our attention on basic instinctual drives rather than on the child's relationships with others in the formation of their independence.

It is crucial to move farther away from biologism, for independence necessitates leaving the primacy of the parental relationship and even introducing other people and other love objects, whether persons or inanimate nonhuman others. For Maxie, this means Victor is a counterpart to the father and the family with the missing mother, even a replacement for the missing mother. These new relations then raise issues of safety, especially for a child whose expressions of nongenital desire may be imposed upon by adult sexuality. Victor indeed acts as a replacement for the mother in his empathy and in boosting Maxie's confidence to seek a different life path through an agentic attunement that cannot be sexual as an inappropriate expression within their search for a mother. In terms of Maxie's attachment to nonhuman others, the feminine inanimate objects they adorn themself with animate their life—the color, the texture, the structure of their clothes bring them joy. The sexual is but part of a larger constellation of love objects.

Preoedipal love speaks to the earliest developmental phase of sensuousness that McWilliams discusses in the infant-parent relationship in Freud, one I also discussed earlier regarding my own maternal relationship with my infant children when breastfeeding them or changing their diapers. The bodily relationship between caregiver and child is indeed sensory in the caregiver's contact with the genital body—in a physical rather than a sexual relation. An example is toilet training, when genital touch by the caregiver discontinues in the cultivation of independence. The sensuous touch is not competitive, but really about the love for the experience of receiving care and, in object relations, the person who is giving care. As I discussed regarding self psychology in the previous chapter, self-esteem is formed from the confidence built on the reliability of the loving touch in an act of parenting that balances indulgence and inhibition. Mourning occurs at the loss of the caregiver's touch, in the loss of the genital connection from the diaper change or weaning from the breast. There is indeed a preoedipal erotic bond that is present in the relationship between Maxie and Victor, such that if any genitalia entered the scene, the child would be shocked. If Maxie's object had been the wrong person, someone who preyed upon the craving for unmet sensual holding, the intimacy could have turned into pedophilic sex that the child would have found vexing, violent, inappropriate, confusing, and wrong. The desire to be held can be misconstrued. Victor does not violate Maxie, nor does he infantilize their very real desire for care and connection. I will argue that the child Maxie wants not sex but the sensual gratification of the caregiver bond—which I define as possessing sensuous and erotic qualities.

Childhood Sexuality: *The Blossoming of Maximo Oliveros*

The Filipino language does not use gendered pronouns but defers to *siya* (they) or *ikaw* (you) rather than her or him. So, throughout *The Blossoming of Maximo Oliveros*, despite its gendered title that says Maxie essentially moves from boyhood to womanhood, they are never referred to as a boy and only thrice as a girl: as *gaga*—a common quip referring to a stupid girl versus *gago* (stupid boy)—or as a "sister" in English, not just a "sibling" or *kapatid*, also not gendered in Tagalog, like the word *anak*, or "child," which is what their dad calls Maxie. It is their brother Bogs who calls them *gaga* when asking them to sew his shorts. The first and only occurrence of *gaga* happens in the first thirty minutes of the film, barely noticeable and not translated in the subtitles. The only time Maxie is directly called a girl is at the police station when visiting the policeman on whom they have a crush. They are gendered female but in a mocking way. "Your girl is here," the other policeman says, laughing as he deliberately uses the term in a teasing and disparaging way. The use of "sister" occurs at the very end of the film, driving home the gendered goal of the story—to render Maxie as blossoming toward womanhood. Yet, this occurs when they are no longer dressed as a girl and no longer walking flamboyantly as genderqueer. They are called sister, yet their comportment reads as a boy and they are dressed in their boy's school uniform, in direct contrast to the rest of the hundred-minute film. The progression of Maxie from boy to woman is actually complicated, for the film ends with their looking like a boy, still bonded with the man who looks over them like a parent.

In terms of a preoedipal polymorphous sexuality, Maxie is not inflicted by shame for their crossing of gender boundaries, nor does their family police them. In her essay "The Development of a Child" (1921), Melanie Klein speaks frankly in encouraging adults to "spare the child unnecessary repression by freeing—and first and foremost in ourselves—the whole wide sphere of sexuality from the dense veils of secrecy, falsehood and danger spun by a hypocritical civilization."[31] She argues that fueling the child with "sexual information" frees the child of repression and avoids "false shame and nervous suffering."[32] This type of education not only lifts a burden that is bothersome to the child and to adults but also creates an "intellectual power."[33] Rather than provoking averted eyes and confusion that prevent full participation in the world, sexual information empowers a child in their larger development into adulthood. The beginning of the film indeed shows us a genderqueer, effeminate, and likely gay child as notably confident. What education did Maxie receive to make them this way? Their familial love. To start a queer film with such a character opens up the possibilities of their story beyond sexuality and sexual identity. They are a grieving child, part of a loving family who shares in their mourning. They are a poor child, aiming to fashion a life outside of the crime that entrenches their family. They are an intensely creative child who plays with their reality in order to thrive.

To be clear, the film represents three important themes alongside Maxie's sexuality: their family's mourning from the death of a mother and wife, their entrenchment in criminality and poverty, and the performance of play that captures their relationship to reality. The family's criminal activity as hustlers in their poor neighborhood is established early in the film when Maxie heads home and we see their dad, Paco, bargaining with a woman during a cell phone transaction in the street. He tells the customer to buy the phone at his price because she will "sell it for more." Maxie also encounters their brother flirting with a young female neighbor—presumably a sex worker who doesn't have a client that night.

Bogs teases her about "looking hot." She is more than amenable to his attention, which he then parlays into selling her a lottery ticket, to her obvious *asar*, or irritation. At home, Maxie's role within the family is quickly established—the men return home hungry and let Maxie know it: "Hey Maxie, I'm starving!" We also see that the family is mourning the death of their wife and mother—the altar bearing her photo and flowers hangs over the table where they eat. And Maxie has taken on the domestic work of cooking and cleaning. In this scene, the father calls Maxie "son" while giving them money to "buy sanitary napkins" in an everyday, casual acceptance of their nonbinary sense of self.

Creativity as a Product of Mourning

Psychoanalyst Melanie Klein survived the death of her closest sister and a beloved brother as well as the death of her own child. In her essay "Mourning and Its Relation to Manic-Depressive States" (1940), she addresses how the loss of a person returns the mourner to the loss of their good objects— their internally archived relations, events, and memories with others. The process of mourning the loss of a loved one initiates a larger process that "reincorporates the person he has just lost and the good objects lost internalized from earliest stages of development."[34] Essentially, in the acknowledgment of death and loss, powerful self-restoration occurs. Grief, then, is an act of creativity, an affirmation of life and its coexistence with death, rather than an admission that things happen for a reason or that there is no accident, thus surrendering to the power of the universe. The recognition that things in the world are out of our control retakes our powerlessness as a site of agency and action toward self-care. To care for the self and others, which Maxie does, is monumental in its power to forge the world, knowing one ultimately can't control the world. In the acknowledgment of the death of his wife, the father demonstrates the importance of mourning a loved one. In doing so, the process of restoring order is encouraged in both the outer world and the inner world, which includes the validation that "good objects existed."[35] In Maxie's world, mourning means there is a place for their mother and the hurt from their loss.

In embracing a life of mourning, Maxie forges a healthy relationship to death. And this act can lead to the acceptance of their own sexuality, for this confrontation with death encourages creativity that they manifest on their body every day in the colors and feminine garb of their preferred gender expression. Melanie Klein describes the process of loss as one related to creativity; when grieving people long for their loved one, they acknowledge their "dependence of a kind which becomes an incentive to reparation and preservation of the object. It is creative because it is dominated by love, while the dependence based on persecution and hatred is sterile and destructive."[36] The suffering from grief, "when experienced to the full and despair is at its height," can become affirming of life itself and therefore productive through the very work of mourning.[37]

Mourning deepens one's relationship to one's inner objects that provide affirmation and strength. This is especially significant for Maxie as a child. As their entire family mourns, the older siblings and father are adults, while Maxie confronts the loss of their mother as a child who has not yet established their good objects inside themself. Klein says the young child "is at the height of his struggle with fears of losing [his mother] internally and externally, for he has not yet succeeded in establishing her securely inside himself. In this struggle, the child's relation to his mother, her actual presence, is of the greatest help."[38] So, for Maxie, the literal loss of the mother is significant, especially when we see that in the openness of their entire family's grief: their father's acts of caring in embracing Maxie to sleep, encouraging their loving nature, and seeing in them an innate goodness; and Maxie's siblings, who also caress them as a thing of beauty and a source of care that they honor and protect, which help Maxie to attain a strong sense of self. We see this in the acceptance of both death and queer sexuality, which results in the enrichment of Maxie's entire personality—exemplified in the defiance of gender restrictions in clothing and comportment as well as pride in their work and their role within the family.

Grief permeates the family, too, as the dad caresses his wife's picture on the prominent altar that overlooks the home and her intimately bound family. The home is a site of intimacy where Maxie decorates the window with Christmas lights, and they all watch a pirated DVD movie with an English title none of them can pronounce—finally deferring to the dad's wrong pronunciation. Maxie is especially loving and sweet, cuddling up to their dad or watching the world go by as the family settles in together after dinner. Maxie is definitely assigned the caregiving role of shopping for and cooking the food, washing the clothes, making the beds, and cleaning the floor. Maxie accepts and takes pride in the gendered role assignation, which they are rewarded for as the most beloved member of the family. This caregiving role extends beyond the confines of their small space, as they wash a little boy in the public bath situated in the entryway of their tenement, receiving thanks from the boy's mom. Part of the mothering in their family extends to this little boy, and later to Victor himself, whom Maxie bathes. Here, in this experience of bathing the boy, we also see a pregenital sexuality that appears in the later scene as well.

Maxie spends their time in their community cinema where kids watch pirated movies together ritualistically. An Italian romance that depicts prevailing love between a handsome man and a beautiful woman is guaranteed to receive a good review from the exhilarated kids. Spending time in the movie theater is part of their family's being outside the economy. We realize Maxie has actually dropped out of school, and their classmate misses them or jealously observes their freedom and alternative life out of school. This fact makes urgent the moment where Maxie's future is threatened by their becoming uneducated as well as entering onto a criminal path. Maxie's classmate, dressed in his boy's uniform and holding on to his plastic bag of iced water, silently and longingly wishes to be with them in their cross-dressing community of other "girls" as they giggle away, happily sloshing their own plastic bags of iced water. In "The Role of the School in the Libidinal Development of the Child" (1923), Klein discusses how "school and learning are . . . libidinally determined for everyone, since by its demands school compels a child to sublimate his libidinal instinctual energies."[39] We see this sublimation in this scene in which the cisgender boy longs to enjoy the freedom that Maxie and their girlfriends have. Instead, he is constrained within his male school uniform. After treating them all to iced water in plastic bags to drink with straws, Maxie calls for her "girl" friends to leave. The boy looks at them with further longing. They are going to play "Miss U Pageant" and perform as various Miss Universe beauty contestants in ornate, over-the-top costumes with umbrellas and other accessories from countries like Thailand, Venezuela, and the Philippines.

The creativity in the performance of the beauty pageant captures Maxie's perception of reality. Klein's "Criminal Tendencies in Normal Children" (1927) describes how the child's "play-life is concerned entirely with the child's impulse-life and desires, performing them and fulfilling them through his phantasies."[40] Fantasies, according to Klein, are unconscious mental images, so to see Maxie's play focused on gendered ideals of beauty and performances of romance is to see their relationship to reality as not a flight but a comfort, a pleasure and an exploration of desire.

To live as genderqueer means experiencing the ongoing threat of violence. To externalize fantasy, then, is to displace violence with pleasure

3.1 Maxie performs as a Miss Universe candidate along with other genderqueer youth in the urban slums who utilize their creativity in fantasy world-making. *The Blossoming of Maximo Oliveros* (Auraeus Solito, 2005).

and to reduce the fear and judgment that befall those who cross policed boundaries of gender. In "Personification in the Play of Children" (1929), Klein says that the displacement of violence with pleasure "affords it various real proofs that the psychic processes, with their cathexis of anxiety and guilt, may have a favourable issue and anxiety be greatly reduced."[41] Maxie's externalization of their fantasies in play and performance shows their attempt to navigate their reality of the threat of violence through grief, poverty, and their genderqueer self.

A montage of materials required to perform the Miss Universe pageant opens the scene: the tiaras, furs, glitter, sparkle, and more worn by the three genderqueer femme contestants. Individually, they parade their elaborate outfits while yelling out their country names to the camera (we serve as their play audience). Three genres compose the talent show: drama, opera, and disco. Moderated and introduced by the cisgender girl, the three over-the-top performances follow each other: a dramatic scene tells the story of a young woman returning home from work with good news about her promotion to find that her mother has died. This is precisely Maxie's story as well: the ongoing grief about their own dead mother. Their friend, the other contestant, cries over the body, begging the mother to rise up and eat *pancit* (noodles). In a highly melodramatic mode, the contestant weeps: "The noodles will get cold and go to waste!

You're even colder than the noodles!" The next candidate sings opera, in direct contrast to Maxie, whose disco song decries falling in love with "hard-to-trust handsome men. My type is one who has hard arms to protect me. Wow, mister, wow!" This stunning performance, though sexual in its lyrics, is performed most innocently.

This is revealed in the next segment: the interview. The cisgender girl emcee asks simplistic beauty contest questions that candidates repeat, then ask her to repeat again in a classic stalling tactic, as the contestant formulates a competitive response. Maxie's question is about love, which they are unable to answer: "Love is like . . . [looks around] Oh no, it's dark!" Maxie then drops the mic on the floor to run home, with their friends yelling that they are missing the swimsuit competition, where they have a "good chance of winning!" Maxie dashes out, yelling back, "It's dark!" to indicate they have a curfew. In their play and performance, Maxie forms images that are "kindly imagos," ones that are beautiful and assuring and provide confidence as a counter to anxiety, while also reflecting their developmental stage.[42] They create a different and pulsating narrative of their desires that, when focused on a real love object, a policeman, show themselves to be directed toward nongenital sex. Their attraction to Victor emanates from the circumstances of Maxie's adult development: choosing between a criminal and a noncriminal adult path.

A New Path: Nongenital Desire

Although Maxie is unable to define what love is during the beauty contest play, they soon undeniably express romantic feelings toward a police officer who is a beefy, burly, and sweet-faced adult man at least ten years older. They meet on the very night when Maxie returns home in the dark, sashaying in the narrow streets of their slum neighborhood. Two street boys tease, grab, and threaten to touch their "smooth skin," provoking Maxie to fight back and scream "Saklolo!" (Help!) and "Rape!" The policeman Victor happens to be walking by and rescues Maxie. Upon Victor's arrival, the boys claim they were just teasing. Maxie, frenzied by very real fear, won't let their claims stand and unabashedly calls them out as "assholes." The policeman takes Maxie home, giving them a piggyback ride. On the way home, the question about love that they were unable to answer during the beauty pageant is answered; it is the trust and safety that agentic attunement allows. They proceed quietly, with Victor whistling a tune while carrying Maxie. Maxie, all of twelve, falls deeply and madly in adulation. It is during this walk home that Maxie glimpses their path to adulthood as one that can be spent safely. While we cannot know if Maxie sees these things at the moment, as they perch on Victor's back, they are literally walking a new path—one that is not going toward criminality, but where they can see themselves in the future making choices about how they wish to live in a noncriminal way. Through this relationship established during the piggyback ride, Maxie is carried toward a new possibility, another kind of life, and perhaps another kind of kinship too. It is not a life free from poverty, merely another way of living in it.

I return to Klein again here to capture how the path of development includes identifying those who can help themselves. In "Love, Guilt and Reparation" (1937), Klein describes how young people seek those they "can look up to and idealize. Admired teachers can serve this purpose; and inner security is derived from the feelings of love, admiration and trust toward them, because, among other reasons, in the unconscious mind these feelings seem to confirm the existence of good parents and of a love relation to them, thus disproving the great hatred, anxiety and guilt which at this period of life have become so strong."[43] Victor serves as this ideal away from the world Maxie currently does not question, even after dropping out of school and having no future beyond illegal activity. The policeman presents an alternate life from the criminality of Maxie's family, rather than simply and only erotic sexual desire.

At home, Maxie's family of criminals welcomes the policeman. Bogs accuses Maxie of flirting in a contemptible way, as if asking for it, an accusation usually made of girls victimized by assault. They also call the boys assholes for assaulting them, for which Maxie says they "will pay in karma!" It is notable that the loving family is not so enraged that they seek vengeance. Maxie does not seem perturbed but instead enters a new phase of development: they cannot stop staring at Victor with fascination and curiosity. Their family studies him, too, but for different reasons, recognizing that he represents a threat to their life of crime. They ask him if he has just arrived in the neighborhood, and if he would be "friends with us." For saving Maxie, the father offers him money and, along with the brothers, takes note when Victor will not accept it.

It is at this juncture that the three elements—criminality and poverty, gender and mourning, and performance and play—collide to constitute the turning point of the film. As Maxie lives a genderqueer life of sexual and gendered confidence from mourning, Victor's arrival shows the conundrum in choosing a path toward adulthood: criminal poverty with abundant fear or law-abiding poverty that cannot afford hospitalizations. Maxie's performance and play shift to a new domain of romance as well.

Romance, in this case, is about turning away from family toward a new love object that also grows the family as a whole—it is one that Maxie resists in the case of Victor's role in their life. Klein discusses how, in childhood, the child's "desires and phantasies are still very much connected with his mother and sisters, and the struggle of turning away from them and finding new love objects is at its very height."[44] To follow the assessment of the psychoanalyst, the death of the mother means the search for love objects is even more amplified because she is no longer present. Klein continues that due to the intensity of opposite-sex relations at this adolescent stage of childhood, "the drive towards people of the same sex tends to become intensified. The love, admiration and adulation which can be put into these friendships are . . . a safeguard against hatred, and for these various reasons young people cling all the more to such relationships."[45] It is here that I examine Maxie's relationship within the context of turning away from family—where their developmental stage involves a struggle with the formation of the self in relation to others in their world.

When Victor leaves the Oliveros house, the family goes to sleep and Maxie cuddles with their dad, almost sleeping on him, in the comfort and safety of their family intimacy. Their brother Boy returns home with bloody clothes—a green shirt that he carefully puts away along with something else in a blue bag. Maxie offers to wash these clothes for him and ultimately burns them. In a neighborhood where public and private space converge, Victor sees Maxie burning the shirt, which he undoubtedly wonders about in terms of Maxie's route to criminality in helping to cover up their family member's crime. In a sense, he witnesses them in their familial and domestic gender role. So, while Maxie's role as caregiver continues, Victor's entry into their life means there is a new element to their experience of gender and family both.

Bogs continues to tease Maxie in gendered ways, including asking them to braid his long hair and expecting them to do laundry, cook, and clean. When the siblings go outside, Bogs continues to tease the sex worker Janet, who is clearly attracted to him. Disappointed and hurt, Janet turns away without missing Maxie's look of empathy. They share this moment of looking at each other, where they recognize their gendered lot of being the object of male teasing that takes a heavy toll.

As the family walks farther into the neighborhood, another gender-queer youth named Leslie appears, and Maxie asks permission from their brothers to join their friend on another movie escapade. This time they agree that it's a "bad movie because they [don't] end up together." When Maxie and their friends leave the theater, they encounter local criminality once again: naked men are waking up in a ditch, bewildered because they don't remember how they ended up there. Among the gathering crowd of neighbors, Maxie perches on a tree overlooking the ditch and spots Victor, who is helping to clear the crowd and round up the disoriented naked men. Maxie's world maps out before them: the shamed naked men and the upright cop creating order. They look at Victor with smiling sweetness, finding his alternative manhood appealing among the available choices of masculinity, but Victor does not notice.

This adulation of Victor from a distance continues when Maxie follows him to a church, where Victor prays, kneeling in the last pew, as Maxie stares at him from across the aisle. Whether they see Victor as a path to upward mobility or the ground for a blossoming sexuality, Maxie uses this opportunity to observe him and gaze on him as a teacher, a model for a different way of life outside criminality and genderqueer aggressions. Yet, the look is not separate from the search for a love object related to their mother or the wider aspects of love to replace her. Klein discusses this phenomenon, where "anything that is felt to give out goodness and beauty, and that calls forth pleasure and satisfaction, in the physical or in the wider sense, and in the unconscious mind take the place of this ever-bountiful breast, and of the whole mother."[46] For Maxie, Victor represents a larger world of continued admiration. They look to him as part of an attachment to their lost mother and as part of their search for good objects, even a romantic one, in the process of their development.

Following Victor to a street café, Maxie offers to sell him a lottery ticket. Victor recognizes them and confirms their name with a question, "Maxie, right?" A romantic friendship that the viewer can easily sexualize ensues. It cannot be denied that Maxie projects romantic idealization upon this man, and it can be denied that it is sexual. Yet, it is also the acceptance of their genderqueerness by their family that leads to an exploration of other love objects. Maxie, in their queerness, is loved without reservation by their family, and it "has been firmly established in the mind, trust in other people and belief in one's own goodness are like a rock which withstands the blows of circumstances."[47] Through this confidence-giving love and devotion, Maxie is free—to explore their grief, their work, their future path, and their sexuality.

So, in the formulation of a future self, when seeking to transfer "interest and love from our mother to other people and other sources of gratification, then, and only then, are we able in later life to derive enjoyment from other sources."[48] Thus, Maxie's nongenital search for love objects is oversimplified by the fear of childhood sexuality and genital sex that the early film reviewers anticipated. If we center the nongenital search for love objects, Maxie's exploration can be more clearly seen as exceeding sexuality without forsaking their queerness—including and going beyond the romantic, the erotic, and the sexual.

To continue in their projection of a romantic life partner, Maxie brazenly tells Victor, "You should try my cooking—you'll forget your girl-friend's name." From across the street, their dad and brother Boy watch this encounter with alarm. They do not know what the two are discussing, but they know Victor is a cop. He is dressed as one at that precise moment as well. Unaware of the father's and brother's gaze, Victor responds to Maxie in nonsexual terms within their relationship of agentic attunement in his watching out for their future. He immediately shifts to a discussion of job security instead of romance and marriage. He asks Maxie to think about finding legal rather than illegal work, suggesting they think about cooking as a legitimate profession and career, "a job you can be proud of." In response, Maxie tells Victor about their aspirations to sell DVDs, which are a source of pleasure in Maxie's life. Victor replies that he hopes they are "not pirated DVDs, so I don't arrest you. I can't make an exception." Maxie responds flirtatiously: "I bet you're ugly when you're angry," while offering to pay for their meal. When Victor refuses and tells them to buy a toy instead, Maxie asserts, "I'm not a kid anymore." In this scene, we see that Maxie occupies their gender and expresses their queerness in the flirtation, but Victor refuses to participate and instead focuses on Maxie's development outside the path of criminality.

In terms of that different path, their next encounter is during a visit at Victor's house, where the theme of family dominates their conversation and physical interaction. Victor talks with Maxie about their family in a parental manner, asking bluntly if their dad hits them. Maxie responds that he "smacks me when I am bad" and that their brothers "tease me but they are cool." They tell Victor about their close relationship with their brothers, sad Boy and playful Bogs. Maxie asks Victor about his family too. For Maxie, good relations in the family are the basis for relating with others. Because Maxie's relationship with their family is "built predominantly upon trust and love," they are "guiding and helpful figures, which are a source of comfort and harmony and the prototype for all friendly relationships in later life."[49] In their conversations and interactions, I see Maxie attempting to gauge Victor's position as a "fantasy parent," a term I coin based on Klein's description of a "helpful, guiding figure . . . loving and protective parents towards us, and we return this love, we feel like parents towards them."[50] That is, rather than an object of genital sexual desire, what Maxie identifies in Victor is an idealized parent who fulfills their intensive needs for safety, pleasure, intimacy, comfort, nourishment, and caring, agentic attunement by the caregiver to the child. Maxie identifies Victor as a source of knowledge and pleasure for a different path in life.

The romantic and erotic cannot be denied, however. Victor is not wearing a shirt, and Maxie touches the cross draped on his chest while asking him about his family. Victor says his father told him to wear it so as not to "become a pot-bellied cop," which I interpret as corruption in the sense of becoming a "fat cat" from bribes rather than an astute and ethically minded policeman. Maxie touches the scar on Victor's cheek while asking him about it. At this second touch by Maxie, Victor offers to go outside, recognizing and recoiling from the intimacy of the gesture as threatening to the parental relation that is fueled by the sensory.

Outside, Victor teaches Maxie how to whistle as they sit on a bench. In psychoanalysis, the lips hold potentiality, "an invitation to silence or secrecy, or exactly *enigma*."[51] They can also be a form of speaking—whether of desire or other feelings. Victor demonstrates by showing Maxie that "you put your lips together then blow." Victor asks Maxie about school, and Maxie talks about how they do well in it, winning contests, and being the teacher's favorite. The conversation turns to an expression of curiosity when Maxie asks if Victor has a girlfriend and what he likes in a girl. When Victor hesitates, Maxie complains: "I'm already twelve! I know so much. My girlfriends already have boyfriends." Victor teases them by asking about their own girlfriend. Maxie says "Kadiri," expressing literal disgust; pushed by the strength of their revulsion, they threaten to walk away. Victor relents, "A boyfriend is what you want." He then shares what he wants in a girlfriend: someone "feminine, beautiful, loving, and simple." Maxie listens intently and reflects on Victor's response while touching their headband. These are lessons in adulthood and growing up that Maxie uses to acquire knowledge in undergoing agentic attunement from this older person. What they know is their relationship with the family they love, and that they live in an untenable situation of criminality and poverty. How does Maxie bring this world together with the one in which Victor lives? Victor is seen as a representative of possibility, both as a potential embodiment of a future partner and, even more so now, as a different parent. But with this burgeoning love, that is not only sexual, comes the possibility of guilt over the betrayal of family that it may imply.

Family Fidelities

Maxie's different fidelities collide when Victor comes to their home to investigate a recent murder. The visits by police tend to be friendly, with apologies from the sergeant that their investigations are *pokpok sa taas*, or pressures coming from above. When Victor comes by with the sergeant while the family is drinking outside, the dad warns Victor that he "won't last long if he does not take the job lightly." Maxie listens while standing behind their dad, lovingly hugging him, yet intent on learning about the world spilling before them. They hear their family explicitly calling Victor an "asshole making life hard." Victor's boss, the sergeant, shows deference to Paco when his charge refuses the offer of a drink. "Perez really doesn't drink!" This collision between Maxie's allegiances continues in Victor's space. When Maxie visits Victor at the police station, Victor's colleague teases him while also gendering the visit as accommodating and servile, "Perez, your girl is here," then turns away to address the other cops, saying, "He's got someone to bring him lunch."

Victor doesn't participate in the teasing or defend himself against the suggestion that he is a child molester. Instead, he accepts Maxie's offer of food and acts on his parenting impulse. As they sit outside, Maxie watches Victor eat and attentively gives him water when he coughs. Victor uses this moment to urge Maxie to keep considering a life of legitimate work to help their family and as an alternative to criminality. He accusingly asks Maxie, "Do you want them stealing and hurting people?" Here, his drive is to veer Maxie's path away from criminality that has harmful consequences for others. When Maxie replies, "They don't mean it, they protect me," Victor encourages Maxie to betray their family and offers the state as an alternative parent: "We are friends, you can trust me. I saw you the other night. You were burning a shirt. Why were you burning it? I won't get you in trouble. Whose shirt was that?" He is holding Maxie's arm as they cry. "It was an accident, he did not mean it," they say, without betraying Boy, their brother who is actually standing in front of Maxie but at a significant distance where he is unable to see Maxie struggling to defend him. Maxie takes off running, recognizing that they can never betray their family to the police. The child has to navigate their love for Victor as a friend and mentor vis-à-vis their loyalty to the family.

At home, they tell their family that Victor knows about Boy's role in the murder. The father unleashes rage onto Boy and accuses him: "I raised a thief and not a killer." This process of child development is ongoing within the family, where the threat of becoming a murderer violates the order the father established. Maxie holds tightly on to Boy, who lands on the ground after their father pushes him. Maxie's embrace prevents further violence. They mediate between their family in a peacekeeping role. The family dynamic within this moment of violence reveals Maxie's role as sacred. The father commands them, "Get away from your brother! Don't touch him!" as Maxie hugs Boy further, not so much in defiance but in genuine protectiveness toward their older brother. The father, whom Bogs is holding down, keeps yelling: "Get away from him! Don't touch him! Stay away from that piece of shit!" But Maxie won't let go even as the father represents Boy as a contaminating threat to Maxie's goodness. The family is so bonded by loss, where they preserve who they are in the face of precarity unprecedented in their life. The scene ends with the father looking at the mother's altar in grief, amplifying how they are together enshrouded by mourning. It is notable, too, that their dying mother's hospital bills led to the father's having to leave his poorly paid company job to resort to thievery and to Bogs and Boy's training as his companions in the profession.

The father and brothers decide to beat up Victor to quell the threat to their family. Here violence is a form of touch that aims to suppress and to silence, unlike the connection Maxie seeks with Victor. After being bloodied and busted up, Victor slowly and painfully walks back to his house. Maxie climbs a tree to enter Victor's room from a window and tend to his wounds. It is crucial to note that they call him older brother, pleading with him to be of help. Victor resists, saying, "Leave me alone. Go home." Maxie kneels by him, mimicking the church scene by now praying over him. Maxie weeps over Victor, before falling asleep by his head. When Maxie wakes up, Victor is in the shower. From the small opening at the doorway, they peer in and see his reddened skin and bruised torso bending down, barely able to raise the pail of water to wash down the caked blood. They begin cooking eggs, gleeful that Victor is awake. They watch Victor emerge from the bathroom, a towel over his hips, bending to put on his underwear. Maxie looks upon him with a mix of curiosity and concern. Curiosity here is both erotic and maternal. Just as Maxie bathed the toddler on the street in their feminized mother-figure role in the neighborhood, in the space of Victor's house, Maxie similarly cares for his injured body. Peering at him in the shower and as he changes clothes, however, adds a different dimension to their curiosity.

In *Three Essays on the Theory of Sexuality*, Freud writes about the power of seeing as "ultimately derived from touching. Visual impressions remain the most frequent pathway along which libidinal excitation is aroused."[52] Here, Freud specifically explores the scopophilic, or pleasure in looking, that includes elements of sexual curiosity. Because Victor is putting on clothes, we are aware that the transition from toweled hips to white briefs is a threatening moment when the genitals may be revealed. Is Maxie looking for that glimpse of their object of desire? This remains possible. The film certainly does not disavow the genital aspect of queer sexuality despite its being inappropriate or unseemly to audiences. The film spends time in this realm of genital sex to make clear the adult's refusal to engage the child's desire, carnal or not.

When Victor looks up, the desire is certainly diverted to the nonsexual realm as would be the practice of agentic attunement where the sexual cannot enter the relation of mentorship. Victor will not entertain any sexual stirrings. Maxie's response is not to stare back but to turn away. It becomes clear that they are not expressing *kilig*, or the intimation of genital stirrings in the presence of a naked man. They deflect it toward the maternal, where Maxie takes care of Victor with the offer of food. As Victor looks up, Maxie turns away, saying in a singsong voice: "Kain na!" or "Time to eat!" or "Let's eat!" Thus, in this reply, another path opens in the sighting of the naked man: the possibility of pleasure in looking as the end of that desire (for the other or for the future self is unclear), rather than its foreplay. Maxie returns their gaze to the frying pan as Victor comes into the kitchen and says, "You're very pretty this morning," a complimentary statement that fulfills a youthful fantasy of family intimacy—where Maxie's role is of concerned caregiver whether wife, sister, or mother. Maxie says, "It was my fault they beat you," to which Victor answers, admitting his own guilt, "I tried to make you confess." This compels Maxie to kiss him on the cheek. Sight turns to touch. The sexual realm opens up. Victor responds by promptly telling them to leave: "Maxie, go home. They are looking for you," showing awareness of them as an inappropriate love object. Indeed, this scene is the closest to acknowledging the sexual dimension of the queer child's desire, but it is not to titillate or to play with the threat of pedophilia. Instead, it illustrates Maxie's larger goals, which include sexuality, indeed, but mourning, family, and companionship too. This is not the Global South's reenactment of the classic Western trope of Lolita.

Maxie expands their family with a new love object in Victor as a fantasy parent from whom they feel the care of agentic attunement to their well-being. As Klein describes, "These phantasy-relationships, based on real experiences and memories, form part of our continuous, active life of feeling and of imagination, and contribute to our happiness and mental strength."[53] In this way, Maxie's joy is overflowing. They leave Victor's place with a big smile, deliberately looking up at the sky with happiness to indicate their bigger world, and they even skip as they turn a corner near home. They return home to a site that seems even more like a criminal space. When Maxie gets to the door, their dad slaps them—which, without lessening its powerful impact and implications, is almost more like a pat on the face. Maxie does not even flinch at the contact, as if there is no pain. "Why, Pa?" The dad says, "I want you to stop seeing that cop." His protest is essentially about loyalty to the family. The father does not see Maxie's being away all night within the framework of sex. "You take care of other people and not your family!" he complains, revealing the nature of his displeasure. Normal life resumes when he instructs Maxie to buy rice for dinner.

But Maxie won't let life go back to normal and resists through their cooking, forgetting to season the meal and eliciting complaints from the family. Bogs tries to draw them back to the family fold with his concerned gaze and invitation to braid his hair. Things are not normal. Maxie tries to contact Victor, to no avail. They return to the police station, meeting further teasing from Victor's juvenile colleagues, who taunt them both: "It's like a movie—a lovers' quarrel!" This is beginning to grate on Victor, who regards Maxie as a ward and an inappropriate sex partner, instructing them to find "someone your own age." Maxie flees home to cry and to seek comfort from their older brother Bogs, who holds Maxie as they cry breathlessly and tearfully. Bogs recognizes their queerness and suffering, telling Maxie, "Forget him. He's not the only guy in the world. Show him you're strong." In feeling for his sibling, he clearly does not question whether the love object is appropriate. Nor does he invalidate the truth of Maxie's feelings. Instead, he protectively advises Maxie, "I won't tell them at home, but you'll swear to stop seeing him. If I find out I will get mad at you!" Thus, the family accepts Maxie's queerness but rejects their care for someone outside the family's criminal activity. Sexual identity and the choice of love object are not challenged.

The relationship itself exceeds queerness, without denying it. Maxie tests the reality of the relationship with Victor, but it does not pass. They may have an intimate attachment, but the impossibility of their relationship means it cannot continue in their reality—where criminality and the law cannot meet harmoniously. Similarly, Maxie cannot expand their parental family due to their queerness, not just their criminality versus lawfulness. Their weeping testifies to their life—their being alive—despite the failure of the fantasy relation.

Maxie's worlds of criminality in their family and legitimacy in their love object converge with the assignment of a new sergeant in the neighborhood precinct. The sergeant arrests Bogs and commands Victor to raid the Oliveros home. The cops harass Maxie—questioning their lack of panties in the chest of drawers—and make a mess of the usually orderly and pristine home when they drag out their mother's clothes, pulling them out of closets and drawers, making a mess all over the cramped quarters. A new order emerges—hateful, homophobic, and without the presence of unsaid respect. Maxie remains concerned about Victor as their father rubs their back, asking, "Why don't you care about us, Maxie? Your

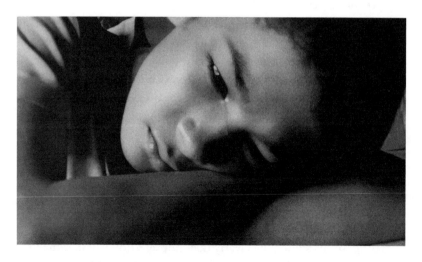

3.2 Maxie cries for the loss of Victor as they experience social teasing and family condemnation. *The Blossoming of Maximo Oliveros* (Auraeus Solito, 2005).

Kuya Bogs could hang." It is at this moment that Maxie's internal struggle is revealed even more so as not sexual but as one involving criminality and poverty itself.

In Closing: A New Family Formation

"Why do we live like this?" Maxie asks their father, capturing their project that exceeds sexuality and encompasses poverty and struggle as well as grief and loss. In response, the father blames the love object for corrupting Maxie's loyalty to the family, stating, "You never complained before. Then that Victor come along and suddenly you're ashamed of us." The father precisely identifies how Maxie struggles with the adult they will become. He accepts their queerness, but not the lessons about poverty and criminality. "If your mom were alive, she'd be angry with you" for questioning the family. To this, Maxie replies, "I just want our life to be peaceful." The father challenges Maxie to be content and to recognize how he "risks [his] life to put food on the table." Maxie's response is central to their internal search: "Is there another way?" For Maxie, this means can they expand their love and attachment outside their blood family? Is the family of birth the only one they can have? The father's response discourages Maxie's exploration, and his reasoning is tied to poverty and the path of criminality: "Get a job in a factory for small change . . . that I cannot use to pay for the hospital? I'm not going to lose another member of this family!" Here, grief—and the fear of losing another family member to poverty—is the central force that motivates and unifies the family. They embrace each other in recognition of their bond. The revelation of the story of their criminality leads Maxie to a kind of peace. They begin to understand what led to their family's life, which in a way enables them to understand the complexity of their love for Victor as not simply romantic but informed by grief, loss, and mourning as well as an exploration of a future outside of criminality that they feel in his agentic attunement to their life choices. In recognition of the multiplicity of their feelings, they no longer understand their emotions as a betrayal to their family but as a matter-of-fact part of their development within the environment of their life.

Boy comes home as the father leaves. Maxie becomes alarmed when they realize their father's gun is gone. Maxie wants to follow him for fear that he will harm Victor. Boy confronts Maxie: "All I hear from you is Victor! Have you done it with him! Have you tasted it?" Here, Boy articulates fear not only of the sex act but also of Maxie's desire that could possibly be carnal. Yet, even here, not just the possibility of sex is condemned but also the perceived disloyalty to the family. Boy is afraid of his own arrest as well.

The new sergeant promises to train Victor to be a real cop in an offer that sounds like a toxic and violent manhood, and so it ends badly. They meet with Paco, and the sergeant shoots him twice in the head at point-blank range, as Victor stands by with Maxie as a witness a distance away. The choreography of the shot is quite striking. Victor is standing extremely close to Paco in the dark; we see them both. We do not see the sergeant, only his gun. The father falls on the ground after the shots are fired. Victor follows his fall by going to the ground himself, then looks up to see Maxie's face across the distance. He is shocked, and fears for Maxie. The death of their dad sends Boy and Bogs into a frenzy of rage. But Maxie's tears calm them so that their brothers set into a new family formation. The siblings return home and choose a different path beyond vengeance, which would have led them to even deeper criminality and fragmentation of the family should they die or be imprisoned. They do not seek revenge. Maxie is saddened by their beloved dad's death and now cooks different amounts of food, putting only three cups of rice into the pot. No longer a family of four, the three nevertheless still eat together.

They encounter Victor, who tries to explain what happened: "This world is full of evil men. Sometimes you have to play their games, or nothing will change." Maxie replies, "There are many evil men. I only had one father," in a full reclamation of their grief and mourning. Here, the feeling of security and peace enabled by the love of their father saves Maxie. Melanie Klein argues that the process of "being able to love . . . in the unconscious mind, [is] closely linked up with keeping loved people safe and undamaged. The unconscious belief seems to run; I am able to keep some loved people intact. . . . I keep them all forever in my mind."[54] For Klein, most powerful is how the "image of the loved parents is preserved in the unconscious mind as the most precious possession, for it guards its possessor against the pain of utter desolation."[55] For Maxie, the death of their father signals the potentiality of their brothers' deaths and the urgency of setting sights on the future: returning to school for themself and leaving the criminal realm of work for their brothers.

As the brothers sleep, Maxie maintains their perch on the windowsill to observe the night. Victor stands beneath the window and begins to whistle the tune from their first meeting. Maxie responds with the same.

It was Victor who taught Maxie to whistle. They each pucker their lips to make a sound that reaches the other, harking back to their first meeting and their subsequent friendship and romance. In "When Our Lips Speak Together," feminist theorist Luce Irigaray refers to how new forms of language develop in order to reach others across distances, in different ways that have not yet been invented by "men [who] have spoken for centuries."[56] Tears run down Victor's face. The rich emotional life between them can be romantic, can be filial, can be friendship—each demonstrates care and commitment—which is central to my reading of this film. Victor walks away. Maxie has already left their perch.

The next day, the pictures of both their parents are now on the altar as Bogs irons Maxie's school uniform. Boy is making their lunch with concentrated effort. They are doing the typically gendered care work for Maxie that was entirely theirs to perform in the past. Bogs is proud of his domestic work, and Boy worries that Maxie will be late—playing the part of parents in their new family roles. Maxie goes to their parents' altar. Boy first gives Maxie a student identification card with someone else's name, indicating that their older brother may not have stopped his criminal activity. Boy compliments Maxie in a gendered fashion: "My sister is so pretty!" Walking in the neighborhood toward school, Maxie, in their male student uniform and carrying a pink backpack, is followed by a police car that drives ahead to park. Victor gets out to watch Maxie go by. Maxie ignores him but stops at a distance after passing him, before forging ahead in their new path. Like Cody in *Driveways*, we do not yet know Maxie's path except for now they have achieved a more balanced and calmer view of the future in the sense of earned secure attachment from the legacy of trauma and loss. They may also have left criminality—or at least the cycle of vengeance and death.

Queerness remains the good object in the film. Maxie's affirmation as queer by their family leads to a larger exploration of alternative adulthoods that is at peace with their growing up. For now, I end with Klein in her meditation on mourning:

> In normal mourning . . . the early depressive position, which had become revived through the loss of the loved object, becomes modified again, and is overcome by methods similar to those used by the ego in childhood. The individual is reinstating his actually lost loved object; but he is also at the same time re-establishing inside himself his first loved objects—ultimately the "good" parents—whom, when the actual loss

occurred, he felt in danger of losing as well. It is by reinstating inside himself the "good" parents as well as the recently lost person, and by rebuilding his inner world, which was disintegrated and in danger, that he overcomes his grief, regains security, and achieves true harmony and peace.[57]

Mourning cannot but inform Maxie's story, which could be overlooked by a focus on their childhood sexuality. But Maxie's queerness cannot be reduced to genital sex, a fact that exposes the moralistic attitudes that can lead to narrow interpretations of childhood sexuality in film. Their development is part of a search for self-sovereignty, which sexuality is a part, that occurs within a larger field of grief and mourning, poverty and criminality. Maxie loses their mom and develops their sexuality without her, while also wrestling with poverty and criminality in grief and mourning. And Victor's integrity and dignity as one who provided agentic attunement for Maxie as a mother, and as an early glimpse of a future partner, cannot be denied.

When my son Lakas died, his aspirations and his ongoing concerns—will he get to wear retainers again, when will his extra teeth grow, will the rash on his cheek go away—all of it brutally and immediately stopped. The jar of Aquaphor ointment that I applied to his cheek remained on his dresser, not to be used. The electric toothbrush head he loved to use was still on our bathroom counter. The deprivation of his life as ongoing hurt. I imagined having to tell him that he died. I would dream of his return. He came back from under the dirt, rising from his coffin, thinned by the lack of food. I would imagine he was living with his godmother. He called me to say he was enjoying himself riding horses, going to the beach, and hiking where he was born in Santa Barbara. Concern for our older child, Bayan, eleven years old at the time, became our focus: how to hold him through the loss, give him strength, and not hold so hard he cannot stand on his own. I recognize the power of mourning, based in love, and the belief in his self-sovereignty, to enable a creative life, make his own attachments, and find his own love objects. It can give him strength to buoy his own navigation through a life we cannot control, where sudden, unexpected death can and does happen, to take so much away and completely redirect the living.

4   The Courage to Compose Oneself

HEALTHY NARCISSISM AND SELF-SOVEREIGNTY

IN *YELLOW ROSE*

The arts provided me love when my parents left me and my siblings in the provinces of the Philippines when I was eight and nine years old. I think about myself then, when I was Lakas's age at the time of his death: my capacity to love and miss my parents, to make friends in a new place, to learn a new language, to feel abandoned, and to experience the meaning of vulnerability as a young girl. I walked into town alone to the library, looking for the poets e. e. cummings and Maya Angelou, whom my mom loved as a young girl and new mother respectively, and to memorize Walt Whitman, much like my dad taught me when he was around. As a second grader, I performed the poem "O Captain! My Captain!" on-stage at the school-wide elocution contest, beating the high schoolers. I won even as my front teeth were broken, jagged, and sharp from a fall, a physical manifestation of the lack of supervision while my parents were thousands of miles away. The temporary silver caps shone blindingly under the lights in the auditorium. I could see the sharp, shiny rays emanate from my own mouth. I did not care, even as the older kids laughed; I emoted how much I missed my parents as if they had died.

By deploying emotion in performance and engaging in the craft, whether music or spoken word or cinema and more, we can use art to show us who we are and who we can be. The arts can provide agentic attunement in helping a child attempt to reach her parents across the oceans, crossing time, space, and other dimensions to express the loneliness and hurt of abandonment. The arts contain powerful emotions that demand feeling for self and others. The high schoolers stopped laughing at me and my teeth as they were silenced by the way I theatrically collapsed at the last word. I know the power of the arts to enable us to assert our subjectivity and demand care from others. This is why books by James Baldwin, Toni Morrison, Art Spiegelman, and more are being banned now, for reading helps expand who is a citizen, who is human and deserving of rights, regard, and recognition. They help us give expression to what is just and right.

We are living in a moment when funding to some libraries is being withheld until books about LGBTQ+ lives are removed.[1] Against this violent erasure, expanding empathy for the marginalized is urgently important, for in 2045 the United States is likely to be a nation composed of a majority of people of color. Who is a citizen, and what grants the right to citizenship? Is it birth? Is it wealth? How does one claim a path, a route, when there is none, especially in terms of citizenship for undocumented youth? In this chapter, I examine a film which argues that citizenship is to be earned; that it is an object that one must take and make one's own—especially as an expression of self-sovereignty, a form of healthy narcissism, for people assigned none in representation or in society. In the path toward establishing citizenship, the care one receives in the form of agentic attunement proves critical—even if it has to be demanded from others and found in the self.

In Diane Paragas's *Yellow Rose* (2019), Rosario "Rose" Garcia (Eva Noblezada), a seventeen-year-old, brown-skinned, wide-eyed, and full-lipped Filipina American girl with a big voice, loves country music and the Texas landscape where she lives. She loves the feeling of the heat and the wind on her face as she bikes home on isolated expansive and even barren roads while listening to her favorite country music. With her short bob and bangs, her proclivity for wearing cowboy hats and boots, Rose presents a spunky, firecracker self to the world. She lives with her mother, Priscilla

(Princess Punzalan), in a small rural town in an apartment behind the front desk of a motel. They have no privacy. Their intimate moments are always under threat of interruption, as evidenced by Priscilla's interacting with motel guests at the front desk while dressed in her nightgown. Despite these constraints, or in the face of them, Rose's attentive mother cossets her. She gives her daughter immense importance—affirming and attending to her. Priscilla checks on Rose's homework and gently nudges her to focus. Attuned to her daughter's preference for composing and playing music on the beat-up guitar left to her by her deceased father, Priscilla shows Rose her recognition of her preferences and predilections but places importance on her role as a mother teaching her to care about school and her responsibilities with an eye toward cultivating her independence.

When Priscilla is suddenly detained and ultimately deported by US Immigration and Customs Enforcement (ICE), Rose discovers that neither she nor her mother possesses legal status to live in the United States. The mother's investment in Rose's care and building her affirmed and secure self comes to be tested. Rose must choose between making her way without documentation in a precarious, threatened, and lonely life alone, as an undocumented and underresourced, underage teen, or forcibly leave her American home for Manila, a place she does not know. Though in Manila she would be with her mother, there would be no guarantee that she could return to the United States. She chooses to stay in her beloved home of Texas and to embrace its culture as her source of belonging. There, in the midst of her struggles, she pursues music to gain a strong sense of self and establish a foothold on belonging, even without formal citizenship. Proving her strength and unleashing her talent gives her the opportunity for freedom from what Filipinx writer and filmmaker Jose Antonio Vargas identifies as the precariousness of undocumented Americans. As Vargas argues, we must define what American citizenship is beyond the accident of gaining it by birth, luck, or privilege.[2]

Yellow Rose is directed by Diane Paragas, a first-time feature filmmaker and Filipina American immigrant who grew up in Lubbock, Texas, as the only Filipina girl for miles around, after immigrating from the Philippines at age four. The film is historically the first by and about Filipinx Americans to be distributed by a major Hollywood studio. My interview with Paragas closes this chapter in order to capture and celebrate this historic first. The film was produced and released during the term of former president Donald J. Trump, when discourses on and occurrences of anti-Asian hate skyrocketed in ways that are depicted in this film and others.[3] In the

4.1 Rose listens to country music while biking home on the deserted streets of her rural Texas home. *Yellow Rose* (Diane Paragas, 2019).

Texas context represented in this film, raids and deportations, as well as family separations at the border, show how state terror leads to familial trauma for children and parents alike. Thousands of children continue to be forcibly separated from their families. Numerous videos of children reuniting with their families show how anguished parents meet their children who have become visibly hardened, indicating the long-term damage inflicted by the violent and frightful experience. In photographs and videos circulating online, the children's faces and their bodily comportment express the foreboding trauma of the lifetime effects of family separation. The demonization of Latinx people as "rapists and criminals" further effectuates far-right extremist hate crimes, such as the 2019 mass shooting in El Paso, Texas, that specifically targeted Latinx people.

It is within this context that *Yellow Rose* specifically contributes a Filipinx American undocumented experience as a story worthy of representation, dramatization, and imagination. Featuring a stellar multigenerational cast of Filipinx American women—Broadway star Eva Noblezada; award-winning Philippine film and television actress Princess Punzalan; and iconic, Tony Award–winning transnational film and theater star Lea Salonga—the film captures a defining yet largely silenced experience within Filipinx communities today: the fear and desperation of being undocumented and the violent dehumanization of incarceration and deportation.

The film especially focuses on the precarity of youth who are abandoned when parents are deported by the state, which is then essentially unwilling to care for them. It traces how parents, extended family, and children manage institutions such as immigration and work, as well as encounters with family and others—Chicanx, Latinx, and white people in Texas—across the racial divide specifically through the nurturing practice of agentic attunement as one worth finding and fighting for. When Rose realizes that her mom's sister, the much richer Tita Gayle (Lea Salonga), who is married to an unsympathetic white American man, cannot take care of her, she asks for the help of her high school friend Elliott and his cousin, an immigration lawyer; Jolene, the owner of a honky-tonk bar; and its star performer, the country singer Dale Watson. All of them have limits in their ability to care for her, which she tests as an immature girl facing imminent danger and significant loss while possessing scant resources. And through her recognition of the limits of her relations, she turns to herself for her own salvation by practicing an attunement to developing her own agency—an ability to act within constraints to secure her freedom. Rose is able to do this because of her mother's efforts at giving her access to a kind of grandiose self, one who is affirmed and showered with love and attention. As she faces disappointments in not receiving that grandiosity from others, she is able to cope. Each time others fail to care for her, she sutures herself, moving away from forces that can destroy her and toward a healthy narcissism that claims herself as deserving of care. The language of the film thus addresses narcissism, creativity, self-sovereignty, and the failures of motherhood within the carceral state, as well as the historical context of immigration and Americana. Rose's insistence on citizenship forces us to reckon with the violence of the state toward her and her mother, as Filipinx subjects whose experiences of racial subjugation organize their lives so thoroughly.

In this chapter, I move from the object relations theory considered in the previous chapter to use self psychology to situate my exploration of Rose's psychic life within social and structural relations. The central question of self psychology is how does one forge and maintain a thriving and strong self in light of the external forces that situate and shape our lives? As I have indicated, Heinz Kohut's theory builds on the work of Sigmund Freud, who understood a subject's personality—their behaviors and desires—as internal, inherent, and bodily, whereas self psychology understands personality more primarily as a dynamic interplay between the subject and their environment. I am particularly interested in the adolescent in *Yellow Rose*, who must form and forge the self while also developing empathy for herself, since others are unable to provide empathy, or can do so only in limited ways. She learns how to listen to herself, much like Lee Isaac Chung, the director of *Minari*, who learned to inventory his own experiences as a child to craft a narrative arc that enabled him to achieve a healthy self. In this context, my priorities are more aligned with Kohut's in moving beyond the intense physical sexual realm and toward self-regard/self-respect/self-recognition, confidence, purpose, ambition, and accomplishment—especially in regard to his spotlight on narcissism, which others in psychoanalysis do not illuminate as centrally as does self psychology.

According to Kohut, narcissism is the intense focus formed as "the cathexis of the self."[4] This refers to the human mind and also its relation to objects. For him, narcissism, when defined as self-centeredness, is often incorrectly assumed to be unrelated to object relations, that is, it is not dependent on others. Narcissism requires others to focus on the self ceaselessly. Instead, he argues that "most intense narcissistic experiences relate to objects . . . which are either used in the service of the self and of the maintenance of its instinctual investment, or objects which are themselves experienced as part of the self."[5] That is, the demand for affirmation from others is ceaseless, frustrating, and sickening to those who receive the demand. In this story about the forging of the self through creativity, narcissism is thus a helpful framework. This is especially the case for the film's seventeen-year-old protagonist, who lives undocumented and largely alone in a hostile state, within a nation that won't recognize her as belonging, as a citizen, even if she feels like a citizen culturally and knows only the United States as her home. A form of healthy narcissism, a love for the self, and a recognition of self-worth in a hostile world are the goals of a self-applied agentic attunement, which is to affirm those incessantly terrorized not only by the state but interpersonally as well.

The selfobject Rose relates to in order to form a positive self-regard is indeed music. She may have no path to citizenship, but through music, the representation of her life makes an argument about cultural citizenship and the importance of developing a powerful, individual, healthy narcissism to assert belonging here through one's craft and one's contributions to the country and community. Psychoanalyst Heinz Kohut makes a distinction between normal narcissism (entitlement) versus healthy narcissism (confidence) in the psychology of children's development. The former is destructive and involves preserving a false self through bad habits; the latter, in contrast, aims for an integrated, worthy subject who achieves full self-actualization through the development of skills and talents. Chapter 1, on Andrew Cunanan, provides an illustration of entitlement in his pathological narcissism—the expectation of deserving grandiose fantasies or that people owe him or that rules do not apply to him. This chapter on Rose Garcia illuminates how confidence in the self enables the pivot to earning self-actualization through the craft of music and honing her talents to achieve citizenship.

If children's needs are met, they have a higher likelihood of developing into adults with positive self-esteem, a theory expanded on by Mary Ainsworth and Mary Main in their methods that show different forms of attachment.[6] Healthy narcissism works differently than self-centeredness alone, in that its goal is self-assertion and self-confidence not only in service of the individual but also in the creation of community. This is especially needed in the case of Rose, whose mother instilled in her a belief in her musical legacy and how the practice of music when she is on her own offers the community not only good, in the sense of epitomizing the highest talent and execution of her music, but also art in the service of bringing people together and making them feel for disenfranchised others, especially those who have no path for formal state-sanctioned belonging. Art thus illuminates injustice, demanding the community to do better.

The struggle Rose faces is how to fill herself with self-belief that is not a form of unhealthy narcissism in grandiosity in order to gain power without her mother, who is physically not present, and without the state, which requires her to be represented by papers that prove legitimate citizenship. When her mother disappears and is unable to take care of her and protect her, how can Rose regain herself in this surge of emptiness that comes from her sudden abandonment, one that feels permanent as her mother is deported to another country, unable to return to her for at least ten years? Rose herself is unwilling to join her because that would mean abandoning her home, the place that centrally composes her feeling and recognition of self as she nears adulthood. Luckily, the mother has instilled in her a secure confidence that enables her to face and rise up from the disappointment of others in a healthy narcissism that buoys her through crisis.

In "The Idealizing Transference," Kohut describes a kind of bliss found in the "idealized object" that is usually the parent. He argues: "The child feels empty and powerless when [s]he is separated from it and [s]he attempts, therefore, to maintain a continuous union with it."[7] This occurs in the film when the mom's disappearance leads to a clarity of vision for Rose—that she can maintain unity with her mother, who gave her confidence-inducing care, even without her physical presence because she must. She harnesses that deep installation of self-belief, so that her mother becomes an eternal presence of affirmation that is secured in what she passed on in raising Rose. What composes the agentically attuned care enshrouding her childhood that should bolster her adulthood includes song, story, and music.

Rose's musical heritage, for one, is a source of strength that builds self-certainty and self-knowledge. In this, she recognizes the insufficiency of the framework of home as a physical place—the motel is not viable, and place does not limit the agentic attunement of parent and child within her inner life. She gathers what she knows. She recognizes the predatory white male proprietor of the motel named Allen, who harasses his workers (including her mom's undocumented Latinx friend, who is a maid at the motel), and her vulnerability in lacking a community. At first, Rose understands the deportation of her mother as a failure and betrayal because her mother did not tell her they were undocumented. This leads Rose to realize her own vulnerability to the state as well as the strength of the inheritance she possesses from her mom's memories and lessons in the experience of agentic attunement. This is a path different from that of Andrew Cunanan, who turns away from his heritage and history and relegates it to shame. Rose here turns to the music of her family, her heritage, and her history to galvanize pride and strength.

Kohut says that the value of objects "does not vanish" even when the child recognizes "more and more details of his environment . . . [that] enable him to love (and to hate) the important figures who surround him."[8] In the case of Rose, her mother and guitar are both selfobjects that she utilizes as sources of power. Rose will encounter disappointment from others who do not love her like her mother does or give her the secure familiarity of her music. The film is thus about the identification of creativity and self-making in the face of loss, the failure of motherhood due to the state, and the community's failure to treat her like family. This leads Rose to use music to assert a sense of self and build a healthy narcissism, which is about self-certainty and confidence that claims belonging in the face of the state's lack of recognition. Her healthy narcissism points to the injustice of the state as that which must be changed.

This is in direct contrast to the destructive narcissism that the former president Trump embodies—a "me first" or an "America first" narcissism that refuses to care for others especially by those with power who do not feel accountable to others. For Rose, receiving affirmation—by performing American music that makes her recognizable as a member of the community (especially when the crowd sings along or dances)—builds what Kohut calls the "grandiose self," which in the context of the arts can be seen as another term for the healthy narcissistic self but has "greater evocative power than the term 'narcissistic self.'"[9] This is especially the case in the way self-attunement and bolstering are practiced to narrate stories to oneself to help achieve self-understanding and the courage to perform.[10] That is, while a kind of grandiosity is particularly essential in the arts when one risks vulnerability in performance, Kohut does not advocate for grandiosity as being ultimately healthy. That is, he finds it developmentally appropriate for small children to experience other people "narcissistically, i.e. [as] selfobjects," but this may not be healthy for adults.[11] I find this relevant here, where Rose has to stand up not only in the vulnerability of her status but also in the revelation and the kind of nudity of the self that performing on-stage demands. This is not a physical nudity but one that requires the self-importance of saying "I have something worth your full attention" in a crowd. Rose needs this self-understanding from the grandiose self and healthy narcissism both before and after her mom's deportation. Especially after her mother's disappearance, she has to "birth herself" as a marginalized person deserving of love from the community touched by her original songs. They recognize her feelings through songs that are made familiar by her performance. Grandiosity—as in the sense of ambition—is a necessity, but grandiosity that requires constant affirmation is not something that adults should practice. It becomes an unhealthy narcissism for adults to need and require constant care. In the beginning of childhood, the receipt of grandiose affirmation from her mother helped Rose to fight for herself. Not having a path toward citizenship makes it an unfathomable dream.

Narcissism and Creativity: Personality Worth Fighting For

Kohutian narcissism is both internal—how one achieves self-regard, self-esteem, and self-recognition in the process of explaining oneself to oneself—and external in how relationships with objects, other people, or material things can help maintain one's self-understanding. The film *Yellow Rose* is about a magnificent and splendid creativity—a birthing of the self as efflorescence—as a means to forge the future for oneself as an abandoned subject and reconstitute what is lost when the state takes away the mother from whom the child secured confidence in agentic attunement. It depicts turning to art as a path to self-love and worth. The child must find that parental love manifested through agentic attunement in herself, the community she creates, and the place of belonging she fashions, which she does through music.

Music is Rose's critical selfobject in the film—the thing that enables her recognition by others. A critical example of a selfobject within music in this film is the guitar Rose totes. When her mother is deported, Rose runs back to their motel-room home. She enters from the external door with her card key and immediately goes to the kitchen, where from under the sink she pulls out a garbage bag that will function as her suitcase. The black garbage bag is the luggage of foster kids. Many nonprofit agencies like Bags of Love and Hope in a Suitcase provide luggage to reduce the stigma associated with the garbage bags, while others say that not having real luggage eases the burden for the children. Still, the garbage bag indicates a life gone awry, as it does here. But the guitar does not go into a garbage bag; it has its own protective case, and it is an object she makes sure to recover. The guitar has a special role in Rose's self-regard; it is a part of her. A gift from her deceased father, it is a lifeline to her family history of wholeness, the strength of her heritage in the prominence of Filipino music in her memory, and how she has learned to be most comfortable: in music and its making. It contains her future self that she knows to be true in the present.

In this way, the guitar captures and communicates not only her personality but also the strength she has inherited from the agentic attunement she received from her parents. Heinz Kohut defines personality as "belong[ing] to a different theoretical framework more in harmony with the observation of social behavior and the description of the (pre)conscious experience of oneself in the interaction with others."[12] Rose's personality is directed toward song, and country music in particular, which is largely understood as music belonging to Black and white people in the South, particularly places like Nashville, Tennessee, and Austin, Texas—where the Broken Spoke honky-tonk bar, the primary setting for *Yellow Rose*, is located. The film makes an intervention in showing that Rose's version of country music is neither Black nor white.

Rose also uses fashion to express herself as a beneficiary of agentic attunement. To establish independence, she changes from a blouse that is appropriate for attending church to clothing more suitable for barhopping. She wears cowboy boots as she finds her performance personality—as one who deserves attention—in relation to the iconicity that describes her geographic location. She establishes her particular way of belonging. In the film *Mosquita y Mari* (2012) by Aurora Guerrero, the character Yolanda, or "Mosquita," spends time looking at herself in the mirror while singing songs that are associated with traditional male roles and donning a particular look with a cowboy-like hat. Mosquita's mother enters the room and interrogates her about the "vaquero" hat—asking if her daughter raided her father's closet for it. They dance together, with Mosquita leading. When the mom catches a glimpse of them in the mirror, all joy dissipates. She is alarmed at her daughter's gender crossing and frowns. While other scholars have interpreted this scene as depicting a loss of the mom's dreams, I read it as fear of sexuality, including queer sexuality and gender crossing, for her child.[13] For Rose, the cowboy hat may not represent a gender crossing for her as a cis high femme brown straight girl but is a similar deployment of path-forging power where there is none. It is an assertion of authorship of country music and a form of belonging in Texas.

When Rose is forced to work as a motel maid, much like her mother before her, she wears her uniform along with Converse high tops as an expression of her youth and her limited resources. The shoes represent the role of maid not as a permanent destination but as a stepping stone along the path to somewhere else and something else as she works her way to freedom. Finally, she wears even more ostentatious Texas gear—an all-frills cowboy hat—when she performs professionally in public. It is white and wide rimmed, donned over her black bangs and bright red lipstick. The hat matches her white cowboy shirt, embroidered with red roses. The red roses match the red silk scarf tied around her neck. It is quite a loud outfit that declares her a star, one who is asking to be seen and noticed. Rose is not hiding herself, even as she lives with undocumented status, always under threat of deportation. Her everyday wear is also Texan—flannel shirts typically associated with cowboys and rugged Americana of the West or T-shirts emblazoned with the word TEXAS. Rose uses these clothes to express herself and assert her belonging and Americanness in a form of self-pride every day off the stage. This contrasts starkly with the orange jumpsuit Rose's mother is forced to wear after she is detained, losing her name and identity when she becomes prisoner N35. Through the expressive culture of clothing, the visibly Filipina American Rose Garcia transforms the undocumented performer into an American cultural citizen, and very assertively so.

Rose's practice of cultural citizenship through the fandom and consumption of live music saves her on the night her mother is arrested and detained by ICE. Curious about Austin and country music, she convinces her mom that she and her friend Elliott (who works at the music supply store she frequents) are going to church. They return late at night, right when ICE is taking her mother out of the motel at 3:00 a.m. If Rose had not gone to Austin for the first time, she would have been caught up in the ICE raid and also detained and deported. The film makes the argument for music as the path for her self-actualization.

Betrayal and Fragmentation: Deportation as Loss of the Mother

When Rose loses her mother, Priscilla, through deportation, fragmentation threatens her sense of self as a blooming adolescent, as had the precarity in which she and her mother lived. Victimized by a predatory immigration lawyer who took her money and ran, Priscilla and likely Rose live with the threat of sexual compromise. As Priscilla discloses to her coworker that she received another letter from immigration authorities, we discover that the white male motel proprietor Allen is attempting to romance her coworker, who describes this as a way for her to remain in the country. In this context, we see the mother-daughter bond between Rose and Priscilla as strong, nurturing, and loving, showing us the importance of agentic attunement provided by the mom in understanding their precarity.

In the very first line of the film, Priscilla says to Rose, who has just returned home from riding her bike and is smelling the steam from the rice cooker she opens, "You have to let me know where you are if you want this freedom to be on your own." Priscilla states this as she cooks Filipino food for dinner, providing sustenance for her daughter with homemade heritage food that Rose loves. Without a doubt, these ingredients were hard to procure in their small, unnamed Texas town.[14] She makes the effort to pass on food and heritage, as well as lessons about how to handle freedom. When Priscilla speaks about responsibility and freedom, she shows awareness of her daughter's burgeoning adulthood, as the child tests her ability to be separate, distant, and mobile. The mother permits this mobility with conditions that demonstrate a conscious and careful loosening of the tether for both of them. She speaks with authority, claiming her position as one who determines and controls a level of freedom that the child must adhere to, and a condition that Rose must earn through her actions. Agentic attunement means attending to the goal of freedom for her child to claim in the nation, while independence is still a privilege to be negotiated with a parent and not a right to be taken within the context of their family.

After dinner, we learn how the mother knows and recognizes her daughter, to whom she is exquisitely agentically attuned. In their motel apartment behind the front desk, Rose occupies the bedroom while her mom sleeps on the living room couch. Their sleeping arrangements indicate a lack of space but also the privileging of the child's need for privacy and the public role of the mother as a worker who interfaces with customers just outside their living room.

Instead of doing homework, Rose plays a country music record while looking at herself in the mirror as she attempts to make her almond-shaped eyes appear larger and rounder. Resigned to not being able to change her face, she instead dons a red cowboy hat, abandons her homework, and picks up her guitar. She sits in the middle of her bed, composing a song about her inability to assimilate—"I never fit in, I never could win"—and feeling out of place, like a "song out of tune" or "a square peg in a round hole." By nasalizing the sounds and murmuring words not yet fully there, she's figuring out the language and sounds of the song, both the words and the music, showing how she, herself, also is in process. At the end of this moment, however, she raises her hand to wave, as if she were performing an already completed song for an audience in public. This is an indication of Rose's dream to perform beyond this room, her wave signaling the anticipation of an audience appreciating her song. We glimpse an impending sense of success in her ability to express herself and reach others so that they recognize both her feeling and her talent.

When her mother knocks on the door and interrupts her, Rose quickly drops her raised arm, not yet ready to reveal her dream. The mother pretends to be upset, asking, "Where are your books?" Rose defends herself, saying, "I was about to start." Here, they both know that Rose prefers to make music not only for comfort but also because it is her passion. They laugh at their performance of discipline and hug instead. Joining her on the bed, Priscilla cradles Rose in her arms like a baby.

This is another moment when Priscilla makes sure Rose not only feels parental love but also knows their family history so that she may understand how to navigate her future as part of practicing agentic attunement.

She tells Rose how much "she is like her father" in playing the guitar, and how the three of them would sing together as part of their family bedtime ritual. The ritual now likely includes the narration of their family's migration as they easily slip into recalling their original home, Manila. Rose asks what it was like there, a place she does not remember or know. "Crowded, hot," her mother responds, explaining how it was her husband, Rose's father, who wanted more for them. Rose acknowledges the hardship of this life in the United States, but Priscilla assures her it has been worthwhile for the opportunity it gives Rose. Here, she reminds Rose of her worthwhile future from the perspective of her parents. They conclude this discussion with a duet of the classic Filipino love song "Dahil Sa Iyo," which they take turns singing, since they both know the lyrics from practice and ritual over the years as a family. The song is not translated but exudes passionate feeling: they sing, "Dahil sa iyo" (Because of you), "Nais kong mabuhay" (I wish to live), and then, as they hug more intensely, "Hanggang mamatay" (until death). A customer interrupts the scene, and Priscilla runs out to the front desk in her nightgown to check her in. The song bonds them through moments of mothering that must occur intermittently due to their circumstances of living where they work. This inheritance—of passing on memory, history, and dreams—is shared by Priscilla to enable Rose to move forward with her heritage as wealth in agentic attunement. It is the same instilling of confidence through the family bond that Gianni Versace's mom passed on, as did Kathy, Cody's mother, in *Driveways*.

"Dahil Sa Iyo" came out in the late 1930s as part of a movie and became a hit in the early 1960s in the United States when renowned American singers Nat King Cole and Jerry Vale recorded it, the former in a recorded concert in the Philippines in 1961 and the latter in 1963. The song is so popular that it is heard across the diaspora and was played when President Barack Obama visited the Philippines. As a love song, it exceeds interpersonal address. The feelings the ballad generates emanate toward the nation. In the 1960s and 1970s, the corrupt politicians Ferdinand and Imelda Marcos played the song during his presidential campaign as a love song to the people. The disgraced former first lady Imelda Marcos performed it regularly as a signature song in her many appearances and when she entered places and stages ceremonially. At the Southeast Asian Games, the song was sung to represent the Philippines—while other Asian singers also performed it there. In this way, the song represents the diaspora for how beloved it is by Filipinos and how it reached Americans as well.

In *Yellow Rose*, it is situated well within the family and, like an umbilical cord, represents the bond between mother and child.

Later that night, as Rose sleeps, Priscilla moves to the couch that serves as her bed and hides a box of papers nearby. She looks over at Rose's bedroom, to make sure her daughter will not see her. The recognition here tilts to one side: Priscilla the mother teaches Rose, and the child Rose trusts the mother to be perfect in caring for her. Yet, Priscilla keeps secrets that undermine the sustenance and agentic attunement she provides—unlike Kathy, who does so with attention to Cody's developmental stage in *Driveways*. Here, Priscilla's not sharing undermines the ability to secure confidence. The daughter, as a child, ultimately does not know the mother. Whether for reasons of precarity or because she has limited options for protecting her daughter, the mother's lies actually lead to feelings of betrayal that cause fragmentation in her child.

We have seen the fragmentation of the child in the face of the loss of their mother throughout this book. In the case of Andrew Cunanan, the mother is separated from him to enable his father's sexual abuse. For Cody in *Driveways*, the absent mother enables the child to develop attachment to a different parental figure. And for Maxie Oliveros, the mother's death leads to their displacement of affection toward the policeman. The attunement for all these children continues across different dimensions and has ramifications in their self-formation and self-esteem. The film *Yellow Rose* also examines the relationship between mother and child as the formative substance in the child's development. This film is different, though, in that it attends to the moment of the mother's disappearance in order to isolate and capture how that relationship constitutes the child's independence.

Rose comes to recognize the limits of depending on her family, as part of a series of large disappointments that nonetheless do not break her due to her secure confidence in childhood: first the death of her father; then the deportation of her mother; and finally the rejection by her Tita Gayle, Priscilla's sister who happens to live in Texas, too, but in a rich part of Austin. When her aunt insists on getting her husband's permission to take Rose in, rather than simply reassuring her niece that she is welcome to stay, Rose encounters another disappointment. She recognizes that Gayle is bound to her white husband, who is indifferent toward his Filipina immigrant wife's family situation. Here Rose is exposed to a different form of precarity than on her own: Gayle's powerlessness in a gilded cage, where she accommodates her husband's racism and sacrifices her kin for the comforts of white domesticity. Her husband, Mark (whose face we do not see, thus presenting him as a monstrous character in the world of the film), won't take in his adolescent niece, who without their help will be homeless. In this way, Rose's idealization of her family breaks into an actual recognition of herself instead as the one on whom she can depend for her own agentic attunement in prioritizing her future.

To recognize the need to care for herself is significant in the development of healthy narcissism for Rose. When she recognizes that it would be harmful to depend on her idealization, she resorts to suturing herself without her aunt and uncle. Thus, she experiences what Kohut refers to as the "parents' gradual revelation of their shortcomings," which "enables the child during the preoedipal phases to withdraw a part of the idealizing libido from the parental imagoes and to employ them in the building up of drive-controlling structures."[15] That is, she determines what constitutes herself apart from her family. The question becomes what composes her self-definition. This is an important break that provides an opportunity to suture or sew herself together in order to access her own agency and her own freedom.

Song certainly becomes illuminating in that process of composing herself: creativity through music is an act of self-making. In Tita Gayle's house, Rose pulls out her guitar when she is unable to explain to her toddler cousin Sophie why her own mom has disappeared. She sings her "Square Peg Round Hole" song, developing it further every time she returns to it. She shows how discipline as an artist is crucial to forming self-respect. She figures out the melody and adds a crucial line, "I run away with nowhere to go." Intercutting this scene with the beginning of her mom's deportation captures how Rose's process of premature adultification, having to take care of herself, is a direct result of her mom's extraction by the state. For mothering to continue across the carceral divide is essentially impossible unless earned secure attachment was achieved earlier.

Later that night, Rose has to endure the ongoing motherhood her cousin Sophie experiences as Tita Gayle sings "Dahil Sa Iyo" to her, the same song Priscilla sang to Rose. This time, however, they sing a different part of the song, with lyrics that reveal an ongoing love, unlike the curtailed and amputated love Rose now holds. Tita Gayle, played by the internationally famous and beloved singer Lea Salonga, sings, "I am happy from loving you . . . and all of this truth is because of you." In contrast, the part of the song Priscilla and Rose sing describes how love is the reason for life, and the reason for death, too, reflecting the violent severing of their mother-child relation in the physical realm. Rose is weeping as she witnesses Tita Gayle and Sophie engage in a mother-daughter relationship—sensuous and physical and something she no longer has in the United States.

Instead of staying at Tita Gayle's, Rose recognizes that the situation of white male supremacy within an interracial marriage that disempowers the brown woman would be destructive for her. In a display of her healthy narcissism, where Rose aspires to self-love and self-respect, she grabs her black garbage bag and declares that she does not deserve to feel unwelcome. She confronts Tita Gayle, telling her that she knows her husband does not want Rose there. Rose can see that Tita Gayle is unable to provide regard, respect, and recognition. The husband yells in agreement, and Gayle commands him to "shut up." Tita Gayle cannot stop Rose's determined decision to depart. Similar to Rose's mom leaving a manila envelope full of cash for her daughter, Tita Gayle gives her a parting gift of her phone number, money, and the offer to keep in contact. It is notable that Rose sets herself up to leave Tita Gayle's by first making sure to get some sleep before she makes her way, on foot and by bus, to the Broken Spoke, where she will cultivate different relationships that she hopes will enable the belonging she needs. The female owner of the Broken Spoke, Jolene, is an adult Rose can trust, hoping this stranger can provide agentic attunement. Rose seeks out that possibility, risking her safety in coming out as undocumented to find out whom she can trust. Thus, Rose leaves her kin, who do not want her, and attempts to establish what she hopes are empowering and enabling relations among Latinx and white communities in Austin's country music scene.

When her mom finally calls Rose from the ICE detention center, Rose explains that maternal betrayal led to this decision. Because Priscilla lied and did not tell Rose that they are undocumented, Rose is now authorized to make her own way. Priscilla can no longer parent her from a distance, and their definitions of safety diverge. Rose is staying in a bedroom behind a bar, which she is accustomed to because it is a site of commerce that has been transformed into a home—much like the apartment she and her mother lived in behind the motel's front desk. Her mom, however, does not recognize her daughter's independence and, specifically, her willfully making a home in a precarious and unfamiliar, essentially public place. Since Priscilla is imprisoned, the fear she feels for her child, the lack of control, and the inability to mother traumatize her. She does not yet see how her daughter is finding her way toward a healthy narcissism to fight for a future that is precisely what she and her dead husband wanted for

Rose when they moved to the United States, and what Priscilla success-fully instilled in Rose: self-confidence even in the face of disappointment. Priscilla does not yet see that the rich home of her sister Gayle would be a destructive place for Rose. The white husband did not want Rose to stay precisely because he feared ICE would come, and he did not want to risk his own family's safety in their mansion. If Rose stayed there, which she could not do anyway, she would not have received love or the agentic at-tunement she needs. Instead, she would have received hostility and would have shriveled. Tita Gayle fails Rose, like she failed her sister, Rose's mom, and in a sense, like Rose's mother fails her daughter at this stage in life. The failure of mothering can lead to the fragmentation of the self—though this failure is not due to any personal shortcomings but results from the structural precarity contextualizing it, which inflects both sisters in rela-tion to Rose. As a child, however, Rose basked in the love of her mother; as a result, the disappointments inflicted even by her mother later in life won't break her down. She learns to take care of herself in a practice of autoagentic attunement.

Community and Creativity: Reconstituting the Self

In the face of abandonment when her mother disappears, Rose must re-constitute herself largely alone by tuning in to her own strength. This in-volves an internal process of narrating her story to herself and an external process to affirm her purpose. She makes sense of her abandonment by paying close attention to herself in the form of walking and moving across the landscape of Texas. She walks in Tita Gayle's wealthy neighborhood, with its picturesque blooming gardens and towering mansions or modern-ist masterpieces with manicured curb appeal; she looks out the windows of the bus at more urban pawn shops and stark sidewalks strewn with gar-bage; and she attends to her feelings when interacting with others.

To attend to one's feelings is a project of agentic attunement in re-constituting the self, especially when living within precarity. To utilize another dimension of Heinz Kohut's argument, the self "is a structure within the mind since (a) it is cathected with instinctual energy and (b) it has continuity in time."[16] To witness the adolescent Rose making sense of her environment in relation to her survival is to see her practice the prevention of injury in the avoidance of danger and in the search for not only sustenance but also affirmation of her personality. Kohut describes this process as the heightening of "pleasure in . . . self."[17] Pleasure is key to this gaining of mastery in her personality at a time when Rose could easily succumb to circumstances that require her servitude and servility. That is, she does not want her responses to fear, worry, and anxiety to surface more than the vitality that comes through her music in her creation of self.

Her mother's disappearance leads to imbalance for Rose, especially since she does not know whether her mother will be "gone forever." Since the relationship with her mom is primary to her "maintenance of self-cohesiveness and self-esteem," her departure means the person attuned to her, attending to her, and nourishing her is no longer there.[18] This means Rose no longer has that mother—representing a parental nurturing of agentic attunement—and that dependency, sustenance, and affirmation are no longer available and she must look elsewhere for them to cultivate a future self. The way she does it is to be observant of her company and to risk speaking in a forthright and truthful way about her limitations—including her illegal status, pursuing country music that is usually exclusively white, and depending on the power of her labor in the low-wage industries available to her, as well as her age, given that she is not yet legally an adult.

Rose's agentic attunement is evident in her encounters with Elliott, a young man who is a year ahead of her in school and works in a music store in her neighborhood. Prior to her mother's deportation, Rose is a regular customer at the store, and they are in sync, sharing musical tastes and finishing each other's sentences about a favorite band or lyric. When he tries to convince Rose to go with him to the Broken Spoke for the show, he says, "You're a senior next year, right?" He wishes to remind her that going is an act of agency and would be part of normal American teen freedom and development at her age. The information he provides is meant to inform her, acculturate her, reminding me of David in *Minari*, who confidently knew how an American grandma looked and behaved. Even as Rose gains courage to ask, cry, and complain to her mother until she gets permission to go, she also compares her lack of freedom to her friend Elliott's freedom, comparing their Americanisms. Her first trip to Austin is nothing compared with what he will be doing this very summer: getting a dorm. He drives himself, and she is not able to do so. He lives more freely and with a future, in contrast with the motel as the place she will rot and die. In the car, Elliott encourages Rose to sing and elicits a powerful and absolutely breathtaking performance from her that reveals her extraordinary gift. To me, the performance is so strong that it breaks the fourth wall when I recognize this actor is indeed the lead in a highly successful Broadway show. Rose Garcia is portrayed by Eva Noblezada, the star of the dazzling box office hit *Hadestown*.[19] The hungry spectatorship for Filipinx American representation rears its head here.

The approval Rose gains from her peer Elliott marks the beginning of finding healthy narcissistic sustenance away from her primary caregiver, even prior to Priscilla's departure. He is the selfobject that expands Rose's self-understanding beyond her mother. He practices agentic attunement much like Victor does to Maxie and introduces a new source of affirmation and validation for Rose. He becomes a source of self-esteem that for Rose does not feel dependent, for he is but one source among many. He is not the primary object, but one of many objects in her present relations as she makes her way, forging her independence by performing to crowds. In the process, she can also begin to see "the unavoidable shortcomings of maternal care" and "replac[ing] the previous perfection (a) by establishing a grandiose and exhibitionistic image of the self: the grandiose self; and (b) by giving over the previous perfection to an admired omnipotent (transitional) self-object: *the idealized parent imago*."[20] In Rose's case, healthy narcissism in the form of a grandiose self is what she needs to harness in order to overcome her fear of sharing song, performance, and making music as the thing that will convince herself and others of her belonging as a way to citizenship. She needs courage and community to access creativity, including in mothering or parenting herself, birthing herself as an aspiration and ambition of seemingly impossible proportions.

Rose's trusted community certainly includes her young white male peer Elliott, who is at first a friend and then possibly a love interest. Elliott expresses his concern for her in a sustained manner, helping her flee the motel as the proprietor Allen chases her, signaling her sexual vulnerability, when she gathers her possessions, including her father's prized guitar. He also drives her to Tita Gayle's and visits her first at the Broken Spoke when she lives there, and then at Dale Watson's when she ends up living there too. He is the consistent person in her life during her stint of houselessness. He affirms her with his presence as she wanders, and he helps her navigate the immigration system with the pro bono assistance of his cousin, an immigration lawyer who helps Rose reunite with Priscilla right before she is deported. And he doesn't take advantage of her when she's completely drunk in her room at the Broken Spoke. Agentic attunement from her friend ensures against harm in respecting Rose's own projects for self and freedom.

Similarly, when Rose returns to the Broken Spoke, after learning that Tita Gayle's husband does not want her in the house, Jolene immediately says, "I recognize you." She follows this affirmation with a direct question, "What's going on, darling, why are you here?" Rose finds comfort in Jolene's Texas drawl, unlike her mom's thick Filipino accent. She interprets Jolene's question as an invitation to disclose the truth of her situation. This is a risk she deems worth taking, as Jolene feeds her and offers her what she calls a "safe space." Rose's forthrightness regarding her immigration status and her mom's deportation, experiences that are usually unspoken, demonstrates an investment and trust in others outside her family. This is a stunning contrast to the lack of trust she has in both her mother and aunt, who see her as a child. Yet this white stranger and her white male peer can be trusted because they see Rose as a self-sovereign person making her own way.

Rose closes this first meeting with the knowledge that she has a community outside her family, a safe place to feel welcome, and that it "feels good to tell someone" about her situation as a forthright expression of her true self. Having decided she won't hide any longer, she takes this risk due to her lack of choices. Doing so enables her to get close to the possibility of freedom. To speak the unspoken as an act of self-validation makes space in the world for others to accept her, even if it's against the law. She deserves kindness, compassion, and her humanity, despite the law. This is unlike the attitude of Tita Gayle's husband, Mark, who won't recognize her humanity. Jolene, on the other hand, actually says, "Put your bag down, you're home." This stranger cuts to the heart of the matter and identifies as well as provides exactly what Rose needs: safety, care and belonging in a form of agentic attunement in attending to the young adult before her. Rose collects sources of strength around her, though disappointment looms in the horizon.

At the Broken Spoke, Rose is supposed to work in the kitchen to pay for her room and board. Her young Latinx male peer and new coworker, Jose, is tasked with training her. He is also a rising high school senior whose parents were deported. Rose once again takes a calculated risk to share her story with Jose. It immediately creates intimacy between them, and they find comfort in recognizing each other as being the same age and in the same situation. While the relationship may have romantic potential, we do not find out if it develops, since ICE soon interrupts their potential relationship by detaining and likely deporting Jose.

This intimacy of full disclosure and the intensity of events also occur between Elliott and Rose. When she says, "I have not known you too long," he answers that it's not a matter of length of time, but the intensity of experiences in how they build a bond of trust—through agentic attunement. That is, in contending with the deportation and the loss of her mother, their relationship as kin is accelerated. Rose also feels community when she befriends the local country music star Dale Watson, played by the musician himself. He meets her on her first night at the Broken Spoke and again when she lives there. Overhearing her playing the melody of her song and hearing it in progress, he helps her find the rest of the music by playing with her and validating her talent and the quality of her musical creation. Rose's talent is similarly affirmed by Jolene, who also overhears her music. She encourages Rose to get over her fear of performing live. The way out for Rose is the validation she receives for the selfobject of music, which creates for her, through talent, an exceptional or extraordinary potential for achievement and distinction that can lead to citizenship. This may be the fantasy conceit that is the right of the film, even if it is a category of entry to the United States that is not available and should be for immigrants.

The safe space of the Broken Spoke is violated by the ICE raid in the middle of the night, like Priscilla's arrest at 3:00 a.m. This is the night when Rose is sleeping, after drunken debauchery with Elliott, while Jose and others work in the kitchen. Officers from ICE arrest the men while one officer, a younger white man, lets Rose go. As she lies on the floor, crying silently, the older white male ICE officers ask him if there is anyone else to round up. He says no. The film won't cast white people, even an ICE officer, in simple terms. The white people in this film are not presented as evil hicks but as people also contending with a world fraught with issues of race and racism.

No longer able to harbor Rose, Jolene sends her to Dale's. Like Elliott, Dale does not prey on Rose sexually but offers her space in an Airstream trailer along with the use of a recording studio to record a demo. Such is his magnanimous faith in her talent. This relationship becomes quite key in how Dale communicates that it is through music that one can find clarity in life. He tells Rose that "all this stuff with your mom, what is on your mind right now" as she figures out what to do, where to go, where to stay, is what she needs to use in her music. He advises her "to stay true to yourself and work it out in song." She listens to this advice, and when things intensify with her mom's impending deportation, she actually seizes the offer and has Dale record her song. She finally finishes it in his studio:

> No matter how apart
> Always here in my heart
> They can take the roof over head
> Won't take freedom away
> Won't quietly go into night
> They can take roof from over my head
> Can't take freedom away
> Won't go quietly into night
> Sing to light of day

When Dale buys Rose a guitar to celebrate making the demo, she interprets this as a replacement of the guitar her father got her and as an offer by Dale to take on the role of father. This response stuns Dale, for he feels unprepared to take her on as a daughter, feeling inadequate as a father to his own daughters. Perhaps this is the risk of healthy narcissism, the expectation of entitlement. Rose yells at him and accuses him of being condescending to her, using her as a kind of low-rent muse because of her undocumented status. He has no words to counter what register to me as unfair accusations, and she storms off. She won't respond to his pleas to talk. She leaves his house and goes out on her own.

As Rose walks around the city, we feel her aimlessness shaped by a lack of freedom, a lack of choices. She happens upon a motel, a familiar place, and situates herself there like her mother, a maid who lives where she works. She finds independence in sustaining herself by working at a motel again, repeating the role her undocumented mother had occupied. Is this her future too? One of arrest and deportation? It seems to be the case as she sells her guitar and no longer sings. Without community, or people who provide agentic attunement, she no longer has the creativity to re-create herself. The process of building the grandiose self toward healthy narcissism halts. She succumbs to bone-weary work, with no distinction between life and work. Her body in full servitude is a mere remnant of capitalism. This is the only place where Elliott does not visit her to check in. She is now alone. When talking with her mom in the Philippines, she is in tears, unable to see a future in the face of how hard her life has become. There is no sustenance, only devastation.

The Road to Freedom: The Purposeful Pursuit of Equilibrium

Rose only gets out of this rut by reconnecting with her mother and realizing she needs music as the selfobject on which she can rely to secure her safety, freedom, and belonging. Music enables her to secure her agency. The film intercuts between the mother wandering the crowded streets of Manila and gazing at the famous sunset over Manila Bay. She is separate from her daughter, longing for her. Rose lives alone, cleans rooms, and solely labors now that she has given up playing music. It is a temporary situation, but she recognizes how music will help create her future path. She returns to Dale's not contrite but proud; she realizes that he recognizes her as a singer deserving of discipline, but one he won't need to father. She must save herself through song and creativity, to enable her to claim her place as a country singer. She approaches Dale as he sits on the porch of his house, tells him to stop drinking, claims the gift of the guitar that he had given her, and invites him to play music with her and record another demo. She finishes her song and even makes a new one. She claims her voice, her experience, and her work in an act of agency. In this, she reaches a healthy narcissism through composing her life of all its parts.

The final scenes of the film occur in a bar more glamorous than the Broken Spoke where Rose now makes her debut. We are able to measure her progress toward success as a singer in the community. Her overall look, such as her makeup and clothes, is elevated to a more professional and glamorous level even as she peers from the dressing room with trepidation. It is a sign of health to be nervous as she is about to embark on a big claim to her citizenship and belonging through her artistry. Dale Watson performs and heartily introduces Rose as his friend, presenting her as a country singer in her own right. She performs her song as a dedication to her mom, and in the audience, we see Tita Gayle streaming the performance to the Philippines for Priscilla, Rose's mom, whom we see on her iPad surrounded by her family. Gayle's husband is not there, just the little cousin Sophie, sharing the booth with her mom. The crowd is accepting and dances to Rose's powerful song—a new one that declares her triumph, her self-composition. The film ends with her voice and a secured confidence through song and music—as extraordinary and worthy of stardom—and perhaps Rose's way into the legibility and belonging of citizenship. The film won't say for sure, but her look clearly stakes a claim to it.

4.2 Rose peers from the dressing room with trepidation even as she wears a glamorous outfit befitting a star. *Yellow Rose* (Diane Paragas, 2019).

In the closing shot, Rose looks at us, the audience, as she finishes, registering with her unflinching gaze on us how she stakes her claim to cultural citizenship through song. It may also secure her legal stay due to an exceptional talent in the 0-1 visa—where those with a distinguished record in the arts can secure a visa. Music is the "only thing she knows how to do," in her words, and through it, she demands that we recognize her as extraordinary. She uses music to invest in herself, outside the idealization of her parents, and builds herself up as deserving of love, regard, recognition, home, and belonging achieved through it. Moreover, music helps her to soothe the pain of abandonment. Through it she "acquires . . . a particle of inner psychological structure which takes over the mother's functions in the service of the maintenance of narcissistic equilibrium, e.g. her basic soothing and calming activities; and her providing . . . warmth and other kinds of narcissistic sustenance."[21] While performance is thus so self-centered, it is also a calling to the activities provided by her mother to establish an earned secure attachment that she wishes for her community to provide now, to support her as she develops her independence. She cannot do this alone. Elliott supports her with love and legal help. They only exchange a kiss when she is finally on her feet, living in the motel where she works, and as she is about to go on-stage dressed like a star who gave birth to herself. Dale will support her, too, as he helps launch her debut. And Jolene, in the audience, also gives what she can. Similarly, Tita Gayle's

4.3 With her unflinching gaze at the camera, Rose stakes a claim to citizenship and belonging through her artistry. *Yellow Rose* (Diane Paragas, 2019).

presence certainly hints at the availability of support. Rose's music enables the formation of community for her necessarily grandiose self in the face of her precarity. She is the one we clearly see and hear on-stage, looking straight at us, demanding us to act on her behalf as well.

In this context, claiming herself as an artist leads to the consolidation of the self, an ever-changing one, yet ready to go into adulthood through proper and healthy development of her independence. Kohut states that the "work of the artist is unconsciously recognized as unalterably bound up with the personality of its creator and it must not be tampered with through the intrusions of another."[22] Indeed, in this developmental stage, the independence that both mother and daughter achieve is a testament to art functioning as a road to freedom for Rose. This idea is in line with the thinking of Kohut, who writes, "The artistic work in which [s]he engaged . . . [became] an important source of external approval and even financial success."[23] It may be the optimistic and unrealistic end of the film—its happy ending that film should allow us and free us to imagine—that the music and performance is so strong. How can it lead to anything but stardom as a route to exceptional citizenship as a particular way in for Rose (though not for all)? It is the film's right to traffic in such a fantasy because there is no path for citizenship for undocumented youth.

So, what we see here is the utilization of music to shift Rose's struggle from involving loneliness, abandonment, confusion, drifting, waiting, and uncertainty to a purposeful pursuit of equilibrium of all kinds—legal, personal, and more—in an important lifesaving healthy narcissism that creativity and the struggle for citizenship and belonging demand. I do not know the legal equilibrium in the film—if extraordinary talent can indeed save her and how uncritical that is of inhumane policies regarding citizenship. It is up to us as audience members to become aware of the undocumented, including in Filipinx lives.

Filipina American first-time feature filmmaker Diane Paragas uses her own creativity in the medium of film to attest to the state's subjection of Filipina women who deserve humanity, love for each other, and creativity even if the laws that govern their movement won't allow it. *Yellow Rose* was the first Filipinx American film to be acquired and distributed by a major Hollywood studio, after more than fifty years of independent filmmaking in the United States. This film insists on registering in the historical record the stories of Filipinx women making themselves in all their strength and creativity, without the pornography of rape and abuse. Instead, it shows the dignity and integrity of composing oneself and being deserving of freedom—not only in terms of mobility but also to express love in what is the most intimate of bonds: the mother-child relation, from birth to breastfeeding to changing diapers and the attachment that lasts for life-times. Paragas encourages us to go on our own walks and sing our own songs. As historian Tiya Miles describes in *All That She Carried*, the creative work of Black women has shown the "valiance of discounted women would be recalled and embraced as a treasured inheritance."[24]

While Rose remains in contact with her mother, who now lives in another country, each of them has already let go. It is at this juncture of my book that I emerge as the mother of my older living son, Bayan, who is now in college, as I write in our home three thousand miles away. I hold on to him at the same time as I let go. Priscilla is not with her daughter, who now enters adulthood. Bayan has let me go too, as he should, in living his own life independently. It is now that my husband and I gather the past ten years as a time to say Lakas was with us, remains with us, and that we could have all died when he died. And yet here we are together with Bayan forging a life where we hold him, honor him, and go on, bringing Lakas along with us wherever we go. I imagine Lakas every day. He would be eighteen now. Ten years since he suddenly died, he lives on in us. He would be driving and off to college soon. And every time he would get in the car, there my heart would go too. Bayan has it the same. This is what I mean by letting go, the recognition of their autonomous grabbing of their own lives. Yet, as the intensive mothering is fleeting, we remain permanently bound to each other in ourselves. Bayan writes with power, moving people to care, to learn. He makes his way in the world with agentic attunement to his development in entering it. Much in the same way, Rose learns to sing as a way to be in the world, to find a place in it. She creates a path for herself where none exists.

Interviewing the Filmmaker Diane Paragas

I interviewed Diane Paragas on January 31, 2022, and immediately asserted that I regard *Yellow Rose* as a classic (much like Mira Nair's *Mississippi Masala* from 1991, which recently received a brilliant tribute from feminist studies scholar Durba Mitra).[25]

CPS: I have heard you say filmmaker Mira Nair inspired you to make *Yellow Rose*. Specifically, if you won't make stories about Filipinx communities, who will? And I love that, for it captures the galvanizing question: "Why not you?" And it's so true since the movie is here when it would not be otherwise.

DP: It took so long, took such a long time! The world had to catch up to it! Once we started doing press, the number one question was why it took so long. Nobody is clamoring down doors for a film with a Filipina protagonist with these sets of circumstances in particular. I first went to the wrong places; I was going to white Hollywood to ask permission. I even went to diverse producers. It was not out of a lack of interest; they did ask me to change [the] ethnicity to Hispanic or Chinese American, but my objective [was] to tell a Filipina story. It was my drive to see myself represented in film. Not seeing yourself represented in film as a cinephile has an effect on how you see yourself. Watching Mira Nair talking about how obligated she was to tell South Asian stories is for me to learn to go back to my own film [after so many obstacles] all this time.

After my film came out, one of the things that broke ground for us was the release of *Crazy Rich Asians*. During our shoot, we took off one day to see *Crazy Rich Asians*, which was number one for the weekend. It was a movie with a cast of all Asian people [and we recognized] we are part of this tradition. We are part of that now. Sony would not have bought our film if that film had not done so well.

CPS: You are using "asking for permission" deliberately in order to point out something important.

DP: After unsuccessfully going to different people "asking permission," we started going to Filipino American producers like ABS CBN who became our primary financier. The way the film got made was we did not have to explain why did it have to be Filipino. We shared the same goals: to see ourselves represented. This past weekend, for example, two Filipino films won at Sundance! With a lot more talent, you will see a lot more stories.[26] So yes, it is a deliberate use of the word *permission*—there is misperception about how everything should be—where we constantly are asking if our stories are worthy. We should not have to think we are worthy; we simply are. The idea that you have to be vetted or given approval from that world? What I learned is that if we build it, they will come. It is a business, [it] takes money. If you have to convince someone so hard, then [they are] not [the] person you should be working with. Eventually, the work will find its way. The industry is more open to stories of diversity, and Asian American stories in particular. What is happening now is I'm getting a windfall of that. Is that where this wave is coming from? After anti-Asian hate crimes? Is it white guilt and wanting to make up for that? There are a lot of diverse stories. And everyone is trying to put Asian characters in their scripts. There is more and more content and more focus. We are getting different opportunities. Is it enough?

For Paragas as a filmmaker, it is important to have as wide an audience as she can, especially to introduce our culture and share our stories within a larger structure. Her goal is to share stories of community. She recalls how she secured the historic distribution of the film.

DP: When Sony offered it to us, it felt like a huge rainbow. Walking under a rainbow. The idea of Hollywood, when I went into the studio building to sign the deal, I saw a picture of the film *Lawrence of Arabia*. It means something to sign this deal, it does. As a little girl in Lubbock, Texas, the biggest thing my mind could absorb was from the movies. To be accepted and championed by one of the five big studios. Unfortunately, we went with the deal that had a theatrical release, then the pandemic happened. We released in twelve hundred theaters, which is a wide release for a small indie film. And nobody went in October 2020 [due to the pandemic]. The community tried to generate attendance, such as Visual Communications, Marie Jamora (of Cinema Sala), and Gold House, who organized a big premiere in Los Angeles. There was nothing in New York City [where she lives].

CPS: Recently, the actor and filmmaker Forest Whitaker said, there is so much we don't know yet until we make it. For me, I understand this in *Yellow Rose* as how the undocumented is a specific Filipinx experience that is so well known in our community; we know people who are hiding because of their undocumented status and we experience their struggles. We know what Jose Antonio Vargas describes as having no path to citizenship, being familiar with the immigration and naturalization system.

DP: It's great you mention Jose Antonio Vargas because he served as a consultant with his organization Define American. Early on, he was on our side, supporting our film and helping us make sure to get it right. Getting it right was very important to me early on. This included reaching out to the Filipino American Legal Defense Fund and interviewing families who have gone through the experience. Through prison gates, we interviewed people who are inside. It broke my heart. There are moments in the film which are a verbatim account of what families go through. ICE comes in the middle of the night to surprise you. They don't tell you where you are going, or even your family. One family was imprisoned for six months and their only help came from the Filipino American Legal Defense in finding their path to stay. This family has a son who was Rose's age [seventeen]. He kept asking what is happening; his family did not tell him.

CPS: Why not tell him he was in that position?

DP: The family was hoping to resolve it, and unfortunately it caught up to them. Definitely very important not to tell him for the family. They did not want to burden him by telling him their lack of legal status. Filipino parents want you to look up to them. We can see this in the ritual of *mano po*, where you physically demonstrate respecting your parents [by taking their hand to your forehead in greeting]. It is embarrassing to them if they failed in any way. It is a kind of undermining authority, so it is not something you do, burden the children.

This is the kind of homework I had to do. I also made a short film with the Filipino American Legal Defense Fund. This is an American story. For non-Americans, I wanted to show this is what America looks like.

My own family told me something after they saw the film. In the scene where Priscilla gets the Immigration and Naturalization Services [INS] letter, my mom said, "We got those letters." We were that close! My dad was a physician. And my mom only brought this up after seeing the movie.

CPS: Regarding your directing process and principles, you cast a phenomenal group of protagonists with Broadway star Eva Noblezada, the global diva Lea Salonga, and well-known Filipina actress Princess Punzalan.

DP: Alfred Hitchcock says 90 percent of directing is casting. You see something in someone, listen to who they are, this is what directing is about. It is about creating moments that feel real. It could go in different ways. We shot the film in nineteen days, where we took lots of first takes and made decisions on the fly. Adjust it when it is not working. Eva is an incredible actor. I used a lot of her personality in her character as a firecracker with this big, passionate, and fiery personality. She gave bigger reactions than in the script. How are you as a teen brat who makes bad decisions at age seventeen? She has never been away, is sheltered.

It was a huge cast with different actors. There was a nonactor who was a musician in Dale. A movie star from the Philippines in Princess. Lea and Eva came from the stage. It was Liam's [Elliott] first major film. Jolene has been in a ton of movies, such as *Boyhood*. Each had varying degrees and levels of acting styles. Your job in this situation is to note the different styles and put everyone in [the] same movie. Some actors want lots of direction; some just let them be! The joy and the fun are to really know what you want.

CPS: Did you choose to move away from the intense sexualization that Filipinas experience in movies?

DP: There are moments in the film where the audience asks, "Is he going to?" and they don't. The threat of it should feel palpable. There are a couple of scenes of the film that were not the best active scenes and not the best written scenes. Too melodramatic!

Too on the nose. In previous drafts, there was sexual assault. It went there. Then it just felt like it would take away from the story. There was a big scene with the detention guard and Rose and her mom. A confrontation between her and all the racist stuff—all of the actors were amazing, but it felt preachy. We have seen the trope of the redneck a million times. To give people more voice is not seeing a kind of aspirational "let us show what makes America great." Rose's experience was compassion and racism in equal parts. I chose to appeal to better angels—following what came out recently in movies that show kindness like *Minari*, which falls in the same category.

CPS: You told a story that is very grounded in the regional geographic, where we must see relations with whites/Latinx people in Texas; where we see policing and being policed, whether in Texas, California, and beyond.

DP: One thing Jose Antonio Vargas talks a lot about is the importance of allies in his life through his book *Dear America: Notes of an Undocumented Citizen* [2018], how he could not have gotten where he is today without them. Teachers and colleagues always coming from [a] place of kindness is a big part of the film. One cannot do Texas without Latino representation. We cut it out at the end when Jose, Gustavo Gomez's character, has a crush on her. Discipline as a filmmaker meant killing your babies. The relationship is touching when Rose asks Jose, "Are you scared?" and his response is "You get used to it." It speaks of survival, and in her choice of speaking of her situation.

In focusing on this kid, she not only chooses to speak, but in doing so, shows her innocence in trusting people. It is endearing yet we are afraid for her. In her trust, she feels disappointed by many people, including her aunt, Tita Gayle, Dale, and Jolene. They do not continue to house her. They make her go. They have kindness but only up to a point, where she ends up on square one, just as her mother, she becomes a maid. She reverts back to what she knows. Tita Gayle is in the prison of her class aspirations. She is so hateful regarding her own people. We all have that Tita Gayle in the family, of wanting to get past the idea of being an immigrant, especially when making it to the upper-middle class and feeling accepted into a white world and they simply don't want to help. Hopefully at the end, she is clearly there for Rose. She reconnects with her and provides that local and global moment at the end of the film.

We got more money. We finished the shoot. We ran out of money. We were cutting the film and needed to feel the distance more between Rose and her mom. Just got enough money to fly Princess out to do these scenes. You cannot fake the Philippines. You have to show it. We show how we love it in a way. It is a beautiful place with trees and the water. She is happier with her extended family, yet the only thing missing is Rose.

CPS: Who refused to go. I really love the intercutting between the two of them with Rose on her own in Texas and her mom walking in Manila.

DP: I cut those scenes to the song "Quietly in the Night" since we needed to do another song in addition to the songs already planned. In this period, she is missing her mom. When Rose walks across the street, Priscilla walks across in the other direction. We had a planned architecture and knew what to cut to when Rose is on the bus and Priscilla is on the jeepney. Or Priscilla walking by the water of Manila Bay, shortly after that walking around, Rose finds the motel, where it is the first time we have total silence in the film, which is very different since Rose is constantly listening to music or playing music. This is the dark night of the soul and there is no sound. We don't hear it. This scene's devoid of sound means something.

CPS: Let us talk about Rose's talent. Is her singing country music the path to citizenship? That is, music enables citizenship. Could you say more about music and citizenship in relation to immigrant identity?

DP: She has this love of country music. A love of culture. It is the same thing. Music is a big part of who she is now at seventeen. What I love about this story is the deep tragedy of what is really going on in her life and how her moments of joy are through music. Through it, we see the interiority of what she is feeling. So much more powerful and expressive than dialogue! There is an added layer you get to use as part of the storytelling. Music was so important to me in conceiving the film, to cast real musicians, for example. And all the girls who auditioned had to play guitar and perform. Eva does compose music too. We had to figure out what is her song. Really write a song—I asked her. Dale is really a musician.

I love the film *Once* [2007], which cast two real musicians. You cannot fake that. *A Star Is Born* [2018] features Lady Gaga and Bradley Cooper performing, the real deal is when that magic comes. When Eva is singing a cappella for the first time with the sun hitting her face, it's movie magic. We did that scene so many times to get the exact right moment with the sun positioned within two minutes. We kept driving until we got it. Every time is better or different. We had to get the right look.

CPS: Tell me about growing up in Lubbock, Texas. Was this the scene for the film?

DP: We ended up there when we were fleeing martial law in the Philippines. We were sponsored by Texas Tech University. My mom grew up in Manila as a very sophisticated woman who traveled a lot. Lubbock is a Texas town. The films set in Lubbock tell racist stories. Like Jose, I had certain allies who believed in me. I immediately moved to New York and have lived here my whole adult life. The film is not set in Lubbock but in another town, one hour from Austin. One thing that happened because financing took so long is Trump just got elected. We leaned more into that story in the mom's experience. There was more to this idea of finding home. A place to hang your hat. There were a lot of shoes shot in the film. The whole idea of constantly putting on and taking off shoes. Rose is this wandering loner. When I thought about the movie, I thought, I am making a modern-day Western, paying homage to John Ford in *The Searchers* [1956] in shooting the sky, going town to town, and how the honky-tonk is about not home, where a cowboy is a roaming person without a home . . .

CPS: Last question, why did you choose to center the story of a seventeen-year-old versus the mom or another more fully developed adult? What was more possible to explore in this creative choice?

DP: I always wanted to tell the story from Rose's, a young woman's, perspective. The character is close to my own age when I left my small-town Texas home. I think the idea of telling a story of a mother and daughter separated by immigration from the daughter's perspective really puts you in the shoes of someone who really didn't make that initial decision to come to the US undocumented.

I think one of the main goals of my film is to shed light on the immigration experience, and placing the audience in the shoes of an "innocent" allows for more sympathy and being open to the story.

She is a vulnerable character but a character with big dreams. Watching her navigate her situation throughout the film and "growing up" in the process just made for a bigger journey, a bigger arc for her to go through.

I love coming-of-age stories for that reason, because our lead character has a long way to go by the end of the story.

I think in many ways it's a love letter to my own childhood and to my immigrant parents who sacrificed so much to give my brothers and I a better life.

But beyond that it is also the story of an artist who is finding her voice. And having a young woman who is not confident in her talents really is a joy to watch as she blossoms through her music.

CPS: Thank you so much for talking with me about your film. It is a real gift to our community and more. It is a real mirror to us. And I am grateful to you for your creativity and your work as an amazing director and filmmaker.

DP: Could you tell me what inspired you to write this book?

CPS: My son Lakas died eight years ago at eight years old. When I think about self-sovereignty and self-determination, I imagine what he would be like growing up and how he would grasp that. So, this book is about imagining him living his life.

5 The Unexpected and the Unforeseen

CULTURAL COMPLEXES IN *THE HALF OF IT*

During the COVID-19 pandemic, a number of television series that focused on young, straight cis Asian American girls' and women's experiences with sex and romance gained popularity, including *To All the Boys I've Loved Before* (2018–22), *Never Have I Ever* (2020–23), and *The Summer I Turned Pretty* (2022). All of these are based on stories by Asian American women such as Jenny Han, the best-selling writer of young adult fiction, and the celebrated film and television writer, producer, and actor Mindy Kaling. Each work acknowledges race differently. In *To All the Boys I've Loved Before*, the mixed-race sisters and their white father mourn the death of their fun-loving Korean mother as a loss of culture without explicitly acknowledging racial dynamics in the social life of romances and intimate desires presented. In *Never Have I Ever*, an Indian American girl, immersed in her cultural community and its expectations for gender propriety, witnesses her father die during one of her school music recitals. The most recent streaming series, *The Summer I Turned Pretty*, de-emphasizes racial hierarchy to render diverse members of a wealthy community where racial differences are subordinated by class belonging wherein some of the wealthiest are African American and wealth also exceeds national borders where transnational citizens are also present. Here, too, a parental figure is under threat of dying from terminal cancer and a father disappears due to divorce. Facing loss, the young mixed-race Asian American girl copes by claiming her autonomy and independence primarily through asserting sexuality and desire in pursuing personal pleasures.

The three-part feature-length television series based on the young adult fiction by Jenny Han, *To All the Boys I've Loved Before*, stars Lana Condor in the role of Lara Jean Covey, the middle daughter of a mixed-race family whose Korean American mother has died. The five love letters her character Lara Jean stashed in her closet get mailed to her five separate crushes. Her declaration of love to five boys leads to a fabricated romance with Peter Kavinsky (Noah Centineo), the most popular boy in school, with a written contract, including rules like watching *Fight Club* and *Sixteen Candles* and no kissing. The contract is cowritten so that the relationship cannot be revealed as fake in how they agree to perform all the rituals of high school romance: picking her and her little sister up to go to school, going to games and parties and the ski trip where couples hook up. Lara Jean uses the letters to assert her sexuality as evidenced in her brazenly running to kiss Peter aggressively and then boldly walking across the lacrosse field to initiate the relationship officially. A video of a sexual make-out session in the hot tub at the school ski trip goes viral, and Lara is embroiled in a high school–level sex scandal. Lara and Peter's relationship moves from false to true when they bond over the social dynamics of grief: her mother's death and its unspoken pain and his parents' divorce and its unspoken shame. Through sharing in their adversities and vulnerabilities, they undo their false ties, emerge in public, and fashion true selves, continually struggling on their way to adulthood.

The four-season series *Never Have I Ever* is similarly celebrated for advancing Asian American, particularly South Asian American, representation through the character of Devi Vishwakumar (Maitreyi Ramakrishnan), an academically competitive valedictorian of her high school whose father's sudden death leads to her losing her ability to walk. Her interest in seeing the swimmer's body of the most popular boy in school, the mixed-race Japanese American Paxton Hall-Yoshida (Darren Barnet), enables her to walk again. She begins pursuing with maniacal bravery her crush

while getting embroiled in another romantic relationship with her closest academic rival, Ben Gross (Jaren Lewison). Paxton and Devi contend
with the social regard for their match, determining their ability to connect
with each other and relate to each other truthfully. When Devi cheats
on Paxton and they resume dating, he won't acknowledge their relationship in public due to her infidelity. Ben suffers neglect from his wealthy
white Jewish parents, who ignore him and are absent from his life, and
instead is cared for by a nanny. He becomes vulnerable to online predation as well as loneliness that prevents him from relating to Devi truthfully as well. Devi continues to navigate her social world by making many
mistakes—especially in lying to her friends and family—for which she
always seeks forgiveness and betterment.

The Summer I Turned Pretty, also based on the work of writer Jenny
Han, is set in the wealthy summer community of the Hamptons, where
biracial Korean American Belly Conklin (Lola Tung) and her family stay
with their white family friend Susannah Fisher (Rachel Blanchard), who
is living with late-stage cancer. Her teen sons, Jeremiah (Gavin Casalegno)
and Conrad Fisher (Christopher Briney), are young, hegemonically attractive cis men for whom Belly feels complicated attraction, for she grew
up with them like siblings. The brothers struggle with the unspoken condition of their mother, not understanding the silence or her lacking wish
to fight her illness. Belly is just sixteen and attempting to socialize with
the older brothers, who aim to protect her but also respond to her growing maturation into womanhood and her eagerness to explore her sexuality. Conrad is particularly grief-stricken by his mother's illness and is
unable to respond to Belly's offering herself to him. She welcomes instead
Jeremiah's bisexuality and his enthusiastic willingness to meet her sexual
desire. She is in the process of becoming, coming of age, and exploring the
multiplicity of her choices.[1]

I begin to close this book to gather what is happening at this moment
within Asian/American films in the first quarter of the twenty-first century.
Gone is the pessimism of the past, and here we see the emotional, intellectual, ethical, and political struggles and dramas of youth contending with
race, death, sex, and grief within their cultural contexts as Asian Americans with particular ethnicities and as gendered beings. As the United
States moves toward being a majority people of color country in 2045, these
films put in place within our popular culture reflections of these new demographics and a hope for a livable future together, including sexual becoming
and sexual choices, even in the face of grief and its inevitability in all our lives.

I began this book with *Minari* and its family dynamics that center the future of children, including their health and their belonging in white communities such as in rural Arkansas. Their family is there to grow familiar food for people of the Korean diaspora. The television series about Andrew Cunanan shows us the power of the true self and in forging a productive and creative life in contrast to the false self, which forges a life of devastation and destruction. Andrew Ahn's *Spa Night* and *Driveways* demonstrate filmmaking that attends to childhood and young adult development that is infinite in possibility once freed from normative constraints. Auraeus Solito's *The Blossoming of Maximo Oliveros* prepares us for a world where we can learn from other cultural sexualities about belonging and sex-positive childhood desires that are not imprisoned by moral panic or constricted by adult sexuality. Diane Paragas's conclusion of *Yellow Rose* contrasts with the opening scenes of the film to offer a world of self-confidence that can charge a path of actualizing freedom rather than incarceration and deportation. Along the way, the children suffer grief and mourning that we recognize in the losses we ourselves have endured in the pandemic. The films give us freedom, releasing us from the persistent accounts of melancholia and pessimism in Asian/American cultural politics with the hopeful generation of these characters forging their paths toward earned secure attachment and the confidence that agentic attunement enables for their futures.

My hope is that the caress of my view as a mother-author-spectator offers a method of self-reflexivity that a reader can follow in situating oneself, gathering one's context when experiencing a film in order to open oneself to unexpected and unforeseen responses. I hope too for this filmmaking to continue in ways that we can find and experience so we may analyze these works and ourselves in an empowering practice of agentic attunement that enables us to see a promising future for Asian American children and youth. Let these films not be made in vain. Let them counter the entrenchment of cultural complexes within the dominant cinema and on television.

In the film *The Half of It* (2020) by Alice Wu, we learn about the importance of self-sovereignty for young people from across a range of backgrounds who are facing different forces (in church, school, class and race hierarchies, and gender roles) that pressure them into shaping their identity in constricting ways. Within these institutions, forces get in the way of fashioning authentic autonomy, true selves, although the young people resist through writing and reading that allow them to reimagine existing and established roles. Adults as arbiters of these institutions can get in the way unless they recognize young people as deserving of agentic attunement and make way for their future autonomy. As such, acknowledgments of both grief and love are recommended pathways for forging healthy lives and confident subjectivities to compose future adult self-sovereignty.

Writer/director Alice Wu's first feature film, *Saving Face* (2004), was the first Asian American lesbian romantic comedy to be released by a Hollywood studio and received multiple festival awards. The screenplay won a contest sponsored by the Coalition of Asian Pacific Americans in Entertainment (CAPE), which led to its production by Hollywood star Will Smith and his production company, including executive Teddy Zee.[2] The film is thus a beneficiary of a fifty-plus-year civil rights movement composed of Asian Americans working in mainstream media and prominent people of color who understand the need for Hollywood's diversification, and it made a significant contribution to the archive of Asian American cinema. In recent years, I witnessed the film's commemoration by major Asian American film festivals in San Diego and twice in San Francisco—in 2011 and again in June 2022 during a Pride Month celebration hosted by the Center for Asian American Media's former film festival director Masashi Niwano, who now leads artist development at San Francisco Film. This acclaim indicates the film's relevance in queer, Asian American, and both independent and industry film circles. The hundreds in attendance and the massive crowd flanking Wu outside the Alamo theater for its June 2022 screening attest to the film's ongoing relevance. Essentially, *Saving Face* was a classic of race and independent media as soon as it arrived and has emerged as a film recognized by LGBTQ+ communities as well. Considering the scant number of women and particularly Asian American and queer women who direct in Hollywood, and how rare it is for them to helm a second feature, it is unsurprising that we waited almost two decades for Alice Wu's sophomore film. *The Half of It* was released on Netflix during the COVID-19 pandemic to highly favorable reviews.

In *The Half of It*, Ellie Chu, an immigrant Chinese American teenager, is the sole Asian American at her predominantly white high school in present-day rural Washington State. Living in an apartment attached to a train depot, she must help her grieving immigrant father pay bills by calling utility companies to explain their delayed payment and assist with his job as a station master. Ellie is grieving too. In the dark sadness of their home is the ghost of a fun-loving mom who loved "the best part" of movies, songs, and life itself. We feel through her husband's and daughter's sadness how she was herself the best part of their lives. It is palpable that "someone is missing" in their family, as if the passive ones were left behind, bereft and not knowing how to move on.

What binds all the films in my study is the loss of a parent through death and the displacement of the family to new places or precarious new situations in search of a home in the face of that loss. In *To All the Boys I've Loved Before*, the death of Lara Jean's mother is the basis for achieving intimacy with Peter Kavinsky when they share their vulnerability and hurt (Peter has lost his father through divorce). Similarly, Ellie in *The Half of It* crosses into a relationship with more gravitas when Paul asks her about the death of her mother. The loss of the mother impedes her normal development: she takes care of her father, who is unable to move on from his wife's death. Although they share the loss of an object, it has different ramifications for Ellie than for her father. She can choose to stay home, forgo her own pursuits, and become stunted. Her father can continue not to change his life if Ellie stays and chooses not to develop.

Twice a day, in the morning and at night, Ellie must physically hold up lights to signal the trains as they pass by. She has settled on a vision of her future as stuck in the fictional small town named Squahamish. Even her favorite teacher calls it "Hellquamish." Ellie bikes to school through a rural forest, then past a welcome sign that reads, "It's Happening in Squahamish." What could be happening in Squahamish? The name may mean nothing or may sound quaint to those not from the Pacific Northwest. But it is important as a choice for the filmmaker because much of the area in the Olympic Peninsula and north of Seattle, and east into the rest of Washington State as well, has rich, complex, and overt Native American roots. Thus, it's not quite the case, for example, that what Ellie bikes down is a country road, insofar as "country" suggests rural whiteness alone.

The rest of Ellie's world is largely determined by her relationships with her peers in high school, where she is an outsider. Nonetheless, she establishes herself as essential to the community. Ellie unifies her need to help her family financially and establish a place in her community through her lucrative yet illicit business of writing papers for her peers. She charges twenty dollars for each paper, with a policy of "It's an A or you don't pay."[3] The English teacher, with whom she is close, turns a blind eye to the setup, encouraging Ellie to apply to college to nurture her as a writer and broaden her world by redirecting her talents and finding people who understand her, unlike in the rural town.

Indeed, Ellie's deepest feeling is one of alienation, despite her connection to her classmates (which is transactional and commercial). Ellie commutes a long distance via a rickety bicycle, with a plastic bin serving as a basket to hold her school bag. First, she trudges up a desolate country road into town, then climbs more isolated and hilly rural paths to school. The only other presence on the road is an old pickup truck filled with a bunch of teenagers who call her "Ellie Chu, Chug-a Chug-a Choo-Choo!" twice daily, to and from school. Their taunts target her odd situation of living at a train depot while also disparaging her ethnic Chinese last name and belittling her big efforts in powering up and down the hill. She ignores them and proceeds with determination every day.

A classmate, Paul Munsky, a white male jock who does not quite fit hegemonic standards of attractiveness and who speaks in a slow drawl that indicates perhaps an unambitious ease with himself, sprints up the hill behind Ellie to try to convince her to write love letters on his behalf. She is appalled at the notion of writing intimate letters versus analytic papers that she can simply churn out. Her immediate response of "That's personal! I can't do that!" is met with his "I'll pay!" She is suspicious of Paul and finds him irritating, although he is earnest, humble, and hopeful toward her. To avoid her family's electricity getting turned off, she agrees to his request. Despite her disbelief that she can write authentic love letters on his behalf, she does so, motivated by the pay but also by her personal interest.

The object of Paul's (and Ellie's) attention is a gorgeous, quiet, and intense Latinx classmate, Aster Flores, with whom Ellie Chu is also intrigued. The only other girl of color in school, Aster is considered very good-looking and thus is at the center of white heterosexual social life, where gender roles for women are limited in ways she resists and even resents, especially as a girl marked by her lack of wealth as well as by difference within a racial hierarchy. In this setting, Aster's beauty, talents, and ability to sing, her gentle kindness, and primarily her rich intellectual life all earn Ellie's regard and admiration. As Aster sings in class, Ellie stares at her, completely riveted. Outside, Paul Munsky runs laps for football practice but stops in his tracks to listen to the siren song of Aster's voice. This triangulation between Aster, Ellie, and Paul exposes the constraint on their personalities due to existing structures of whiteness, wealth, religion, heterosexism, and ableism regarding speech and literacy.

The way the three young people behave within these structural constraints breaks open archetypes that hold back their true selves, their grandiose and healthily narcissistic selves, and their healthy paths toward adulthoods. This is much like how Andrew Cunanan fabricates worlds in his desire to exceed his circumstances, David pursues gay same-race sex in the spa, Maxie pursuing the older policeman as a replacement for their mom and to redirect their destiny of a life of criminality, and Rose pursues her grandiose self in order to perform and find an exceptional path to citizenship. Ellie narrates at the beginning of the movie, "In case you have not guessed, this is not a love story, not one where anyone gets what they want"—that is, in the short-term aims of the conventional teen romantic comedy. Instead, this story is about developing healthy narcissism and true selves—which is the thematic thread that ties together all chapters of this book. The characters each do this through the power of learning their personal projects—sexual or otherwise—and their autonomy as belonging to them and in acknowledging others' self-sovereignty as well. And in becoming friends, in failed romantic relations, they learn the value of agentic attunement in caring for each other.

Aster possesses hegemonic beauty (what Ellie describes as "classic bone structure") yet struggles with race, gender, and class constraints in their town. In their subsequent conversations via letters and texts, where Ellie writes as Paul, she diagnoses what Aster endures as "the oppression of fitting in" while "sitting on the mountaintops of popularity." Ellie recognizes Aster and reflects that understanding to her in ways that Aster feels deeply through their constant texting. Alice Wu depicts this connection in matching shots—where late at night they lean on their bedroom windows longing for the other's intimate communication—the words get inside each other's heads, leading to recognition and yearning for that recognition. Their letters connect them so that their communication becomes essential to their lives as a source of affirmation and closeness in what they call "finally being understood." Ellie (as Paul) and Aster write to each other about the philosophies and practices of abstract art, the boldness of brushstrokes as they physically work together on a mural at separate times, and the loneliness of living in a small town where Aster's beauty and her family's lack of fortune limit her future to marrying the town's most popular and richest boy. This epistolary romance, the love letters, really enters Aster's life as a different path that opens suddenly, and she becomes interested in exploring it. At first, she calls it a friendship to make her exploration acceptable in a town where she is not invisible—she is already partnered with its most eligible bachelor whom others target. But the texts and letters become something else for her, an expression of her polyamorous desire. Her queer self is born.

Ellie considers the intimacy of writing each other "dating," while Paul Munsky insists on going on an actual date with Aster as having "hamburgers and fries, and a second order of fries" and "hanging out." Ellie asks what hanging out actually entails. For her, letters and texts convey the affective power of love, intimacy, and desire along with and expressive of physical desire, as a way to navigate the various "cultural complexes" of their worlds. And along the way, Alice Wu is saying that films do this work too.

Cultural complexes are collective ideas present in individual psyches and collective psychic structures, and what lies in between. That is, in the "vast realm of human experience that inhabits the psychical space between our most personal and our most archetypal level of being in the world," there exists the "'cultural level' of the psyche."[4] Jungian psychoanalyst Thomas Singer defined the term *cultural complex* as "the heart of the conflicts between many groups [that] are expressed in group life all the time: politically, economically, sociologically, geographically, religiously."[5] Cultural complexes unify varying communities in their shared assumptions and are felt in individual experience psychically with real ramifications, emotional and otherwise. In the case of Squahamish, these complexes include navigating gender and race politics in high school, compulsory heterosexuality, the domination of religion in town life, and class inequality that limits people's futures.

Films and literature populate young people's psyches and have the potential to frame their interactions as an intervention to the entrenchment of cultural complexes. Although film can intervene in the entrenchment of cultural complexes, they also have the power to further entrench them. First, Ellie and her father ritualistically watch films together every evening while eating dinner, even after Paul Munsky starts coming around to join them daily. Together they watch classic films by Wim Wenders and Howard Hawks while eating from their own trays and bowls. One way in which the cultural complex of whiteness is felt is in the isolation of Ellie's father, who hardly speaks English and is unable then to integrate himself in society. He participates in it and communicates with his daughter through the consumption of movies. Ellie's ability to depend on her father enables her secure attachment. Despite his lack of power outside the home that requires her taking on parental roles such as paying bills and finding money to pay them, Ellie is able to go to literature to gain a strong sense of self and go to movies in a dependable companionship first with her father and then later as they are joined by Paul. When the father makes known his support of her going to college, he affirms her self-sovereignty. It is a practice of agentic attunement in forgoing his dependence on her and enabling her to reach for a future of freedom and self-determination.

In terms of literature infusing their lives as young people, Ellie's English teacher assigns Plato on love and Sartre on "thwarted desire," and in class and in their assigned papers students discuss "barely repressed longing" in Kazuo Ishiguro's *Remains of the Day* (1989). These stories inform and make their daily lives grander. When Paul and Aster meet in person, it is, as she describes, "confusing." Paul struggles to speak beyond phrases and one-word sentences. "Yeah, talk, ugh" is one line that he delivers almost as a grunt. Another is, "Oh, friend" when Aster says she is delighted to pursue friendship with him. And another: "Reddi-wip. It's from a can, but it's OK," when milkshakes are delivered to their table.

In a different scene, Ellie and Aster meet in person and travel to a secret hot spring in the forest. They take off their clothes with different attitudes. Aster casually removes hers, shocking Ellie, who quickly turns away. Ellie, in turn, hides as she takes off her outerwear and remains in her long johns even when in the water. Ellie's sensations are heightened in the scene as she watches Aster's every move. Aster is at ease. Together in the isolated wilderness, the act of listening to music and feeling the sensations of sound while almost entirely immersed in water depicts the cerebral and physical dimensions of intimacy and interconnectedness that bind them. This scene expands our definition of adolescent sexuality beyond the act of touching bodies, in a direct challenge to hookup culture that defines the dating experiences of many young people today. Hookup culture is largely understood in popular culture as millennial ways of dating, which include emotionless sex. Sociologist Lisa Wade argues that this is but a sliver of the interactions she observes among college-age young people where students of color also opt out of such interactions that do not reflect their specific cultural values.[6] We see this in the landscape of *The Half of It*, where Aster and boyfriend Trig's crowd subscribe to gendered norms of elevating cis-patriarchal white macho, but Paul and Ellie's crowd follow more wide-ranging practices of what is considered fun. Aster and Ellie's romance queers teen sexuality beyond the physical in ways that show the wide range of relations that young people enact today.[7] In this scene, the sensations of listening to each other and to the music while floating in water are entirely sensuous. They float on their backs and listen very closely to a song, waiting for its "best part." In a wide image shot from above, we see their full-length bodies in the water as they unify in listening. They are not touching, yet their senses are most alert and attuned to each other and the environs through the sound. The film cuts to a close-up of their heads floating on the water as

5.1 Ellie and Aster float in the hot springs seeking the "best part" of the song and, by chance, of their lives, as they listen to the music and experience pleasure in each other's bodily proximity. *The Half of It* (Alice Wu, 2020).

the music rises. In recognizing this as the part they have been waiting for, their sensations unify in pleasure.

In a twist, Paul falls in love with or begins to desire Ellie, not knowing about her feelings for Aster. At a football game, Paul runs the full length of the field to make a touchdown. Until now, the Squahamish team has not scored in more than a decade, and the entire town goes wild. We see that it is Ellie who has inspired this heroic achievement. Paul finds her in the locker room and attempts to kiss her. Aster discovers them in the act of kissing—even if Ellie is resisting—and runs away. As Ellie calls for Aster, Paul looks at her disappointed face. Ellie's feelings for Aster are revealed to Paul when she brazenly looks at Aster with longing. Paul, completely vexed, admonishes Ellie for the sin of queer desire but uses this confusion as an opportunity for learning. He researches what it means to be gay, to realize one's queerness, since Ellie, whom he loves, clearly and matter-of-factly is queer.

Attesting to the complexity of her sexuality, Aster already has a boyfriend and is open to polyamory with Paul; she has kissed him twice and is perpetually available to text with Ellie (as Paul). She is at the cusp of a decision too—about who she is, what her sexual project will be, and what

5.2 Ellie kisses Aster with the promise that they will see each other again after they return from their first years in college. *The Half of It* (Alice Wu, 2020).

defines her autonomy. When Aster's rich boyfriend Trig proposes to her at church, Ellie and Paul both speak up to interrupt them, exposing their triangular entanglement.

The film ends with Ellie kissing Aster as they say goodbye, which Ellie gets the courage to do when Aster says that the possibility of getting together romantically did cross her mind. They promise to see each other again in a year or two after Aster returns from art school. Paul and Ellie reunite as friends as she departs for Grinnell College, while he stays home in Squahamish to be with her dad and his own family. So, both girls leave for college and the white male romantic lead stays home with his family in the small town. Self-sovereignty here is available to the young people that these three characters represent—queer Latinx, straight Polish, and queer Chinese immigrant—and the three of them have divergent desires when centering themselves.

"Not a Love Story Where Anyone Gets What They Want"

Ellie takes care of her widowed father in a premature adultification that befalls teen girls living with a lack of privilege but also missing mothers, like Maxie in *The Blossoming of Maximo Oliveros* and Rose in *Yellow Rose*. At school, Ellie has no friends except for her white female English teacher who admires her writing and helps direct her departure from Squahamish. In the classroom, we see the buzz of social media functioning as a realm of its own, another world, another layer to reality. Party planning and asking others out for dates receive in-real-life outbursts of collective laughter that compel the teacher to demand the students pay attention to class. Within this world, Ellie quietly distributes papers from her corner perch of the orchestra room. It seems that she has written papers for most of her classmates, and soon we hear the sounds of the app notifying her of their various payments. Ellie stands out in her community not only because of her race but also because of her ability to write and think, reflecting on what relationships mean and how they fit in history. She is then multiply aware of herself in comparison to her less conscious classmates who farm out their opportunity to learn and reflect on themselves through their writing and reading.

As the only Asian American student in school and perhaps in the entire town, Ellie has to contend with thoughtless comments as she finally enters the social world, which she only does with nudging from her friend Paul. Even Paul's mom says, "Oh, here's Paul's Chinese friend." Along with the daily taunts making fun of her situation of living at a train depot and her Chinese name, these words remind her of unbelonging and continually position her as an outsider. Through the language and word choices of others, her alienation is based on the magnification of her racial difference, presenting it as a barrier of otherness.

We see the prominence of Ellie's racial difference at the party she attends, where she is welcomed with a greeting yelled by an unknown partygoer who confirms her hypervisibility: "The Chinese girl came!" The party is primarily composed of white kids. One of them approaches Ellie to say they've been in math class together for four years and invites her to play "Drinkers of Catan," a board game they have converted to a drinking game. Here, the racial exclusion her father lives extends to his daughter, who does not participate in the white kids' social rituals. Ellie leaves her isolation, her intense thinking through of things, and her self-protection to abandon caution. She drinks too much and loses control and the conscious ability to make choices. Paul chooses to remain sober and stays close to Ellie in her vulnerable state. He takes her home safely, to his house actually, where she wakes up the next day, fully clothed and safe.

Unlike Ellie, who does not participate in femme practices of beauty, Aster experiences the demand to perform gendered archetypes befitting her looks. A group of five blonde girls who occupy normative gendered roles that compose what is popular at school adopts Aster as a kind of mascot, manipulating her to dress like them and talking behind her back about her luck being the rich boy's girlfriend, even as they look down on her family as mere renters. "Aster's so lucky," one of the girls says, because her boyfriend Trig's "family owns half of Squahamish" while she "does not even own her house." It is arresting—in racial terms—that Trig's family "owns half of Squahamish," a fact that marks settler colonialism, while Aster's is a migrant family of Latinx descent who moved there from Sacramento and subsequently feel discomfort and unbelonging. As an indictment of Aster's lack of choices as a poor girl who should deem herself lucky to be the object of the privileged boy's desires, Trig already treats her like a trophy—an accessory to his debauchery and his ascendancy to community stature via his family's wealth. Aster, while at the center of these events that maintain whiteness, wealth, and heterosexuality, always sits at its periphery, barely acknowledging Trig when he speaks to her. Aster actually refuses to participate in queen bee culture and resents her status as a trophy girlfriend. She uses this feeling of displacement to pursue her queer relationships with Paul and Ellie as more worthwhile.

The Half of It indeed rewrites and recasts the premise of *Cyrano de Bergerac*, a popular nineteenth-century play by Edmond Rostand. The play has endured for more than a hundred years, traveling in various iterations all over the world, including the Philippine production *Cyrano: Isang Sarsuwela* (2010) to the more recent feature film *Cyrano* (2021) starring Peter Dinklage, who describes himself as a dwarf, in the title role for which he was nominated for multiple acting awards. In this latest version of *Cyrano de Bergerac*, Dinklage's dwarfism stands in for the disadvantage that prevents Cyrano from being a viable romantic partner. In *The Half of It*, Cyrano's mythical large nose is replaced by queerness and Asianness in an American high school setting where whiteness, heteronormativity, conventional gender roles, and wealth prevail as the restraining norms.

Speaking of Sexual Projects and Sexual Autonomy

In *Sexual Citizens: A Landmark Study of Sex, Power, and Assault on Campus* (2020), public health scholar Jennifer Hirsch and sociologist Shamus Khan argue that "men's uncritical acceptance of a gendered and sexual script where their job is to pursue sex and women's job is to convey agreement or not renders them susceptible to sexually assaulting someone."[8] The film *The Half of It* shows us how young people should learn to speak their desires and wishes even to themselves, in order to make them known to others in a world where not all desires and subjectivities are welcome, and social scripts can feel firmly entrenched. Hirsch and Khan argue that college students do not know how to articulate their desires or recognize others'. This inability to describe their sexual aims and goals, or what the authors call the "sexual projects" of students, contributes to cultures of assault that are further enabled by structures of space and money that deepen inequality for marginalized people in ways that appear acutely in sexual relations.[9] Indeed, this landmark study makes an important intervention we must implement in requiring an attunement to each other's projects and the power dynamics involved when becoming sexually engaged.

We see this organization of social spaces according to privilege in *The Half of It* as well. Trig, whom his peers refer to and treat as the "Big Man," is a beloved figure at school. When he performs on-stage, applause erupts without his being introduced at all. Everyone knows who is meant. Parties center his drunken shenanigans as he is flanked by the five fawning blonde girls. A photo shoot features him as the heir to his father's company, and he formally asks for Aster's opinion on what to wear, without expecting a response for any of the questions. They are performative, since her answer does not really matter; that she looks the part of his girlfriend suffices. Aster is at the periphery of these events that focus on Trig; she literally does not participate, indicating her resistance to her secondary status, though her lack of enthusiasm and her retraction seem invisible to Trig. Her response to her status as the queen bee is negligible. Similarly, in terms of the charmed elite acting without regard for the autonomy of others, Trig assumes, in what is the opposite of attunement to others, that Ellie desires him even if she is completely oblivious of him. Along with Paul, she interviews him to gather information to help their project of pursuing Aster. Trig simply assumes Ellie is in love with him within such a setting. He even attempts to kiss her by going to her house, demonstrating intense narcissism, that is only prevented by Ellie's dad chasing him away by spraying him with a hose.

Like Aster and Ellie, the athlete Paul Munsky is similarly ambivalent about his status. Unlike Trig, he is not conventionally attractive as a white man and is not patriarchal in his demeanor. He does not get wildly drunk like Trig and is regarded as a "good guy" or "safe" by Aster, as is apparent in how he protects Ellie at the party when she is drunk. Within the hierarchy of young men, he is indeed an athlete with a truck, but he "works part-time" (as he describes in his first attempt at a love letter to Aster) at his family's ethnic business selling sausages. He also has a disadvantage in the way he speaks—literally, he grunts, delivers phrases versus complete sentences, and uses incorrect grammar in addition to not being conversant in current events or literature. Unlike Aster and Ellie, who communicate with precision utilizing a wide vocabulary and frequent literary referents, Paul expresses bare and simple feelings, much like Trig, who texts Aster: "Don't let me eat carbs today." Meanwhile, Paul texts Ellie to ask, "When does the dating start?" as she and Aster share profound thoughts when Ellie texts on his behalf. In talking about the mural that Ellie and Aster paint separately but together in the sense that it is on the same canvas, Ellie remarks, "Everything beautiful is eventually ruined." Ellie and Aster simply understand each other in their long reflections that secure the intimacy of their texting.

The conversations between Ellie and Paul about Aster do turn into a kind of dating (in Paul's perception) as well, as their intimate knowledge about each other grows. Paul asks bluntly why Ellie's family stays in Squahamish when she and her father both seem so unhappy. When she won't answer and throws the question back to him petulantly, he provides his own honest response. As a nod to Ellie's literary influence, he credits Jean-Paul Sartre's existentialist play *No Exit* (1944) with enabling him to articulate his wish to run his own shop, with his signature invention of the taco sausage, but doing so would break his mother's heart. This is why he stays. Under Ellie's influence he has learned how to use literature as she and Aster do: to achieve consciousness about themselves, their desires, and the wishes on the path to autonomy and self-sovereignty.

Paul's openness in his response moves Ellie to disclose her family's circumstances as immigrants. Squahamish was supposed to be a "jumping-off point" for her dad, who has a "PhD no less." But "speaking good English trumps a PhD, one from China at least." Paul identifies with this inability and says he "does not speak very good English" either. To which Ellie challenges that he has "no excuse," as Paul laughs. Paul and her father indeed bond through cooking as their primary language of expression. In a different kind of multiculturalism from Alice Wu's first feature film, the father makes his daughter's favorite dish of braised pork and teaches Paul recipes to meet the teen's perpetual wish to learn about spices and other aspects of cooking. Her father begins to think of Paul as Ellie's boyfriend, since he visits so much and eats meals with them. Paul actually prefers the quiet of their home to his own large, rambunctious, and loud household where he and Ellie won't get a chance to talk.

As they continue to work together in writing love texts to send to Aster, Paul and Ellie not only get to know each other's backgrounds but also interrogate the meaning of love. When Ellie asks Paul why he loves Aster, his response is that she's "pretty, smart, and kind." In contrast, Ellie's explanation for why someone would love Aster impresses and confounds Paul. She says, it's because of "how her eyes look right into yours . . . how her laugh busts out like she can't help herself and she stops being perfect for a few moments. She has five different voices. And one can drown in an ocean of her thoughts." Paul recognizes Ellie's ability to use words to describe an intense and keen observation of Aster as superior to his inability to access language. He says, "I am so dumb" in response to the perfect way Ellie captures their shared love object. Speaking to each other is important, but it is actually speaking of the self that is crucial in identifying one's sexual project, which then becomes a demand for its recognition by the other who listens. Listening is a key element of agentic attunement in learning about the other. When listening to the speaker, the recognition of their sexual aims, goals, and desires can be transformative for those participating in the intimate relation.

Ellie's description frightens her, too. She recognizes she is in love with Aster and that this is not an acceptable feeling in the culture and community of Squahamish's religious environment, where queerness is neither visible nor allowed. Speaking of her own desire to Paul visibly takes Ellie aback, awakening her to the truth of her wishes, the fact of her sexual project. Perhaps to rescue herself from the spotlight on her feelings, she affirms in Paul how hard he works to win Aster's love and how effort is precisely what composes love, much like her father's love for her mother. She says, "If love is not the effort you put in, then what is it?" Her words touch Paul, and slowly he starts to see Ellie differently, looking up at her window with longing as the focus of his feelings begins to change from Aster to Ellie.

On Paul and Aster's second date, the question of what composes a romantic relationship is confronted. Because the two are awkward and unable to connect with each other through words spoken in each other's physical presence, Ellie begins to text Aster from the car outside the window of the restaurant. So, Paul (via Ellie) and Aster are texting each other while sitting across from each other. But it is actually Ellie speaking as Paul from the parking lot. She does so as Paul says he's "not good with words" in Aster's physical presence. He says he's intimidated to speak. The texting between Ellie (as Paul) and Aster only goes on for so long before Paul stands up with an outburst stating he does not just want to be friends. Ellie is cut off from texting soon after through the physical expression of his bodily desire interrupting the cerebral connection between the two women.

The next day, Paul tells Ellie that he and Aster held hands and kissed. They connected physically. Ellie is genuinely curious about how people physically connect—how consent happens. Paul's explanation that it is intense attunement through body language, and particularly the expression of the face that invites the kiss. In this explanation, he pivots to another language, one in which he is more conversant, expressive, and effective. And if one does not rise up to it, he says, one becomes "a putz." Hirsch and Khan describe how this lack of language tends to be common in contemporary relationships between young people today, who "rarely use direct language to elicit or grant consent" or to "talk about their own sexual projects."[10] Essentially, such a system of communicating consent depends on "careful attention to whether kisses are enthusiastically reciprocated."[11] Consent is crucial to recognizing the sovereignty of the other in relation to one's own sexual project. It must be secured in ways that are as certain as can be.

So, while consent is important in that young people are trying to be agentially attuned to the other person, the inability to speak of desire is unreliable in gauging what is sexually mutual, especially when one considers that drunken sex is the norm and nondrunk sex is called "serious sex."[12] This is when self-sovereignty is most clearly needed—one needs to be able to say "no," this is not what I want (rather than "I let it happen" or "I wanted to get it over with"). But even more important, for the one who is not hearing the "no," they must listen in recognition of the other's different sexual project and their autonomy. That is, one's sexual aims must be met with consent and willingness. The texting is in the dating, the speaking, the conversations, the friendship that recognizes the autonomy and the different desires of the other, the partner. The terrain of the physical is where consent must happen because of the bodies there.

Sober relations of intimacy occur in this film through talking as intimate disclosure. It begins in written speech via love letters and text (between Aster and Ellie) and spoken interaction (between Ellie and Paul) that both convey growing intensity. In their real-life interactions, however, Paul increasingly feels attracted to Ellie and makes efforts to support her, whether in helping her dress more properly for the senior talent show performance or encouraging her to perform her song that he has listened to from under her window (in a reverse serenade). He discovers envelopes she has addressed and stamped to send to food critics with his sausage recipe on his behalf and interprets this advocacy for him as a love that goes beyond mere friendship. When he assumes she collects the Yakult (Asian drinks) from the vending machine as a gift for him, after he scores a touchdown for the first time in fifteen years for the town of Squahamish, he actually misinterprets her desire to consume them (since the closest Asian store is "three hours by bike"). Ellie is completely unaware of his misinterpretation that she wishes to kiss him, directly countering his earlier description that he can read when and what girls desire from him in terms of sexual acts.

Ellie doesn't make the mistake of assuming desire. When Aster invites Ellie to her "favorite secret spot," hot springs on the outskirts of town, she won't look at Aster taking off her clothes and demands the same prudence. She fears being touched by Aster as an act that would unleash desire, even if Aster is simply reaching past her to turn on music. In the water, Aster says it is strange to be with a girl and not talk about boys, which is one of the criteria of the Bechdel test, that women talk with each other about topics beyond men. In a sense, the Bechdel test transpires in the screenwriting of this film in itself. They do not actually talk about Paul at length, but instead talk about music and movies—their own tastes and preferences. Aster does express that Paul confuses her because when they are physically together, she feels safe. But when reading his letters and texts (written by Ellie), she feels unsafe. In this way, her talking about Paul is actually talking about Ellie. Laden with intense emotion, those feelings inform Ellie's fear of expressing desire that Aster glimpses from the words that have constituted their interaction for so long. Both Ellie and Aster describe "never having felt so understood" until those words, letters, and texts that they exchange as Paul and Aster.

The triangle of their relationship is broken apart when Aster actually witnesses Paul kissing Ellie. And when Paul's attempt fails, he realizes Ellie is not there for him and instead sees she is in love with Aster. What comes next is the barrier of religion that constrains them all. Gayness is a sin, according to Paul, but he cannot reconcile his respect for Ellie with this belief. He begins to learn about queerness and asks Google: "How does one know you're gay?" At church, where Paul attends with his family and Ellie is the "resident heathen" who serves as the one-person choir, Trig proposes to Aster during the service. While the proposal makes Aster's father, the pastor, happy, it triggers protest from both Ellie and Paul. Ellie essentially argues that Aster cannot stay in Squahamish and settle for heteronormativity, wealth, and whiteness—and a religion that says queer desire is bad. Ellie declares that unlike in the Bible where "love is 'humble,' it is actually bold." The church scene clarifies not only the bond among the three young people but also the ways in which speaking can reorganize the world. At church, Ellie and Paul's unified plea to Aster not to settle for less as inauthentic is the opposite of what they supposedly value—the real, actionable, and changeable. Aster is enraged at this claim, for Paul has been represented by Ellie this entire time. Aster slaps Paul for deceiving her, and she runs away from Ellie too.

The film ends with two scenes that celebrate the potentiality of fleeing whiteness that hierarchizes difference, religion that condemns queer sexualities, gender norms that limit women's futures, and a small white town that others people of color. Aster and Ellie stand on the street with two yellow lines between them. When Aster declares that a relationship or attraction did cross her mind, it gives Ellie a confidence in the consent of her object for the love she has available. Consent appears to be verbally given. Ellie pushes down her bike and kisses Aster, who reciprocates with curiosity and enjoyment. Both smiling, they promise to see each other in two years. Then Ellie rides away on her bike, standing, open-faced, with a future full of possibilities that include Aster. Her face looks different from how it appeared during all the other bike rides in the film, when she was moving toward a ritual alienation. Instead, she looks forward to a wider future.

At the train station where Ellie is about to leave for college, she is no longer simply raising flags to the trains every morning and night. There, Paul promises to take care of her father with whom he has bonded through cooking. He follows the train, running alongside it to wave to Ellie as she rides away, defying her instructions not to chase her like moronic characters in movies. He does anyhow, and she cries in response to his act of authentic and genuine love that she returns, as friends, in the film's insistence on the sovereignty of young, racialized subjects.

Ending the film with references to tropes in other films asks us to see the mythologies being broken in our understanding of young people in the movies. *The Half of It* contends with the racialization of Latinx childhoods, white ethnic childhoods, and Chinese American immigrant childhoods in a town full of cultural complexes that limit young people's everyday lives and constrain their imaginings of the future. In addressing the cultural specificities of each, a framework of American childhoods emerges that is simply not white, not wealthy, not sexist, not heterosexist, and not heterosexual. These characters seek an adulthood with more meaning through self-determination that honors their own self-defined desires. The film ends with a patient recognition of waiting for the surprises of what can lie ahead. And in involving this diverse range of childhoods, Wu's film shows how everyone needs self-sovereignty. In her culture, Aster faces the pressure to marry early, perhaps to redeem the family and offer them a path toward a more secure financial future. Paul feels the pressure to stay home and agrees to it, to preserve the family business and cultural identity of what they make with pride. Ellie's father tells her to go to Grinnell, to fulfill her mother's wishes and render their immigrant path more open-ended and aspirational. It is also a vow against his own deterioration—and her continued development and growth. Parents get out of the way to support the project of self-sovereignty, as they should and as the method of agentic attunement shows.

My hope for this book is that it can demonstrate the importance of young people owning their bodies and desires—indeed, how they can establish a path toward healthy adult selves with the help of movies, which can also clarify adults' roles as readers and viewers in helping to ensure this path and remove ourselves as obstacles. This means enabling young people to want for themselves, respecting the sovereignty of their desires and the autonomy of their bodies, and teaching them to recognize those of others.

Too often racialized childhoods are ignored, and white childhoods go unmarked, even in recent studies, rendering other films that represent white childhoods as a default.[13] Nonetheless, the pursuit of self-determination and self-sovereignty here is not framed as family versus individual self, but as the removal of obstacles that have defined family in ways that limit the child's true self as one that can be encouraged by agentic attunement. The individuals remain in the family and revise it by asserting their needs.

In addition to arguing for children and young people to speak of their desires, a more expansive understanding of film can happen in the relation between the viewer and the film. I aim to transform that relationship through this book, which has centered the child in a world of adults who speak about experiences that are far in their past but continue to shape them. They make films about childhood to address their experiences and in turn shape our understanding of this fleeting time and of generations in certain epochs and eras. To argue that films can help us in our regard and recognition of children, and in the practice of watching films as parents agentially attuned to their needs and desires, more precisely as a grieving mom, I present them as significant objects and experiences—especially those that represent childhood. As parents, the central cultural role in our relationships is to understand children as autonomous subjects even if and especially because they demand and need our care—our agentic attunement that should help them find themselves in their own terms and not ours.

I examine films about childhoods because the site of family is where we can help launch children whose self-sovereignty we must value from the very beginning and throughout their lives. We need to give children the space that they demand, to separate them from our preconceived hopes that are too much like our own dashed dreams, so they may grow up valuing who they are and their true senses of self.

Love for my children and my family sustains me in the act of writing as a grieving mother. Through it, death in life is not inevitable. There is a path to develop a self that keeps the child living, as this book aims to hold space for Lakas in this world. I claim his days. He would have been eighteen now, ready to launch, joining his brother, Bayan, to show us all what we've done to make space for their growth, to develop a sovereign self that can withstand obstacles and find expression in ways they wish and want. Make way.

In Closing

THE POWER OF FILMS ABOUT RACIAL CHILDHOODS
IN THE TIME OF RAMPANT DEATH

When my younger son, Lakas, died, numerous people told me I would become a shell of myself. The message was I would die while remaining alive.
They had seen death in life before. It happened to other grieving mothers
in their families. We left the country the summer after Lakas died, as a
first foray into resuming work while on fellowship. I remember walking
deliberately up the hill from our home in Sydney, Australia, one foot then
the other super-intensely, so I literally would not fall on my face. It was a
plain old street. Yet I was really learning how to walk without falling on
my face every day. I could feel the force of the ground pulling me down,
or was it my own heavy feelings? I remember not being able to read (I
literally could not make sense of words) or watch movies (their sensorium
overwhelmed me and made me want to bolt up and flee). These acts are
what I do for work. Text blurred, images felt too sharp and jarring. I could
not see in front of me; no matter my efforts, the screens and pages became

opaque. Emotions took over thought. Heart, soul, and body over mind. I remember stupefying rumination. Everything is nothing. Thinking in endless circles about things I could not control. His death. My life. Did the common virus that killed him within twenty-four hours come from the hamburger he ate for lunch on Sunday? Was it fully cooked? Was it from touching the buttons at the video game arcade right before that? Was the virus airborne from crowds at the miniature train exhibit in the small, cramped museum? These are all the things we did on the Sunday before he suddenly died, in living a full family life that centered our children who were there with cousins hanging out with us for the day. Was it the burrito for dinner on Monday? Was it the shrimp on Tuesday in preparation for Christmas dinner? My family and I would warn each other to get out of the crippling cogitations. Then, out in the world, I remember being asked if I was all right, incessantly. And if I would make sure to see a doctor then and there. How could people see how deep the pain was, how hard?

I do remember despair. Then I remember consciously working on grief's unbeatability because I needed to live. To choose to live, to organize memory to make life possible. Let the pain come. I would tell myself not to turn away from it so it would not kill me. Our whole family—me, my husband, and our older son, who was only eleven at the time—had to fashion a life where Lakas remained with us. Could we still thrive? His death could have killed me. I could have stopped living. I left my tenured full professorship at the University of California at Santa Barbara. I began to teach again, at San Francisco State University, where I resumed my tenured full professorship with a different set of students and colleagues. There, I noticed a different compassion: boundless in ways different than before. I always loved to teach, loved my students and collaborating with my colleagues, but this was something else. Was it that I could now move deadlines in the face of life and death in beginning to understand students outside the classroom? Was it the students, 60 percent Pell Grant eligible, 80 percent students of color, hungry to learn and struggling financially? Was it me in how I bore my pain? What was this open and curious invitation I extended to collaborate with my colleagues across all our differences? It became simple somewhat, the importance of connection and community and in bringing Lakas to my work.

I began all my classes with Lakas, not to ask my students to take care of me. It was simply important for me to say who and what I carried, and in doing so, a new relation in my classes was born, a courage that bound us because I began with a powerful vulnerability that invited their honesty too. When they shared their pain, I extended compassion. This is how I behaved with my colleagues as well. I requested we rise up to do great things together. While I did not raise my hand to lead, I was unanimously elected as director of the School of Cinema at San Francisco State University, a major film school globally. I was its first woman of color permanent leader, and the priority to serve with empathy and unflinching clarity became an emblem of my leadership.

I am now the first woman of color academic dean at the University of California at Santa Cruz. As a faculty member, I am a distinguished professor, having led dual careers as a scholar and filmmaker in the academy, where I would achieve tenure, promotion, and acceleration based on my record in either track. While my career looks like a powerful ascendancy, especially in the university system where very few women of color lead and very few rise to the highest of ranks, the grief I bear never leaves. It grows and remains with me and guides me in public schools with few resources, and where dynamics of power rupture and surge constantly. My own mothering guides my leadership: I know that no one can avoid the certainty of death—its pain, loss, and grief—and my singular goal is to help our community harness our creativity and analytic power so we can get so strong we survive it, fight it, and find purpose for a meaningful life.

As a mother who worked throughout the intensive time of caregiving, despite the demands I faced rising up as an ambitious and assertive professional, I committed to attending to my children, aware of the power of their regard and reliance on me as someone they could depend on. This is very important to me as a child who was largely neglected by my parents. What I call agentic attunement can be aspirational, in nodding to the imperfections in parenting that come from the conditions and circumstances of capitalism and colonialism that prevent us from being precisely and consummately around or being perfect as caregivers. These expectations are brutal to parents. I learned that there are ways mistakes can be overwhelming but need to be understood within the larger context of parenting. If the child can count on you, their confidence builds not only in your relationship but in themselves as well, which is critical as children become adults and sovereign selves.

When I refer to self-sovereignty in this book, I refer to the way in which children and young people must resist disciplinary control of their bodies and psyches by others if it is not for their good, as well as by the structures that organize their identities as not for themselves. Imagine if Andrew Cunanan in *American Crime Story* did not turn away from the abundance of healing that could have made less prominent the voice of his father and the method of lying and killing others who did not cooperate with his delusions. So many lives would have been saved. David in *Spa Night* found affirmation via the redeployment of selfobjects to serve him as queer and Asian while maintaining his family and community. In *Driveways*, Cody similarly found affirmation from selfobjects that mimicked parental care and nurturing so he could build a strong self in his new environment. *Blossoming*'s Maxie expanded our ideas about childhood sexuality, demoting genital sex and pleasure for the wide expanse of desire, including maternal love and the alleviation of suffering from grief. Rose in *Yellow Rose* taught us the power of healthy narcissism in forging belonging, exposing the power of film to imagine freedom within impossible circumstances. And Ellie, Aster, and Paul in *The Half of It* gave us examples of navigating cultural complexes to find their autonomous selves within a limiting environment. Each of these young people established their power and self-sovereignty within their contexts and constraints. They became the centers of their own stories, agents in their own lives.

Foucault defines disciplinary power as one that "centers on the body, produces individualizing effects, and manipulates the body as a source of forces that have to be rendered both useful and docile."[1] The self-sovereignty that children must possess resists that cultivation of docility and their use by others in a way that is not in the child's self-interest. Thus, we as adults have a role in supporting that project for children, rather than controlling them and worsening their situations. My hope for this book is to expand the relation between the viewer and the film, to transform that relationship through my analysis of agentic attunement, which centers the child and young people in a world of adults who speak about experiences that have long passed them yet continue to shape them. In arguing that films can help us in our regard and recognition of children, adolescents, and youth, and in the practice of watching films as parents, I present them as significant objects and experiences that shape our adult relationships.

I conclude this book with two aims: I wish for young people to identify their bodily desires and psychic identities as their own. Doing so is crucial to determining their self-sovereignty, which I have defined as self-recognition and regard that honors oneself in ways inseparable from community. And I have identified filmmakers who use films to examine childhood in order to undo harm and to strengthen all of our paths forward toward healthy selves. Self-sovereignty does not mean splitting the individual from the family. It means honoring the interior life as deserving of the dignity of articulation in the face of others' claims on it—whether family or other structures, such as religion, or social forces such as race, gender, and sexual normativity. Through the concept of the cultural complex, I explore how the realm of the psyche that is between the individual and the collective, which is shaped by culture, influences the integrity of childhood aims as belonging to them alone. Cultural complexes influence the expression of behaviors/thoughts/feelings. In asserting the self, we all benefit in expanding who the child is, lambasting the way childhood is understood as white and heterosexual along the way.

Films can help us identify the importance of autonomy in forging our childhood paths to a healthier adulthood, precisely through a redefinition of sovereignty for the individual. This recognition of the cinema as crucial to redefining self-sovereignty has been particularly important in a shut-down world, where I wrote from within the repetition and isolation of daily life at the height of the COVID-19 pandemic. Like other grieving mothers who are triggered and traumatized by the mass death and suffering we are undergoing still, and for me as a mom whose son was killed by a common virus, I do not want to endure the suffering from the death of anyone else in my immediate family from this novel virus, so strong that millions of people have died and even more have been infected.

Films give hope, make the world big—they connect us with each other intimately when we need it most. The necessity of film to our survival is now an undeniable and proven fact. The worlds films represent help us to understand our own, including the fundamental need to be around each other. To write this book helps me see Lakas as he could be now, and through the growing up in the past decade that he could not do. These are the ages of the children in this book—the years he could not have. This book enabled me to hear him, see him, feel him, and imagine him here with me—watching these movies and growing together from them. I hope this book clarifies the powerful work film does to help us live. This book, too, is an attempt to touch you and help you live in the face of so much death.

notes

Preface

1　I use both *Asian/American* and *Asian American* many times throughout the manuscript. In the case of *Asian/American*, I refer to films, characters, identities, and locations inclusive of Asian films that I interpret in my American context. And in the case of *Asian American*, I refer to the Asian American identities born from the struggle of 1960s civil rights movements to capture particular experiences of Americans with Asian ancestry and racializations as people of color in the United States. David Palumbo-Liu, in his book *Asian/American* (1999), encourages us to use the slash so as to draw attention to the fraught space between Asian and American identities and identifications, while David L. Eng, in the epilogue to his book *Racial Castration* (2001), explores the psychic life of the space between, including their linkages and dependencies.

2　Quoted in de Lauretis, "Becoming Inorganic," 548.

3　Quoted in de Lauretis, "Becoming Inorganic," 548.

4　De Lauretis notes how Sabrina Spielrein's essay "Destruction as Cause of Becoming" "argued that the instinctual drive for the preservation of the species, the wish to procreate or give birth [*das Werden*, becoming or coming into being], contains a destructive impulse: 'As certain biological facts show, the reproductive instinct, from the psychological standpoint as well, is made up of two antagonistic components and is therefore equally an instinct of birth and one of destruction' (qtd. in *SS*, p. 142)" (de Lauretis, "Becoming Inorganic," 551).

5　Pine, *Drive, Ego, Object, and Self*, 18.

6　De Lauretis, "Becoming Inorganic," 555.

7　Winnicott, *Playing and Reality*, 16.

8　Pine, *Drive, Ego, Object, and Self*, 28.

9　Pine, *Drive, Ego, Object, and Self*, 29.

Introduction

1　A24 and Plan B, special panel on *Minari*.

2　A24 and Plan B, special panel on *Minari*.

3　Pine, *Drive, Ego, Object, and Self*, 35.

4　Pine, *Drive, Ego, Object, and Self*, 3.

5　Pine, *Drive, Ego, Object, and Self*, 5.

6   De Lauretis, "Becoming Inorganic," 554.

7   Pine, *Drive, Ego, Object, and Self*, 4.

8   Pine, *Drive, Ego, Object, and Self*, 31.

9   Pine, *Drive, Ego, Object, and Self*, 29.

10 Hall, *Representation*.

11 De Lauretis, "Popular Culture, Public and Private Fantasies."

12 Stewart, *Migrating to the Movies*; Ahmed, *Cultural Politics of Emotions*, 10.

13 Bhabha, "The Other Question," 107.

14 Miyao, *Sessue Hayakawa*.

15 Eng and Han, *Racial Melancholia, Racial Dissociation*; Cheng, *Melancholy of Race*; Hong, *Minor Feelings*.

16 Ding, "Strategies of an Asian American Filmmaker"; Peña, "Lotus Blossoms Don't Bleed"; Collins, *Black Sexual Politics*, 69.

17 Hamamoto, *Monitored Peril*.

18 Vargas, "Incensed and Empowered."

19 Ho, *Consumption and Identity in Asian American Coming-of-Age Novels*; Shankar, *Desi Land*; Martin, *The Child in Contemporary Latin American Cinema*; Shary, *Cinemas of Boyhood*.

20 Mahmood, *Politics of Piety*, 31.

21 Mahmood, *Politics of Piety*, 31.

22 Bowlby, *Attachment and Loss*, 245.

23 Ulaby, "Youn Yuh-jung Is First Korean to Win Oscar for Best Supporting Actress."

24 "*Minari* Q&A."

25 "*Minari* Q&A."

26 Bowlby, *Attachment and Loss*.

27 Main, Kaplan, and Cassidy, "Security in Infancy, Childhood, and Adulthood."

28 Ainsworth et al., *Patterns of Attachment*.

29 Main and Weston, "Quality of the Toddler's Relationship to Mother and to Father"; Main, "Ultimate Causation of Some Infant Attachment Phenomena."

30 See preface note 1 on the use of *Asian/American*. In this case *Asian/American* is a shorthand for "Asian" and "Asian American," which are distinct spaces, yet in both, devastation and exploitation as well as a wider range of experiences including joy and resistance are common themes.

31 Roberts, *Killing the Black Body*.

32 Fleetwood, "Raising a Black Boy Not to Be Afraid."

33 Wong, "Little Noticed."

34 Shimizu, *The Hypersexuality of Race*; Shimizu, *Straitjacket Sexualities*; Shimizu, *Proximity of Other Skins*.

35 Freud, "Three Essays on the Theory of Sexuality."

36 Associated Press, "Officer Defends Giving Boy Back to Dahmer."

37 Lim, *Brown Boys and Rice Queens*.

38 Bernstein, *Racial Innocence*.

39 Miller, "Lesson in Moral Spectatorship," 710.

40 Miller, "Lesson in Moral Spectatorship."

41 Bernstein, *Racial Innocence*, 50–51.

42 Taylor, *The Archive and the Repertoire*, 20.

43 Deborah Martin studies the representation of children in various Latin American countries to assess their status and significance in national politics and history. She is interested in how narrative representations aim to present the perspective of the child, or whether they present only adult concerns. Martin, *The Child in Contemporary Latin American Cinema*.

44 Freud, *Three Case Histories*, 164.

45 Frankenberg, "Mirage of an Unmarked Whiteness," 72.

46 Frankenberg, "Mirage of an Unmarked Whiteness," 72.

47 Miller, Rodríguez, and Shimizu, "Unwatchability of Whiteness"; Shimizu, "Gnawing at the Whiteness of Cinema Studies."

48 Pine, *Drive, Ego, Object, and Self*, 31.

49 Pine, *Drive, Ego, Object, and Self*, 67.

50 Pine, *Drive, Ego, Object, and Self*, 61.

51 Psychoanalysts Melanie Klein, Jacques Lacan, and Sigmund Freud have commented on the power of film, as discussed in Heath, "Cinema and Psychoanalysis." Klein preferred other cultural practices to the cinema, while Freud was "dimly amused" and "disinterest[ed]." Lacan, however, was "astounded by the 'female eroticism' in the 1976 film by Nagisa Oshima, *Empire of the Senses*," according to Heath, who quotes Lacan as saying, "I began to understand the power of Japanese women" (25), referring to a seminal film about sexuality. In Heath's interpretation, psychoanalysis expressed "intellectual and class disdain for the upstart popular entertainment" (26). Yet we cannot deny that unlike other art forms, cinema best mimics the processes of the mind, whether these early psychoanalysts wish it to or not. Heath captures how the cinema can visualize the work of psychoanalysis: "Indeed, the ready appeal of cinema as an analogy for mental processes—cinema regarded from the start as a good way of imaging the workings of the mind . . . —brings exactly by its readiness the danger of the loss of the specificity of psychoanalytic understanding" (26). Conversely, I argue that psychoanalysis and its focus on sexuality help us understand real-life phenomena represented in cinema, whose scenes permeate the everyday and that patients themselves use to understand life itself.

52 Silverman, *Acoustic Mirror*; Silverman, *Male Subjectivity at the Margins*; Silverman, *Threshold of the Visible World*.

53 Van der Kolk, *The Body Keeps the Score*, 186.

54 Van der Kolk, *The Body Keeps the Score*, 188.

1. A Deluge of Delusions and Lies

1 Foo, *What My Bones Know*, 69.

2 Sánchez-Eppler, "Playing at Class," 40, 42.

3 Winnicott, *Maturational Processes*, 148.

4 Winnicott, *Maturational Processes*, 143.

5 Winnicott, *Home Is Where We Start From*, 66.

6 Winnicott, *Home Is Where We Start From*, 22.

7 Winnicott, *Playing and Reality*, 15.

8 Winnicott, *The Child, the Family and the Outside World*, 165.

9 Winnicott, *Playing and Reality*, 136.

10 Winnicott, *Playing and Reality*, 139.

11 Winnicott, *The Child, the Family and the Outside World*, 162.

12 Winnicott, *Playing and Reality*, xv.

13 Zelizer, *Pricing the Priceless Child*.

14 While we do not know the facticity of pedophilic incest, the makers of the film seem to be following the example of the author Gary Indiana, who imagines what could have happened to lead Andrew Cunanan to the life of pathological lying and more. Indiana, *Three Month Fever*.

15 Winnicott, *Home Is Where We Start From*, 22.

16 Winnicott, *The Child, the Family and the Outside World*, 165.

17 Orth, "Assassination of Gianni Versace, Revisited."

18 Winnicott, *Home Is Where We Start From*, 40.

19 Winnicott, *Home Is Where We Start From*, 33.

20 Winnicott, *Home Is Where We Start From*, 40; Winnicott, *Home Is Where We Start From*, 39.

21 Winnicott, *Home Is Where We Start From*, 39, 40.

22 Bernstein, *Racial Innocence*, 15.

23 Winnicott, *Maturational Processes*, 143.

2. The Inner Life of Cinema and Selfobjects

1 Lee, *Koreatown, Los Angeles*.

2 Warner, *Publics and Counterpublics*, 9–10.

3 Palumbo-Liu, *Asian/American*; Lee, *Orientals*; and Chow, "How the Inscrutable Chinese Led to Globalized Theory."

4 Xiang, *Tonal Intelligence*, 10.

5 Erbland, "'Spa Night' Review."

6   Oishi, "Bad Asians."

7   Anderson, "Director Andrew Ahn."

8   Kohut, *Analysis of the Self*, 11.

9   Wolf, *Treating the Self*, 26.

10 Wolf, *Treating the Self*, 63.

11 Wolf, *Treating the Self*, 30.

12 Hüser and Silverman, "Crossing the Threshold," 4.

13 Wolf, *Treating the Self*, 13.

14 Wolf, *Treating the Self*, 29.

15 Wolf, *Treating the Self*, 13.

16 Shimizu, *Proximity of Other Skins*.

17 West, "New Cultural Politics of Difference," 93.

18 Kohut, *Kohut Seminars*, 5.

19 Wolf, *Treating the Self*, 53.

20 Similarly, Linh Thuy Nguyen's "Unwatchable Violence" studies the ways three forces of the state, as well as white and Vietnamese patriarchy, controlled the Vietnamese American woman's ability to express and define her own desires and pleasures.

21 The spa or bath house occupies a special space for gay sexual and social cultures. Historian George Chauncey describes it as a space that "outlasted bars," offering a "protected" site for sex compared to other sites more vulnerable to arrest and harassment; "forthrightly sexual," it was also "social" and thus enabled community building for a targeted and often closeted group (*Gay New York*, 224).

22 Williams, *Screening Sex*.

23 Kohut, *Kohut Seminars*, 64.

24 Kohut, *Kohut Seminars*, 64.

25 Kohut, *Kohut Seminars*, 65.

26 Lacan, *Écrits*, 95.

27 Silverman, *Threshold of the Visible World*, 37.

28 Hüser and Silverman, "Crossing the Threshold," 5.

29 hooks, "Homeplace as a Site of Resistance."

30 Main, Kaplan, and Cassidy, "Security in Infancy, Childhood, and Adulthood."

31 Metzi, "Reproduction of Mothering"; Chodorow, *Reproduction of Mothering*.

32 Wolf, *Treating the Self*, 125.

33 Berlant and Warner, "Sex in Public," 547.

34 Kohut, *Kohut Seminars*, 35.

35 Gaffney, *Transgressions*.

36 Kohut, *Kohut Seminars*, 42.

37 Kohut describes the critical "stage" of the "baby experiencing separate processes in mental and physical body parts. In this developmental phase

it is enormously important for the maternal environment to respond according to the baby's needs. I do not mean necessarily the biological mother but whoever the mothering adult may be" (*Kohut Seminars*, 34).

38 Kohut, *Kohut Seminars*, 70–71.

39 Mahmood, *Politics of Piety*.

40 Wolf, *Treating the Self*, 25.

41 Stockton, *Queer Child*, 4.

42 Ahmed, *Queer Phenomenology*.

43 Anderson, "Director Andrew Ahn."

44 Cuby, "What Happens When Queer Characters Stop Coming Out."

45 Cuby, "What Happens When Queer Characters Stop Coming Out."

46 Connell, *Masculinities*.

47 Anderson, "Director Andrew Ahn."

48 Fear, "'Driveways' Review."

49 Wolf, *Treating the Self*, 36.

50 Wolf, *Treating the Self*, 52.

51 Wolf, *Treating the Self*, 53.

52 Kohut, *Kohut Seminars*, 81.

53 Kohut, *Kohut Seminars*, 31.

54 Anderson, "Director Andrew Ahn."

55 Catsoulis, "'Driveways' Review."

3. Adolescent Curiosity and Mourning

An earlier version of this chapter was published in the *Journal of Cinema and Media Studies* 62, no. 3 (2023): 170–75.

1 Tolentino, "On Pinoy Indie Digi Cinema."

2 Qin, "Filipino Filmmakers."

3 J. B. Capino in conversation with author, September 3, 2020.

4 Klemm, "Secret Worlds."

5 Quito, "Acclaimed Movie."

6 Cine Malaya, "Philippine Film Foundation."

7 For a famous reference to flowers as vaginas that the painter Georgia O'Keeffe found frustrating, see Ellis-Petersen, "Flowers or Vaginas?"

8 Tadiar, *Remaindered Life*.

9 Uhlich, "Review: *The Blossoming of Maximo Oliveros*."

10 Harvey, "The Blossoming of Maximo Oliveros."

11 Lee, "Floating above the Slums of Manila."

12 Dawson, "The Blossoming of Maximo Oliveros."

13 Anomalilly, "Film Review: *The Blossoming of Maximo Oliveros*."

14 Anomalilly, "Film Review: *The Blossoming of Maximo Oliveros*."

15 Freud, "Three Essays on the Theory of Sexuality."

16 Freud, "Three Essays on the Theory of Sexuality," 191.

17 Freud, "Three Essays on the Theory of Sexuality," 191.

18 Uhlich, "Review: *The Blossoming of Maximo Oliveros*."

19 Walters, "The Blossoming of Maximo Oliveros."

20 Walters, "The Blossoming of Maximo Oliveros."

21 Klemm, "Secret Worlds."

22 Klemm, "Secret Worlds."

23 Fairbairn, *Object Relations Theory of the Personality*; Klein, *Collected Works of Melanie Klein*.

24 McWilliams, *Psychoanalytic Diagnosis*, 23.

25 McWilliams, *Psychoanalytic Diagnosis*, 31.

26 McWilliams, *Psychoanalytic Diagnosis*, 31.

27 McWilliams, *Psychoanalytic Diagnosis*, 31.

28 McWilliams, *Psychoanalytic Diagnosis*, 32.

29 McWilliams, *Psychoanalytic Diagnosis*, 24–25. What is also interesting here is this observation: "Freud's own work was not inhospitable to the development and elaboration of object relations theory. His appreciation of the importance of the child's actual and experienced infantile objects comes through in his concept of the 'family romance' in his recognition of how different the oedipal phase could be for the child depending on the personalities of the parents, and also in his increasing emphases on the relationship factors in treatment" (32).

30 McWilliams, *Psychoanalytic Diagnosis*, 33. McWilliams states: "Object relational concepts allowed therapists to extend their empathy into the area of how their clients experienced interpersonal connection. They might be in a state of psychological fusion with another person, in which self and object are emotionally indistinguishable. They might be in a dyadic space, where the object is felt as either for them or against them. Or they might see others as fully independent of themselves" (33).

31 Klein, *Collected Works of Melanie Klein*, 1.

32 Klein, *Collected Works of Melanie Klein*, 1–2.

33 Klein, *Collected Works of Melanie Klein*, 2.

34 Klein, *Collected Works of Melanie Klein*, 353.

35 Klein, *Collected Works of Melanie Klein*, 353.

36 Klein, *Collected Works of Melanie Klein*, 360.

37 Klein, *Collected Works of Melanie Klein*, 360.

38 Klein, *Collected Works of Melanie Klein*, 362.

39 Klein, *Collected Works of Melanie Klein*, 59.

40 Klein, *Collected Works of Melanie Klein*, 180.

41 Klein, *Collected Works of Melanie Klein*, 205.

42 Klein, *Collected Works of Melanie Klein*, 209.

43 Klein, *Collected Works of Melanie Klein*, 329.

44 Klein, *Collected Works of Melanie Klein*, 330.

45 Klein, *Collected Works of Melanie Klein*, 330–31.

46 Klein, *Collected Works of Melanie Klein*, 330–33.

47 Klein, *Collected Works of Melanie Klein*, 341.

48 Klein, *Collected Works of Melanie Klein*, 342.

49 Klein, *Collected Works of Melanie Klein*, 339.

50 Klein, *Collected Works of Melanie Klein*, 340.

51 Heath, "Cinema and Psychoanalysis," 27.

52 Freud, "Three Essays on the Theory of Sexuality," 157.

53 Klein, *Collected Works of Melanie Klein*, 340.

54 Klein, *Collected Works of Melanie Klein*, 330.

55 Klein, *Collected Works of Melanie Klein*, 330.

56 Irigaray, "When Our Lips Speak Together," 69.

57 Klein, *Collected Works of Melanie Klein*, 369.

4. The Courage to Compose Oneself

1 V. Nguyen, "My Young Mind Was Disturbed by a Book"; Gibson, "When Should My Kids Read 'Maus'"?

2 Vargas, *Dear America*.

3 The producers of *Yellow Rose* were also involved with Isabel Sandoval's *Lingua Franca* (2020), a trans, Filipinx American, immigrant filmmaker's film about a trans immigrant care worker in New York fearing for her safety in the Trump era.

4 Kohut, *Analysis of the Self*, xiii.

5 Kohut, *Analysis of the Self*, xiv.

6 Ainsworth et al., *Patterns of Attachment*; Main, Kaplan, and Cassidy, "Security in Infancy, Childhood, and Adulthood."

7 Kohut, *Analysis of the Self*, 37.

8 Kohut, *Analysis of the Self*, 38.

9 Kohut, *Analysis of the Self*, 26.

10 Kohut, *Analysis of the Self*, 26.

11 Kohut, *Analysis of the Self*, 26.

12 Kohut, *Analysis of the Self*, xiv–xv.

13 Diaz-Sanchez, "Re-mapping Queer Desire(s) on Greater Los Angeles," 105–6.

14 In 2022, there were a whopping two Filipino restaurants in Lubbock, Texas, where the filmmaker hails from, even if Filipinx people settled in the state in the early 1800s and Tagalog is the fourth most widely spoken language in that state today. UTSA Institute of Texan Cultures, "The Filipino Texans," 2019, https://texancultures.utsa.edu/wp-content/uploads/2019/08/TxOneAll_FilipinoCombined2019-1.pdf.

15 Kohut, *Analysis of the Self*, 41.

16 Kohut, *Analysis of the Self*, xv.

17 Kohut, *Analysis of the Self*, 17.

18 Kohut, *Analysis of the Self*, 21.

19 New York Theatre Workshop, *Hadestown* (2019–present).

20 Kohut, *Analysis of the Self*, 25.

21 Kohut, *Analysis of the Self*, 64.

22 Kohut, *Analysis of the Self*, 310.

23 Kohut, *Analysis of the Self*, 314.

24 Miles, *All That She Carried*, 6.

25 Mitra, "'Mississippi Masala' at 30."

26 Policarpio, "2 Filipino Indie Films Bag Historic Wins."

5. The Unexpected and the Unforeseen

1 Before the COVID-19 pandemic, from 2015 to 2020, Nanatchka Khan created the television series *Fresh Off the Boat*, about a Taiwanese American family moving from Washington, DC, to Orlando, Florida, in search of economic opportunity. While the television series did not focus on Asian American young women's sexual and gender experiences, it was a landmark historical achievement for Asian American representation. Based on the real-life celebrity chef Eddie Huang's autobiography, the show was successfully produced for six seasons and was the first television sitcom featuring an Asian American family since the cancellation of Margaret Cho's single-season program *All American Girl* twenty years prior. *Fresh Off the Boat* enabled us to witness three young boys growing up from childhood to their teen years, navigating racial otherness in the forging of home. By depicting the family opening a cowboy restaurant called Cattlemen's Ranch rather than a Chinese restaurant, the series emphasized assimilation as a goal. While no parental loss besieged the family, the loss of a familiar home framed their search for belonging. The love of the main character, Eddie, the oldest child, for hip-hop at the time of its emergence in the 1990s also felt quintessentially American and current. As a situation comedy, the series enabled Asian American multigenerational presence in a genre of popular culture that entered American homes.

2 Holden, "Juggling Her Chinese Clan"; Morris, "Supporting Cast's Vibrancy Saves 'Face'"; Rooney, "Saving Face"; Gregory, "The 200 Best Lesbian, Bisexual, and Queer Movies of All Time."

3 It is notable that the Asian American teen film *Better Luck Tomorrow* (2004) by Justin Lin deploys the same premise of turning the model minority myth on its head, as high-performing Asian American kids monetize their known talents in criminal enterprise.

4   Singer, "Archetypal Defenses of the Group Spirit," 19–20.

5   Singer, "Archetypal Defenses of the Group Spirit," 20.

6   Wade, *American Hook-Up*.

7   Wade, *American Hook-Up*.

8   Hirsch and Khan, *Sexual Citizens*, 124.

9   Hirsch and Khan, *Sexual Citizens*, xiv

10   Hirsch and Khan, *Sexual Citizens*, 122, 268.

11   Hirsch and Khan, *Sexual Citizens*, 122.

12   Hirsch and Khan, *Sexual Citizens*, 91.

13   Beebe, "The Child in 21st Century American Film."

In Closing

1   Foucault, *Society Must Be Defended*, 249.

bibliography

A24 and Plan B. Special panel on *Minari* featuring Sandra Oh and cast and crew on January 13, 2021. https://www.youtube.com/watch?v=ofUy2STaRXQ.

Ahmed, Sara. *The Cultural Politics of Emotions*. Abingdon, UK: Routledge, 2004.

Ahmed, Sara. *Queer Phenomenology*. Durham, NC: Duke University Press, 2006.

Ainsworth, Mary, Mary C. Biehar, Everett Waters, and Sally M. Wall. *Patterns of Attachment: A Psychological Study of the Strange Situation*. London: Psychology Press, 2015.

Al-Kassim, Dina. *On Pain of Speech*. Berkeley: University of California Press, 2010.

Anderson, Tre'vell. "Director Andrew Ahn Is Challenging the Definition of Queer Cinema." *Xtra*, May 8, 2020. https://www.dailyxtra.com/andrew-ahn-driveways-spa-night-172437.

Anomalilly. "Film Review: *The Blossoming of Maximo Oliveros* by Auraeus Solito." *Asian Movie Pulse*, October 3, 2019. https://asianmoviepulse.com/2019/10/film-review-the-blossoming-of-maximo-oliveros-2005-by-auraeus-solito/.

Associated Press. "Officer Defends Giving Boy Back to Dahmer." *New York Times*, August 26, 1991. https://www.nytimes.com/1991/08/26/us/officer-defends-giving-boy-back-to-dahmer.html.

Beebe, John. "The Child in 21st Century American Film." In *Cultural Complexes and the Soul of America: Myth, Psyche and Politics*, edited by Thomas Singer, 239–54. Abingdon, UK: Routledge, 2020.

Benjamin, Jessica. *The Bonds of Love*. New York: Pantheon, 1988.

Berlant, Lauren, and Michael Warner. "Sex in Public." *Critical Inquiry* 24, no. 2 (Winter 1998): 547–66.

Bernstein, Robin. *Racial Innocence: Performing American Childhood from Slavery to Civil Rights*. New York: New York University Press, 2011.

Bhabha, Homi. "The Other Question: Stereotype, Discrimination and the Discourse on Colonialism." In *The Location of Culture*, 94–120. Abingdon, UK: Routledge, 1994.

Bowlby, John. *Attachment and Loss*. Vol. 1, *Attachment*. New York: Basic Books, 1969.

Bridges, Khiara. *Reproducing Race: An Ethnography of Pregnancy as a Site of Racialization*. Berkeley: University of California Press, 2011.

Catsoulis, Jeannette. "'Driveways' Review: What Friends Are For." *New York Times*, May 7, 2020. https://www.nytimes.com/2020/05/07/movies/driveways-review.html.

Chauncey, George. *Gay New York: Gender, Urban Culture, and the Making of a Gay Male World, 1890–1940*. New York: Basic Books, 1994.

Cheng, Anne Anlin. *The Melancholy of Race: Psychoanalysis, Assimilation and Hidden Grief*. Oxford: Oxford University Press, 2001.

Chodorow, Nancy. *The Reproduction of Mothering: Psychoanalysis and the Politics of Gender*. New Haven, CT: Yale University Press, 1979.

Chow, Rey. "How the Inscrutable Chinese Led to Globalized Theory." *PMLA* 116, no. 1 (2001): 69–74.

Collins, Patricia Hill. *Black Sexual Politics: African Americans, Gender, and the New Racism*. New York: Routledge, 2005.

Connell, R. W. *Masculinities*. Berkeley: University of California Press, 2005.

Cuby, Michael. "What Happens When Queer Characters Stop Coming Out (and Start Getting Real)." *Them*, May 15, 2019. https://www.them.us/story/films -beyond-coming-out.

Dawson, Tom. "The Blossoming of Maximo Oliveros." *BBC*, May 28, 2007. http://www.bbc.co.uk/films/2007/05/28/the_blossoming_of_maximo _oliveros_2007_review.shtml.

de Lauretis, Teresa. "Becoming Inorganic." *Critical Inquiry* 29, no. 4 (2003): 547–70.

de Lauretis, Teresa. "Popular Culture, Public and Private Fantasies: Femininity and Fetishism in David Cronenberg's 'M. Butterfly.'" *Signs* 24, no. 2 (Winter 1999): 303–34.

Diaz-Sanchez, Micaela Jamaica. "Re-mapping Queer Desire(s) on Greater Los Angeles: The Decolonial Topographies of Aurora Guerrero and Dalila Paola Mendez." *Chicana/Latina Studies* 17, no. 1 (Fall 2017): 94–117.

Ding, Loni. "Strategies of an Asian American Filmmaker." In *Moving the Image: Independent Asian Pacific American Media Arts*, edited by Russell Leong, 46–59. Los Angeles: UCLA Asian American Studies, 1991.

Ellis-Petersen, Hannah. "Flowers or Vaginas? Georgia O'Keeffe Tate Show to Challenge Sexual Clichés." *Guardian*, March 1, 2016. https://www .theguardian.com/artanddesign/2016/mar/01/georgia-okeeffe-show-at -tate-modern-to-challenge-outdated-views-of-artist.

Endo, Jun. "Philippine Film Foundation Flipped the Script for a 'Dead' Industry." *Nikkei Asia*, April 29, 2019. https://asia.nikkei.com/Spotlight/Nikkei-Asia -Prizes/Philippine-film-foundation-flipped-the-script-for-a-dead-industry.

Eng, David L. *Racial Castration: Managing Masculinity in Asian America*. Durham, NC: Duke University Press, 2001.

Eng, David L., and Shinhee Han. *Racial Melancholia, Racial Dissociation: On the Social and Psychic Lives of Asian Americans*. Durham, NC: Duke University Press, 2019.

Erbland, Kate. "'Spa Night' Review: Gay Korean Coming-of-Age Drama Finds Resonance in Unlikely Places." *IndieWire*, August 17, 2016. https:// www.indiewire.com/2016/08/spa-night-review-andrew-ahn-sundance -1201717645/.

Fairbairn, W. R. D. *An Object Relations Theory of the Personality*. New York: Basic Books, 1954.

Fanon, Frantz. *Black Skin, White Masks*. New York: Grove Press, 2008.

Fear, David. "'Driveways' Review: Won't You Be My Neighbor." *Rolling Stone*, May 14, 2020. https://www.rollingstone.com/movies/movie-reviews/driveways-movie-review-brian-dennehy-990230/.

Fleetwood, Nicole. "Raising a Black Boy Not to Be Afraid." *LitHub*, October 3, 2018. https://lithub.com/raising-a-black-boy-not-to-be-afraid/.

Foo, Stephanie. *What My Bones Know: A Memoir of Healing from Complex Trauma*. New York: Ballantine Books, 2022.

Foucault, Michel. *Society Must Be Defended*. London: Picador, 2003.

Frankenberg, Ruth. "The Mirage of an Unmarked Whiteness." In *The Making and Unmaking of Whiteness*, edited by Birgit Bander Rasmussen, Irene J. Nexica, Eric Klinenberg, and Matt Wray, 72–96. Durham, NC: Duke University Press, 2001.

Freud, Sigmund. *Three Case Histories*. New York: Touchstone, 1996.

Freud, Sigmund. "Three Essays on the Theory of Sexuality" (1905). In *The Standard Edition of the Complete Psychological Works of Sigmund Freud*, vol. 7: *(1901–1905): A Case of Hysteria, Three Essays on Sexuality and Other Works*, 123–246. Mansfield Center, CT: Martino Fine Books, 2011.

Gallop, Jane. *The Daughter's Seduction: Feminism and Psychoanalysis*. Ithaca, NY: Cornell University Press, 1984.

Garbes, Angela. *Essential Labor: Mothering as Social Change*. New York: Harper Wave, 2022.

Gibson, Caitlin. "When Should My Kids Read 'Maus'? How Parents Can Help Children Learn about the Holocaust." *Washington Post*, February 3, 2022.

Gregory, Drew. "The 200 Best Lesbian, Bisexual, and Queer Movies of All Time." *Autostraddle*, January 18, 2022. https://www.autostraddle.com/100-best-lesbian-queer-bisexual-movies-285412/?all=1.

Hagedorn, Jessica. *Pet Food and Tropical Apparitions*. San Francisco: Momo's Press, 1981.

Hall, Stuart. *Representation: Cultural Representations and Signifying Practices*. London: Sage, 1997.

Hamamoto, Darrell. *Monitored Peril: Asian Americans and the Politics of TV Representation*. Minneapolis: University of Minnesota Press, 1994.

Harvey, Dennis. "The Blossoming of Maximo Oliveros." *Variety*, January 30, 2006. https://variety.com/2006/film/markets-festivals/the-blossoming-of-maximo-oliveros-1200518990/.

Heath, Stephen. "Cinema and Psychoanalysis: Parallel Histories." In *Endless Night: Cinema and Psychoanalysis, Parallel Histories*, edited by Janet Bergstrom, 25–56. Berkeley: University of California Press, 1999.

Hirsch, Jennifer S., and Shamus Khan. *Sexual Citizens: A Landmark Study of Sex, Power, and Assault on Campus*. New York: Norton, 2020.

Ho, Jennifer. *Consumption and Identity in Asian American Coming-of-Age Novels*. Abingdon, UK: Routledge, 2005.

Holden, Stephen. "Juggling Her Chinese Clan, Gay Lover, Pregnant Mom." *New York Times*, May 27, 2005. https://www.nytimes.com/2005/05/27/movies /juggling-her-chinese-clan-gay-lover-pregnant-mom.html.

Hong, Cathy Park. *Minor Feelings: An Asian American Reckoning*. New York: One World, 2020.

hooks, bell. "Homeplace as a Site of Resistance." In *Yearning: Race, Gender, and Cultural Politics*, 41–49. New York: Routledge, 2014.

Hüser, Rembert, and Kaja Silverman. "Crossing the Threshold: Interview with Kaja Silverman." *Discourse* 19, no. 3 (Spring 1997): 3–12.

Indiana, Gary. *Three Month Fever*. New York: Harper, 1999.

Irigaray, Luce. "When Our Lips Speak Together." *Signs* 6, no. 1 (Autumn 1980): 69–79.

Ishiguro, Kazuo. *Remains of the Day*. London: Faber and Faber, 1989.

Kaufman, Amy. "Depiction of Latino Character in 'Boyhood' Is Assailed by Some Critics." *Los Angeles Times*, February 23, 2015. https://www.latimes.com /entertainment/movies/moviesnow/la-et-mn-boyhood-latino-controversy -20150223-story.html.

Klein, Melanie. *The Collected Works of Melanie Klein: "Love, Guilt and Reparation" and Other Works, 1921–1945*. London: Hogarth Press, 1975.

Klemm, Michael D. "Secret Worlds." *CinemaQueer*, March 2009. https:// cinemaqueer.com/review%20pages%202/blossominglaleon.html.

Kohut, Heinz. *The Analysis of the Self*. Chicago: University of Chicago Press, 1971.

Kohut, Heinz. *The Kohut Seminars on Self Psychology and Psychotherapy with Adolescents and Young Adults*. Edited by Miriam Elson. New York: Norton, 1987.

Lacan, Jacques. *Écrits*. New York: Norton, 2006.

Lahiri, Jhumpa. *The Namesake*. New York: Mariner Books, 2004.

Lane, Christopher. *The Psychoanalysis of Race: An Introduction*. New York: Columbia University Press, 1998.

Lau, Evelyn. *Runaway: Diary of a Street Kid*. Toronto: Coach House Books, 1989.

Lee, Lela. *Angry Little Asian Girl*. Accessed July 15, 2022. https://www.angry littleasiangirl.com/.

Lee, Nathan. "Floating above the Slums of Manila on a Current of Love." *New York Times*, September 2, 2009. https://www.nytimes.com/2006/09/22 /movies/22blos.html.

Lee, Robert G. *Orientals: Asian Americans in Popular Culture*. Philadelphia: Temple University Press, 1999.

Lee, Shelley Sang-hee. *Koreatown, Los Angeles: Immigration, Race, and the "American Dream."* Stanford, CA: Stanford University Press, 2022.

Lim, Eng Beng. *Brown Boys and Rice Queens: Spellbinding Performances in the Asias*. New York: New York University Press, 2013.

Linmark, R. Zamora. *Rolling the R's*. New York: Kaya Press, 1997.

Mahmood, Saba. *Politics of Piety: The Islamic Revival and the Feminist Subject*. Princeton, NJ: Princeton University Press, 2004.

Main, M. "The Ultimate Causation of Some Infant Attachment Phenomena." *Behavioral and Brain Science* 2 (1977): 640–43.

Main, Mary, Nancy Kaplan, and Jude Cassidy. "Security in Infancy, Childhood, and Adulthood: A Move to the Level of Representation." *Monographs of the Society for Research in Child Development* 50, no. 1/2 (1985): 66–104.

Main, Mary, and D. Weston. "The Quality of the Toddler's Relationship to Mother and to Father: Related to Conflict Behavior and the Readiness to Establish New Relationships." *Child Development* 52, no. 3 (1981): 932–40.

Mani, Lata. *Myriad Intimacies*. Durham, NC: Duke University Press, 2022.

Martin, Deborah. *The Child in Contemporary Latin American Cinema*. London: Palgrave Macmillan, 2019.

McClintock, Anne. *Imperial Leather: Race, Gender and Sexuality in the Colonial Conquest*. Abingdon, UK: Routledge, 1995.

McWilliams, Nancy. *Psychoanalytic Diagnosis: Understanding Personality Structure in the Clinical Process*. New York: Guilford Press, 2011.

Metzi, Marilyn Newman. "The Reproduction of Mothering; Feminism and Psychoanalytic Theory; Femininities, Masculinities and Sexualities; The Power of Feelings (Book Reviews)." *Division 39 Society for Psychoanalysis and Psychoanalytic Psychology* (Winter 2003): 55–60. https://www.apadivisions.org/division-39/publications/reviews/chodorow.

Miles, Tiya. *All That She Carried: The Journey of Ashley's Sack, a Black Family Keepsake*. New York: Random House, 2021.

Miller, J. Reid. "A Lesson in Moral Spectatorship." *Critical Inquiry* 34, no. 4 (2008): 706–28.

Miller, J. Reid, Richard T. Rodríguez, and Celine Parreñas Shimizu. "The Unwatchability of Whiteness: A New Imperative of Representation." *Asian Diasporic Visual Cultures and the Americas* 4 (2018): 235–43.

"*Minari* Q&A with Lee Isaac Chung, Steven Yeun, Yeri Han, Yuh-Jung Youn, Alan Kim & Noel Cho." *Film at Lincoln Center*, December 21, 2020. https://www.youtube.com/watch?v=9A25kc9rgdg.

Mitra, Durba. "'Mississippi Masala' at 30: Revisiting a Film Classic in Authoritarian Times." *Public Books*, February 3, 2022. https://www.publicbooks.org/mississippi-masala-at-30-revisiting-a-film-classic-in-authoritarian-times/.

Miyao, Daisuke. *Sessue Hayakawa: Silent Cinema and Transnational Stardom*. Durham, NC: Duke University Press, 2007.

Morris, Wesley. "Supporting Cast's Vibrancy Saves 'Face.'" *Boston Globe*, June 10, 2005. https://www.boston.com/tag/entertainment/.

Nguyen, Linh Thuy. "Unwatchable Violence: Historical Affects and the Legacy of the Vietnam War in Vietnamese American Film." In "The Unwatchability of Whiteness: A New Imperative of Representation," edited by J. Reid Miller, Richard T. Rodríguez, and Celine Parreñas Shimizu, special issue, *Asian Diasporic Visual Cultures and the Americas* 4, no. 3 (September 2018): 262–79.

Nguyen, Viet Thanh. "My Young Mind Was Disturbed by a Book. It Changed My Life." *New York Times*, January 29, 2022.

Oishi, Eve. "Bad Asians." In *Countervisions*, edited by Darrell Hamamoto and Sandra Liu, 221–44. Philadelphia: Temple University Press, 2000.

Orth, Maureen. "Assassination of Gianni Versace, Revisited." *Vanity Fair*, January 11, 2018. https://www.vanityfair.com/hollywood/2018/01/gianni -versace-murder-andrew-cunanan-maureen-orth-vulgar-favors.

Orth, Maureen. *Vulgar Favors: Andrew Cunanan, Gianni Versace, and the Largest Failed Manhunt in U.S. History*. New York: Random House, 1999.

Palumbo-Liu, David. *Asian/American: Historical Crossings of a Racial Frontier*. Stanford, CA: Stanford University Press, 1999.

Pellegrini, Ann. *Performance Anxieties: Staging Psychoanalysis, Staging Race*. Abingdon, UK: Routledge, 1996.

Peña, Renee Tajima. "Lotus Blossoms Don't Bleed." In *Making Waves: An Anthology of Writings by Asian American Women*, edited by Asian Women United of California, 308–17. Boston: Beacon Press, 1989.

Pine, Fred. *Drive, Ego, Object, and Self: A Synthesis for Clinical Work*. New York: Basic Books, 1990.

Policarpio, Allan. "2 Filipino Indie Films Bag 'Historic' Wins at Sundance." January 30, 2022. https://entertainment.inquirer.net/435657/2-filipino-indie -films-bag-historic-wins-at-sundance.

Qin, Amy. "Filipino Filmmakers Shed Light on the Forgotten. They Hope It Can Last." *New York Times*, November 28, 2006. https://www.nytimes.com /2016/11/28/movies/filipino-filmmakers-shed-light-on-the-forgotten-they -hope-it-can-last.html.

Quito, Gil. "Acclaimed Movie: Ang Pagdadalaga . . . / The Flowering Returns to NYC on Dec. 9." *Philippine Daily Mirror*, December 6, 2022. https:// www.philippinedailymirror.com/acclaimed-movie-ang-pagdadalaga-the -flowering-returns-to-nyc-on-dec-9/.

Roberts, Dorothy. *Killing the Black Body: Race, Reproduction, and the Meaning of Liberty*. New York: Penguin Random House, 1997.

Rooney, David. "Saving Face." *Variety*, September 19, 2004. https://variety.com /2004/film/markets-festivals/saving-face-1200530945/.

Sánchez-Eppler, Karen. "Playing at Class." In *The American Child: A Cultural Studies Reader*, edited by Caroline Field Levander and Carol J. Singley, 40–62. New Brunswick, NJ: Rutgers University Press, 2003.

Seshadri-Crooks, Kalpana. *Desiring Whiteness*. Abingdon, UK: Routledge, 2000.

Shankar, Shalini. *Desi Land: Teen Culture, Class, and Success in Silicon Valley*. Durham, NC: Duke University Press, 2008.

Shary, Tim. *Cinemas of Boyhood: Masculinity, Sexuality, Nationality*. New York: Berghahn Books, 2021.

Shimizu, Celine Parreñas. "Gnawing at the Whiteness of Cinema Studies: On Asian American Media Now." *Cinema Journal* 56, no. 3 (Spring 2017): 119–54.

Shimizu, Celine Parreñas. *The Hypersexuality of Race*. Durham, NC: Duke University Press, 2007.

Shimizu, Celine Parreñas. *The Proximity of Other Skins: Ethical Intimacy in Global Cinema*. New York: Oxford University Press, 2020.

Shimizu, Celine Parreñas. *Straitjacket Sexualities*. Stanford, CA: Stanford University Press, 2012.

Silverman, Kaja. *The Acoustic Mirror: The Female Voice in Psychoanalysis and Cinema*. Bloomington: Indiana University Press, 1988.

Silverman, Kaja. *Male Subjectivity at the Margins*. New York: Routledge, 1992.

Silverman, Kaja. *The Threshold of the Visible World*. Abingdon, UK: Routledge, 1996.

Singer, Thomas. "The Archetypal Defenses of the Group Spirit." In *The Cultural Complex: Contemporary Jungian Perspectives on Psyche and Society*, edited by Thomas Singer and Samuel L. Kimbles, 13–33. Abingdon, UK: Routledge, 2004.

So, Anthony Veasna. *Afterparties: Stories*. New York: Ecco Press, 2022.

Spillers, Hortense. "Mama's Baby, Papa's Maybe: An American Grammar Book." *Diacritics* 17, no. 2 (1987): 64–81.

Stewart, Jacqueline. *Migrating to the Movies: Cinema and Black Urban Modernity*. Berkeley: University of California Press, 2005.

Stockton, Kathryn Bond. *The Queer Child*. Durham, NC: Duke University Press, 2009.

Tadiar, Neferti X. *Remaindered Life*. Durham, NC: Duke University Press, 2022.

Taylor, Diana. *The Archive and the Repertoire: Performing Cultural Memory in the Americas*. Durham, NC: Duke University Press, 2003.

Tolentino, Rolando. "On Pinoy Indie Digi Cinema." September 26, 2007. https:// rolandotolentino.wordpress.com/2007/09/26/on-pinoy-indie-digi-cinema/.

Uhlich, Keith. "Review: *The Blossoming of Maximo Oliveros*." *Slant Magazine*, March 8, 2006. https://www.slantmagazine.com/film/the-blossoming-of -maximo-oliveros/.

Ulaby, Neda. "Youn Yuh-jung Is First Korean to Win Oscar for Best Supporting Actress." NPR, April 25, 2021. https://www.npr.org/sections/live-updates -oscars-2021/2021/04/25/989638064/youn-yuh-jung-is-first-korean-to -win-oscar-for-best-supporting-actress.

van der Kolk, Bessel. *The Body Keeps the Score: Brain, Mind, and Body in the Healing of Trauma*. New York: Penguin, 2014.

Vargas, Jose Antonio. *Dear America: Notes of an Undocumented Citizen*. New York: HarperCollins, 2019.

Vargas, Jose Antonio. "Incensed and Empowered." *Washington Post*, October 9, 2005. https://www.washingtonpost.com/wp-dyn/content/article/2005 /10/08/AR2005100801286.html.

Vuong, Ocean. *On Earth We're Briefly Gorgeous*. New York: Penguin, 2021.

Wade, Lisa. *American Hook-Up: The New Culture of Sex on Campus*. New York: Norton, 2017.

Walters, Ben. "The Blossoming of Maximo Oliveros." *Time Out*, May 29, 2007. https://www.timeout.com/london/film/the-blossoming-of-maximo -oliveros.

Walton, Jean. *Fair Sex, Savage Dreams*. Durham, NC: Duke University Press, 2001.

Warner, Michael. *Publics and Counterpublics*. Brooklyn, NY: Zone Books, 2002.

West, Cornel. "The New Cultural Politics of Difference." *October* 53 (1990): 93–109.

Williams, Linda. *Screening Sex*. Durham, NC: Duke University Press, 2008.

Winnicott, D. W. *The Child, the Family and the Outside World*. London: Perseus, 1964.

Winnicott, D. W. *Home Is Where We Start From: Essays by a Psychoanalyst*. New York: Norton, 1986.

Winnicott, D. W. *The Maturational Processes and the Facilitating Environment*. Abingdon, UK: Routledge, 1974.

Winnicott, D. W. *Playing and Reality*. Abingdon, UK: Routledge, 1971.

Wolf, Ernest. *Treating the Self*. New York: Guilford Press, 1988.

Wong, Tiffany. "Little Noticed, Filipino Americans Are Dying of COVID-19 at an Alarming Rate." *Los Angeles Times*, July 21, 2020. https://www.latimes.com /california/story/2020-07-21/filipino-americans-dying-covid.

Xiang, Sunny. *Tonal Intelligence: The Aesthetics of Asian Inscrutability during the Long Cold War*. New York: Columbia University Press, 2020.

Young-Breuhl, Elisabeth. *Mind and the Body Politic*. Abingdon, UK: Routledge, 1989.

Yu, Phil. *Angry Asian Man*. Accessed July 15, 2022. http://blog.angryasianman .com.

Zelizer, Viviana. *Pricing the Priceless Child*. Princeton, NJ: Princeton University Press, 1985.

Films and Television

Ahn, Andrew. *Driveways*. USA. Brooklyn, NY: FilmRise, 2019.

Ahn, Andrew. *Spa Night*. USA. Culver City, CA: Strand Releasing, 2016.

Cho, Margaret, Gary Jacobs, and American Broadcasting Company. *All American Girl*. Los Angeles: ABC Television, 1994–95.

Chung, Lee Isaac. *Minari*. USA. Manhattan, NY: A24, distributor. World premiere: Sundance, 2020.

Gaffney, Stuart. *Transgressions*. Los Angeles: LA Freewaves. Accessed July 13, 2022. https://vimeo.com/45329024.

Guerrero, Aurora. *Mosquita y Mari*. USA. Wolfe Releasing, 2012. Los Angeles, CA: The Film Collaborative, distributor.

Khan, Nanatchka. *Fresh Off the Boat*. USA. Twentieth Century Fox Television, 2015–20.

Lin, Justin. *Better Luck Tomorrow*. USA. Los Angeles: MTV Films, 2004.

Murphy, Ryan. *The Assassination of Gianni Versace*. USA. Los Angeles: FX Network, 2018.

Paragas, Diane. *Yellow Rose*. USA. Los Angeles: Sony Pictures, 2019.

Riggs, Marlon. *Tongues Untied*. USA. San Francisco: Frameline Films, 1989.

Sandoval, Isabel. *Lingua Franca*. USA. Los Angeles: Array Releasing, 2020.

Shimizu, Celine Parreñas. *80 Years Later*. Digital video. World premiere: Los Angeles Asian Pacific Film Festival, 2022.

Shimizu, Celine Parreñas. *The Fact of Asian Women*. Digital video. Berkeley: Progressive Films, 2004.

Solito, Auraeus. *The Blossoming of Maximo Oliveros*. Philippines. Philippine Independent Film Festival, 2005.

Wu, Alice. *The Half of It*. USA. Los Gatos: Netflix, 2020.

Wu, Alice. *Saving Face*. USA. Los Angeles: Sony Pictures, 2004.

index

van der Kolk, Bessel, 31

Variety magazine, 124

Versace, Gianni: childhood of, 49–52, 164; class and context for, 43–49; Cunanan's encounters with, 74–76; murder of, 34–35, 78–80; self-development of, 60

Vietnamese culture, state and patriarchy in, 217n20

violence of whiteness, casual, 18–19

Vulgar Favors: Andrew Cunanan, Gianni Versace, and the Largest Failed Manhunt in U.S. History (Orth), 44, 64

Vuong, Ocean, 27

Walters, Ben, 126

Walton, Jean, 30

Warner, Michael, 84, 103

Watson, Dale, 155, 170, 172–74

Wenders, Wim, 194

West, Cornel, 89

What My Bones Know (Foo), 31–32

"When Our Lips Speak Together" (Irigaray), 149

whiteness: American Dream and, 57–60; in American film, 25–26; casual violence of, 18–19; Cunanan and role of, 66–67; disempowerment and, 167–68

Whitrock, Finn, 73

Winnicott, D. W., xv; false self and good mother theories of, 44, 63; good enough mother paradigm and, 49–52; on lying, 63–64, 67–69; object relations theory of, 6–8, 35; psychoanalysis and work of, 28–29; on representation and emotions, 12; true and false selves and, 48–49, 70–72, 78–80

Wolf, Ernest, 87–88, 90, 113

Wong, Anna May, 9–10

work, creativity and, 51–52

World Cinema Dramatic Competition, 124

Wu, Alice, 38, 189–90, 193–94

Xiang, Sunny, 84

Yellow Rose: actualization of freedom in, 189; betrayal and fragmentation in, 162–68, 197–98; community in, 170–73; creativity and narcissism in, 159–62; distribution of, 177, 179; healthy narcissism in, 152–59, 170–73, 211; Paragas's discussion of, 178–85; pursuit of equilibrium in, 174–78; self-reconstitution in, 168–73

Ye-ri, Han, 2

Yeun, Steven, 2–3, 8, 15–16

Young-Breuhl, Elisabeth, 30

Yu, Phil, 11

Yuh-jung, Youn, 2–3

Zee, Teddy, 190

Zelizer, Viviana, 56